Software Engineering in the UNIX®/C Environment

William B. Frakes
Software Productivity Consortium

Christopher J. Fox
AT&T Bell Laboratories

Brian A. Nejmeh
Instep Incorporated

Prentice Hall, Englewood Cliffs, New Jersey 07632

Library of Congress Cataloging-in-Publication Data

Frakes, William B. (William Bruce)
  Software engineering in the UNIX/C environment / William B.
Frakes, Christopher J. Fox, Brian A. Nejmeh.
    p.   cm. — (Prentice Hall software series)
  Includes bibliographical references and index.
  ISBN 0-13-829763-0
  1. Software engineering.   2. UNIX (Computer operating system)
3. C (Computer program language)   I. Fox, Christopher John.
II. Nejmeh, Brian A.   III. Title.   IV. Series.
QA76.758.F73   1991
005.1—dc20   90–24191
                                                    CIP

Editorial/production supervision: *bookworks*
Cover design: *Ben Santora*
Manufacturing buyer: *Kelly Behr and Susan Brunke*
Acquisitions editor: *Greg Doench*
Cover photo: *Courtesy Trustees of the National Maritime Museum.*
  (A cosmographer at work. Drawn by J. Stradanus, late sixteenth century.)

Prentice Hall Software Series, Brian W. Kernighan, Advisor

 Published by Prentice-Hall, Inc.
A Division of Simon & Schuster
Englewood Cliffs, New Jersey 07632

The publisher offers discounts on this book when ordered
in bulk quantities. For more information, write:
  Special Sales/College Marketing
  Prentice-Hall, Inc.
  College Technical and Reference Division
  Englewood Cliffs, NJ 07632

UNIX® is a registered trademark of UNIX System Laboratories, Inc.

Printed in the United States of America
10 9 8 7 6 5 4 3 2 1

ISBN   0-13-829763-0

Prentice-Hall International (UK) Limited, *London*
Prentice-Hall of Australia Pty. Limited, *Sydney*
Prentice-Hall Canada Inc., *Toronto*
Prentice-Hall Hispanoamericana, S.A., *Mexico*
Prentice-Hall of India Private Limited, *New Delhi*
Prentice-Hall of Japan, Inc., *Tokyo*
Simon & Schuster Asia Pty, Ltd., *Singapore*
Editora Prentice-Hall do Brasil, Ltda., *Rio de Janeiro*

For Gloria—Bill Frakes

For Susan—Chris Fox

For my wife and friend Laurie and our children
Mary Elizabeth and Emily Elise—Brian Nejmeh

Contents

Preface

This is a book about software engineering in the UNIX®* programming environment using the C programming language. There are already many books about software engineering, about the C language, and about the UNIX operating system. This book is different because it puts the tools and techniques offered by the UNIX/C environment into the context of a software engineering life cycle. This approach, based on software engineering courses we have taught at Rutgers and Columbia, has several advantages. First, it helps to make clear how these tools and techniques contribute to the overall goals of a software engineering project. Second, it clarifies the relationships among the tools and techniques. Finally, it shows which parts of the life cycle have strong tool support and which do not.

In selecting texts for software engineering courses, we found that many failed to provide examples of life-cycle products such as requirements documents and design documents. Students using these texts were often confused when given the task of creating life-cycle products for class projects, and we have been asked by practitioners for examples of life-cycle products as well. In this book, we present life-cycle products we created in building **ccount**, a small C metrics tool.

One question a reader of a book like this one might ask is: How much of the large and diverse field of software engineering does the book cover? This book is aimed primarily at those software engineers responsible for generating, testing, and documenting elegant, reliable, efficient, and maintainable code. Our bias, therefore, is strongly toward the *technical* rather than the *managerial* aspects of software engineering, a distinction we make as follows:

---

*UNIX is a registered trademark of AT&T. Hereafter we will use the abbreviation UNIX/C to stand for UNIX system C programming language.

- The managerial side of software engineering is concerned with project planning and scheduling, software cost estimation, project monitoring, project organization, and staff management.
- The technical side of software engineering is concerned with software design and implementation, software testing and quality assurance, and software maintenance.

In addressing the technical side of software engineering, we do not mean to belittle or slight software engineering managers. In fact, we believe that managing a software project is among the most difficult and important of all software engineering tasks. There is more than enough to be said about the technical aspects of software engineering in the UNIX/C environment to fill this book, however. In addition, managerial practices are inherently more generic than technical practices; managing a project in the UNIX/C environment is not very different from managing a project in other programming environments. Consequently we have little to say about software project management not already discussed in other excellent books. [1] [2] [3] [4] [5] [6] [7]

We hope that this book will be useful as both a tutorial and a reference for anyone building systems in C under some version of the UNIX operating system. The book should be of interest to designers, C programmers, and testers. Despite its technical orientation, this book should also be useful to managers responsible for products developed in the UNIX/C environment because it provides a catalog of the methods, tools, techniques, and practices available to their staff. This book should also be useful to students of computer science and engineering studying software engineering.

In our discussion we assume that our readers know how to program, and are at least novice users of the C programming language and the UNIX operating system. We do not assume any familiarity with software engineering, although, again, our survey of the field purposely neglects management issues, so our discussion of software engineering is incomplete.

One decision we faced in writing this book was whether to discuss UNIX tools that are not generally available. We decided to discuss the best tools we know of for UNIX/C development regardless of their availability. These tools demonstrate technologies to solve certain problems; a reader familiar with a technique for solving a problem can build the tool for himself or herself if necessary. For similar reasons, we also discuss needed tools that seem feasible but do not currently exist.

ACKNOWLEDGMENTS

Many people have contributed to this book. We would like to thank the following at Bell Laboratories: Tom Beattie, Susan Crocker, Nancy Firestone, Ed Fuchs, Judith Grass, Jeff Hooper, Brian Kernighan, Jim Krist, David Lubinsky, and Dave Neal. Our thanks to Steve Simmons at SUN Microsystems and P. J. Plauger of Plauger Associates for their helpful reviews. A special thanks to all our students at Rutgers and Columbia, especially Fritz Henglein, Maria Leone, and Bud Moore.

Chris Fox
Bill Frakes
Brian Nejmeh

REFERENCES

1. Boehm, B., *Software Engineering Economics*. Englewood Cliffs, N.J.: Prentice Hall, 1981.

2. Brooks, F. P., *The Mythical Man-Month*. Reading, Mass.: Addison Wesley, 1975.

3. DeMarco, T., *Controlling Software Projects: Management, Measurement and Estimation*. Englewood Cliffs, N.J.: Yourdon, 1982.

4. DeMarco, T., and T. Lister, *Peopleware: Productive Projects and Teams*. New York: Dorset House, 1987.

5. Fairley, R. E., *Software Engineering Concepts*. New York: McGraw-Hill, 1985.

6. Pressman, R. S., *Software Engineering: A Practitioner's Approach*. New York: McGraw-Hill, 1987.

7. Vick, C. R., and C. V. Ramamoorthy (eds.), *Handbook of Software Engineering*. New York: Van Nostrand, 1984.

1

Introduction

1.1 SOFTWARE ENGINEERING

On 15 January, 1990, AT&T's nationwide long-distance network was crippled for nine hours by a software fault. Millions of calls were blocked. Businesses such as travel agencies that depend on telephone service were virtually shut down. This was yet another demonstration of the importance of software in our lives and the sensitivity of our society to software errors.

The discipline that deals with such problems is called *software engineering.* Software engineering has been a recognized discipline only since the late 1960s. Still in its infancy, software engineering lacks a firm scientific basis. Indeed, software engineers disagree about the definition of the field itself. We define software engineering as the technical and managerial discipline concerned with the systematic invention, production, and maintenance of high-quality software systems, delivered on time, at minimum cost.

Software engineering has borrowed from many fields including computer science, mathematics, economics, and management theory. We focus on one part of this broad field—how to use a programming environment to produce high-quality software systems. Specifically, we discuss how to write such systems in the UNIX®* System C language environment. Our focus is thus on the technical rather than the managerial side of software engineering.

*UNIX is a registered trademark of AT&T.

1.2 UNIX SYSTEM AND C LANGUAGE

UNIX is a time-shared operating system originally written by Ken Thompson of Bell Laboratories in 1969. UNIX has two main parts. The UNIX kernel is a set of frequently used functions that are kept in main memory. The kernel schedules jobs, controls hardware, and manages input and output. The UNIX shell interprets commands sent to the system. "UNIX" is also often used to denote the set of tools and utilities—editors, compilers, software engineering support tools, and so forth—that typically come with the system. Many versions of UNIX exist. The best known are AT&T UNIX System V, and Berkeley UNIX—officially known as UCB 4.xBSD. Versions of UNIX are similar, but differ in their implementations and in the tools and utilities they provide. For example, several UNIX shells are available: the Bourne shell, the C shell,[1] and (our favorite) the Korn Shell.[2] All these shells can be used with different kernels.

The C language was written in 1970 by Dennis Ritchie. Thompson and Ritchie rewrote the UNIX kernel in C in the early 1970s, and since then, UNIX and C have been linked. C was originally written as an alternative to assembly language for systems programming. As such, it allows a programmer great freedom—it is lax, for example, in its handling of data types. It also allows low-level access to the machine. C is known for producing fast, efficient code.

C has become enormously popular. Besides systems programming, C is used to build large-application software systems. The latest generation of large switching systems at Bell Laboratories, containing millions of lines of code, for example, is written in C. Whether C is a good language for large-system software engineering is the subject of heated, often religious, debate. Until enough empirical data are gathered to answer this question, all we can say is that it has been used successfully to build large systems.

One indication of the popularity of UNIX/C is the many books about them. These books describe both the C language and the UNIX system, and give detailed guidance to their use. In this book we do *not* provide detailed guidance to the use of the tools and techniques we discuss. Our purpose is to put UNIX/C in a large software engineering system context—to show how UNIX/C can be used throughout the life cycle to support a software engineering project.

1.3 STATE OF THE ART IN SOFTWARE ENGINEERING

Although many important technical contributions have been made to software engineering (for example, the development of high-level programming languages) the state of the art is far from what software engineers would like. Common practice is worse. Software development projects often have low productivity, and software products are often full of faults and do not meet user needs. To illustrate the extent of the problem, consider the findings of a study of nine Department of Defense software development contracts totaling $6.8 million:[3]

- On software that was delivered but never successfully used, $3.2 million was spent.

- On software that was paid for but not delivered, $1.95 million was spent.

- On software that was delivered and used, but had to be extensively reworked or later abandoned, $1.3 million was spent.
- Out of the $6.8 million, $119,000 was spent on software that was used as delivered.

Unfortunately, such waste is common. Most large technical organizations can chronicle legendary software disasters.

Although software project failures are often attributed mainly to managerial problems, technical sources of waste and inefficiency contribute to project failures, and certainly contribute to high costs. For example, one well-known source of waste attributable in part to technical problems is failure to reuse software. DeMarco estimates that the average project reuses only 5 percent of code, despite evidence that much more code could be reused.[4] Technical problems about how to design, catalog, store, and retrieve reusable software components are not yet solved. One reason the UNIX/C software development environment is important for software engineering is that UNIX contains many small reusable tools. Reusable function libraries are a staple of the C language. We discuss these issues in greater detail in Chapter 6.

What can be done about the poor state of software engineering? One approach is better education about the problems of software engineering, and about the best available tools and techniques to solve them. This task is not adequately addressed by academic and industrial courses in programming and software engineering. In our experience doing and teaching software engineering, hiring and supervising software engineers, and interacting with developers on many projects, we have observed a widespread lack of knowledge about software engineering problems, and a host of bad practices. Some unfortunately common observations follow:

- Managers with no background in software engineering responsible for technical work in major software projects.
- Employees with little software engineering experience responsible for difficult technical tasks, such as the design or implementation of major portions of software systems, with inadequate technical training and guidance.
- Graduates of computer science programs at major universities who have never heard of software engineering, let alone the tools and techniques for producing high-quality software products. Many computer science programs do not offer courses in software engineering, or if they do, the courses are optional and focus on programming.

1.4 SOFTWARE PRODUCTS, PROJECTS, AND METHODOLOGIES

Software is some executable object such as source code, object code, or a complete program. A *software product* is software plus all the supporting items and services that together meet a user's needs.† A software product has many parts including manuals,

---

†Some authors refer to what we have called "software products" as simply "software." We prefer our terminology because it more closely reflects common usage.

references, tutorials, installation instructions, sample data, educational services, technical support services, and so forth. Software engineers produce software products, not just software.

Anything produced by a *software project* is a *work product*. Work products include (1) engineering documents used to define, control, and monitor the work effort; (2) executable objects like prototypes, test harnesses, and special purpose development tools; and (3) data used for testing, project tracking, and so forth. Software engineers help produce most work products because they have technical content. In fact, software engineers often spend more time working on nonsoftware work products, especially documents, than they do working on software.

1.5 SOFTWARE PROJECT SIZE AND TYPE

Software projects come in many sizes. One way to classify them is by lines of code[‡] as in Table 1.1.

Table 1.1:   Project Size Categories

Category	Programmers	Duration	Lines of Code	Example
Trivial	1	0–4 weeks	<1K	Sort utility
Small	1	1–6 months	1K–3K	Function library
Medium	2–5	0.5–2 years	3K–50K	Production C compiler
Large	5–20	2–3 years	50K–100K	Small operating system
Very large	100–1000	4–5 years	100K–1M	Large operating system
Gigantic	1000–5000	5–10 years	>1M	Switching systems

The largest software projects employ thousands of programmers, managers, and support personnel. System files and functions number in the tens of thousands and may be distributed across many machines. Changes made to one file may affect hundreds of others—and all the people who work on them. It is the complexity of the interrelationships among all these system elements that distinguishes software engineering in the large. It is difficult for someone who has not worked in a large project environment to appreciate this complexity. This is one barrier to teaching software engineering. People familiar with software engineering techniques for small projects may think that these techniques will scale up to large projects. This is usually not so. Software engineering tools, for example, sometimes do not work for large or distributed systems. Informal change management techniques adequate for a group of five developers will be disastrous for a group of fifty.

[‡] A *line of code* is a common measure of program size, but there is not a standard definition of what a line of code is. In this book, a line of code is a source code file line containing at least one language token outside a comment.

Software engineering practices are important for projects of every size. For large, very large, or gigantic projects, they are indispensable, because systems of such size could not be built without them. There is empirical evidence that project size has a major effect on important project attributes, such as individual programmer productivity, which decreases exponentially as system size and development team size increase. The reason for this effect is probably the need for more coordination and communication on a big project. Conte et. al.[5] provide a good discussion of empirical studies of factors affecting software projects.

Another factor that varies with project size is the amount of required project documentation. A trivial project, say a simple source code metrics program like **ccount**, may not need any engineering documents, and no more user documentation than a manual page. In contrast, a medium-sized project, such as a C compiler, should have a set of engineering documents that includes at least a concept exploration and feasibility document, a requirements document, a project plan, design documents, a test plan, and a project summary. The user needs at least a manual, and typically also tutorials, quick reference cards, installation instructions, and so forth. It would be wasteful (and discouraging to the developer) to require as much documentation for the metrics utility as for the C compiler. Nevertheless, such demands are sometimes made. This is a common example of software engineering practices inappropriately applied.

Projects differ in type as well. The performance requirements, designs, implementation strategies, testing methods, and problems encountered differ substantially for operating system programs, scientific application programs, business application programs, and embedded real-time systems. Productivity differences between different types of software projects have frequently been observed.[5] Software engineering practices must be adapted to projects in different domains.

The set of tools, techniques, and methods used by software engineers in a software project is called a *project methodology*. Choosing the right methodology for a project is difficult. The lead software engineer must form a project methodology by selecting from the available tools, techniques, and methods those appropriate for his or her project.

1.6 SOFTWARE LIFE CYCLE AND LIFE-CYCLE MODELS

Project methodologies are applied within the context of a *software life cycle*—the series of developmental stages, called *phases*, through which a software product passes from initial conception through retirement from service. A *life-cycle model* is a representation of the software life cycle that may also include information flows, decision points, milestones, and so forth. We stress that a life-cycle model is only that: a model. No real project will behave exactly as specified by a life-cycle model, and the divergence may be large.

The phases of a life-cycle model may be *temporal phases*—forming a sequence in time—or *logical phases*—representing steps not forming a temporal sequence. For example, implementation logically precedes testing, but parts of the implementation and testing phases may occur simultaneously. Thus a life cycle model using logical phases may have an implementation phase before a testing phase, whereas a model using temporal phases may have these phases overlap. A life-cycle model may be used *prescriptively* to mandate life-cycle events or *descriptively* to record life-cycle events. Many software life-cycle models have been proposed.[6] Most models agree on the fundamental phases of the life cycle, but differ in terminology, emphasis, flexibility, and scope. A detailed prescriptive temporal model is useful in a project plan because it maps the project's intended course. Descriptive temporal models are useful in documenting the life cycle and analyzing a project when it is over.

The life-cycle model we use in this book is a general prescriptive logical model. It is general in that it presents only the logical sequence of life-cycle phases. Although it would be better to present a specific temporal model, no such model will fit all software projects. Like other parts of a software methodology, specific life-cycle models must be constructed for specific software projects.

Our model is a standard waterfall model[7] consisting of the following logical phases:

- *Concept exploration and feasibility analysis phase.* Identify a need to automate a process and analyze project feasibility.
- *Requirements specification phase.* Analyze and document system requirements. The requirements document must clearly state *what* the projected system will do, what elements the software product will have, and what characteristics the product elements must have.
- *Design phase.* Design the system and document the design. The design document specifies *how* to build a software system to satisfy the requirements.
- *Implementation phase.* Write the software.
- *Testing phase.* Exercise the software to verify that it satisfies its requirements.
- *Maintenance phase.* Following deployment of the software product, correct faults; change and enhance the system.

This model, like any other, only loosely represents how a project actually works (Figure 1.1). Too many unforeseen things happen on a software project for any model to be more than a general guide. The waterfall model is often criticized as having little to do with project realities. Despite this, it is still the model most often used on large projects. Furthermore, it is a useful pedagogical framework, which is why we adopt it here.

1.7 ATTRIBUTES OF SOFTWARE QUALITY

Quality is linked to meeting user needs. One way to link quality with user needs is to follow Juran[8] in defining quality as *fitness for use*. Juran distinguishes two aspects of fitness for use: the collection of product features that meet user needs and freedom from deficiencies. A product with a collection of features that enables it to meet a user's needs makes for customer satisfaction. Freedom from deficiencies avoids customer dissatisfaction. Together these aspects of a product make it fit for use, or of high quality.

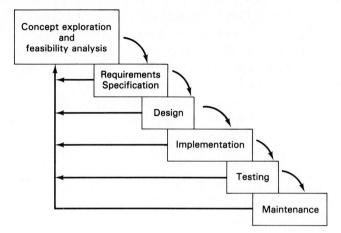

Figure 1.1   Waterfall Model of Software Life Cycle.

The quality of finished software products depends largely on the quality of the work products generated during development and maintenance. The notion of quality as fitness for use yields attributes for evaluating the quality of work products based on the needs of the users of the work product. For example, requirements specification documents are used by customers and developers to record decisions and agreements about the product to be built, by designers as a definitive source of information about the product to be designed, by documenters as a source of information about how the product will behave and how it should be used, and by testers as a source of information about how the system should behave in response to test data, and about its performance parameters. These needs motivate specific quality attributes for requirements specification documents—for example, that all requirements be testable, precise, and clear; that performance constraints be explicitly stated; and so forth. Similar quality attributes can be generated for all work products; it turns out that most work products share a core set of quality attributes that includes the following:

- *Correct.* The definition of correctness varies. For example, a requirements document is correct if it accurately describes needed functions and properties of a product; software is correct when it meets its input-output requirements; program documentation is correct when it accurately describes a program.
- *Efficient.* This attribute refers to how well software uses computational resources. For example, quicksort is more efficient than bubblesort because it can sort a list with fewer machine instructions.
- *Maintainable.* This attribute can be applied to any work product but is most often applied to software. Maintainability is how easily a work product can be corrected, changed, or enhanced.
- *Portable.* Refers to how easily software can be moved to a variety of environments.
- *Readable.* This attribute applies to any textual work product. It refers to how easy it is for a person to read and understand the work product.

- *Reliable*. This attribute is usually applied to software and refers to the ability of software to operate according to its requirements for an extended period of use.
- *Reusable*. This can be a characteristic of any work product and refers to how easily a work product, or its components, can be incorporated into systems other than the one for which it was developed.
- *Robust*. This attribute is usually applied to software and refers to how well a program continues to operate correctly in the face of invalid input.
- *Testable*. This attribute refers to how easily a work product can be fully, accurately, efficiently, and systematically exercised to see whether it satisfies its requirements.
- *Well documented*. This attribute refers to how well a software product is supported by material (other than source code) that adequately describes its installation, operation, maintenance, repair, development, construction, and evolution.

These quality attributes have complex inter-relationships. For example, highly optimized code is often concise but not very readable. Less readable code is usually less maintainable. Conversely, optimized code is usually more efficient.

Programmers are able to increase certain quality attributes of their programs, though usually at the expense of others.[9] Software engineers must decide which quality attributes are most important for their projects. For instance, if a system is expected to have a long life, maintainability and portability may be most important, whereas efficiency may be somewhat less important. Software engineering practices, standards, and techniques could then be put in place to promote maintainability and portability, though perhaps at the expense of efficiency. This point illustrates once again the importance and difficulty of choosing an appropriate project methodology.

1.8 GOALS AND ORGANIZATION OF BOOK

Software engineering problems are formidable, and much remains to be discovered. Still, many valuable tools, techniques, and methods are available for building high-quality software products. As we noted earlier, one shortcoming of current software engineering practice is that many software engineers and managers are unaware of what is available. This is true of software engineering practices in general. It is also true of software engineering practices in particular software development environments. For example, many software engineers who develop C programs under the UNIX system are unaware of the tools available to them in the UNIX environment, and of the techniques, methods, and practices that can be used to build high quality software products with the C programming language. The main goal of this book is to provide a guide to the tools and methods of the UNIX/C environment, within the context of a software life cycle. It is not meant to provide detailed instruction in the use of these tools and methods. The book can serve both as a tutorial introduction to software engineering in the UNIX/C environment, and as a reference when forming methodologies for UNIX/C development projects.

The book is organized according to the waterfall life-cycle model. It discusses tools, techniques, and methods for each life-cycle phase. Chapter 2 discusses both the concept exploration and feasibility analysis phase, and the requirements phase. Chapter 3 discusses the design phase. Because most of the tools, techniques, and methods in the UNIX/C environment are for the implementation and testing phases, our longest discussions deal with these phases. Chapters 4 to 6 discuss C coding practices: Chapter 4 is about program readability, Chapter 5 is about low-level programming, and Chapter 6 is about high-level programming. Chapter 7 surveys UNIX/C coding tools. Chapter 8 discusses methods for software quality assurance, including testing. Chapter 9 discusses change management practices and the maintenance phase. Chapter 10 presents some thoughts on the future of UNIX/C as a software engineering environment.

We develop a small software product to illustrate our discussion. The system, called **ccount**, is a C source code metrics tool that reports counts of commentary and noncommentary source lines, and comment-to-code ratios. All **ccount** material is collected in appendices. The **ccount** program is neither powerful nor complex; in practice it would not merit the attention we lavish on it. However, **ccount** provides a simple but interesting example that is not so complex that it overwhelms the material it is supposed to illustrate.

REFERENCES

1. Thomas, R., L. R. Rogers, and J. L. Yates, *Advanced Programmer's Guide to UNIX System V*. New York: McGraw-Hill, 1986.

2. Bolsky, I. M., and D. G. Korn, *The KornShell*. Englewood Cliffs, N.J.: Prentice Hall, 1989.

3. Cox, B. J., *Object Oriented Programming*. Reading, Mass.: Addison-Wesley, 1986.

4. DeMarco, T., and T. Lister, *Controlling Software Projects: Management, Measurement, and Evaluation*. Seminar Notes. New York: Atlantic Systems Guild, 1984.

5. Conte, S., H. Dunsmore, and V. Shen, *Software Engineering Models and Metrics*. Reading, Mass.: Benjamin/Cummings, 1986.

6. Agresti, W. (ed.), *Tutorial: New Paradigms for Software Development*. Los Angeles: IEEE Computer Society Press, 1986.

7. Royce, W. W., "Managing the Development of Large Software Systems: Concepts and Techniques," *Proceedings WESCON* (August 1970), 1–6.

8. Juran, J. M., *Juran's Quality Control Handbook* (4th ed.). New York: McGraw-Hill, 1988.

9. Weinberg, G., *The Psychology of Computer Programming*. New York: Van Nostrand Reinhold, 1971.

2

Concept Exploration and Requirements Specification

Many projects fail because of insufficient early analysis. Significant resources are expended before the system developers realize that the system is infeasible. The concept exploration and requirements specification phases address these issues. These phases are the least tractable and least formal portions of the life cycle, and have the weakest support from tools and techniques. Perhaps because of this, they are often treated lightly by software engineers. The early phases of the life cycle are vitally important to the success of software projects, however, because decisions are made in these phases determining the viability of the finished product, and because errors made in these phases are far more difficult and expensive to fix than errors made later. In this chapter we consider the problems that must be dealt with early in the life cycle, and discuss the tools and techniques available to help solve them.

2.1 CONCEPT EXPLORATION PHASE

Software systems are conceived when a process needs to be automated. If the projected software system is substantial, then the need for it and its feasibility must be established. All too often, software products are developed that amount to solutions looking for problems, or that solve minor problems while major problems go unaddressed. Software development projects are often begun without any hope of ever being completed because it is not technically nor politically feasible to complete them. Careful groundwork in the concept exploration phase of the life cycle can help avoid these problems.

Technical people sometimes underestimate the importance of human interaction in the software engineering process. To answer the questions raised in the concept exploration phase, for example, one must often interact extensively with potential clients for the system, with managers who control needed resources, with other organizations that might be affected by the work, and with many others. Failure to interact effectively with these groups can easily doom a project.

2.1.1 Concept Exploration Process

In the concept exploration phase, a proposed system is analyzed and investigated to determine its merits. The analysis consists of defining what problem the new system will solve and, at a high level, how the system will solve it. The investigation consists of considering whether the new system should be built, whether it must be built (rather than bought), and whether it can be built.

The first step in concept exploration (problem and solution clarification) should include the following:

- The problem to be solved by the new system should be stated precisely. This exercise usually leads to better understanding of both the problem domain and the projected system.
- The system constraints should be explored and stated explicitly. For example, there may be limits on the computational resources available to the system because of other demands on the computer.
- The target operational environment should be stated.
- The goals for the system and project should be stated. System goals include desired nonfunctional aspects of the system, such as the level of user documentation, or the robustness of the system. Project goals include desired benefits to the organization, such as increased productivity, or software development experience.
- The features and functions of the new system should be sketched at a high level of generality. Acceptance criteria for the new system (the essential tasks it must do) should be stated.

Once the new system has been specified in some detail, one should investigate whether the system should, must, and can be built. Start by considering whether the new software system *should* be built. Software development is an expensive business: Building the wrong system leads to disaster no matter how well the development process is implemented. In general, a software system should be built only if it provides a cost-effective solution to an important problem. Four considerations implicit in the last sentence follow:

- *Is the problem solved by the new system important?* An important problem is one that requires a solution crucial to the major work of an organization or an individual. If the solution can only be reached through tedious, error-prone, or time-consuming effort, automation may help.

- *Does the problem solved by the software arise frequently?* A problem that arises once every few years, for example, may not warrant the expense of a software development project.

- *Is the potential user population for the new system large enough?* This is a marketing question. Probably more software products have failed because their markets were too small than for any other reason. Market determination is a difficult process often requiring extensive research and systems engineering. One useful method is to profile typical potential users. Such information can lead to changes in what the new system does or in its constraints. For example, it may be necessary to add more extensive help facilities to a program intended for inexperienced users. Another factor that makes market determination difficult is that markets are constantly changing. A market that looks lucrative at the beginning of a long development process may not be when the product is completed.

- *Does the automated system provide a better solution to the problem?* Computers are not the best answer to every problem—less technical solutions are sometimes better. A good example is the mechanized appointment calendar. Mechanized calendars, particularly for personal computers, are commonly available. Few people use them much, however, because they are inconvenient. Appointment calendars are needed at meetings, at lunch, at public telephones, as well as at one's desk. A paper pocket calendar provides a more useful solution than does a computer in this case.

The concept exploration phase frequently leads to changed ideas about the new system, new understanding of system constraints, and altered goals for the system and the project. If the new product should be built, the next point to consider is whether the new system *must* be built. Perhaps there is already a software system to solve the problem. If so, then it will almost certainly be cheaper, faster, and easier to buy it than it will be to build it.

The final task in concept exploration is feasibility analysis, which is an investigation of whether the new system *can* be built. Feasibility includes two major components: technical feasibility and political feasibility.

- A system is *technically feasible* if there are proven hardware and software methods, tools, and techniques to build the system. For example, a software system to comprehend natural language fully is not currently technically feasible. Sometimes long and expensive studies, themselves requiring a large software component, are required to investigate technical feasibility. In investigating technical feasibility, insights about the development strategy may also arise. For example, a sophisticated prototype may solve the problem without the need for a larger development effort. The computing environment needed to support development and maintenance is also likely to become clear at this stage.

- A system is *politically feasible* if there is adequate organizational support for it, and adequate resources available to complete it. Political feasibility depends on factors like the stability of funding and personnel, management commitment to long-term research and development efforts, the existence of clear organizational goals, and so forth.

Again, feasibility discoveries for the new system may lead to changes in its features and functionality, the constraints governing the system, and the goals of the project and the system.

The need for a software system, and its feasibility, change over time—often rapidly. These questions should be re-examined throughout the software life cycle. Although many projects fail because of an inadequate job in the concept exploration phase, many others fail because the conclusions and decisions made during this phase are never reconsidered later in the life cycle. It is probably wise to build re-reviews of the concept exploration and feasibility document into the life cycle.[1]

2.1.2 Concept Exploration Document

The final task in the concept exploration phase is the preparation of a *concept exploration document* that records the findings of the concept exploration phase. This document serves as a basis for decisions about proceeding with the project and input to the requirements specification phase of the life cycle.

As an illustration, we have written a concept exploration document for a simple C source code metrics program called **ccount**. We will use **ccount** as an example throughout the book. In doing so we will produce a requirements document, a design document, prototypes in the UNIX shell language and **awk**, a C program, a test plan, and test results. In terms of our project size categories **ccount** is trivial and therefore unrepresentative of typical software projects, which are medium to large in size. We needed a small example for the purposes of illustration. Furthermore, **ccount** has been found useful in larger development projects. Similar documentation for a large project has been published by the Naval Research Laboratory.[2] The engineering documents for our tool are collected in Appendix A. The source code is listed in Appendix B.

2.1.3 Concept Exploration Phase Tools and Techniques

There are virtually no UNIX tools and few formal techniques specifically designed to help with the concept exploration portion of the life cycle. Text editors can be used to write and change the concept exploration document, and the "writers workbench"[3] can be used to help with spelling, grammar, punctuation, and writing style. Version management tools like **SCCS** (see Chapter 9) are useful in maintaining successive versions of concept exploration documents.

A template for our concept exploration document appears in Appendix C.

2.2 REQUIREMENTS SPECIFICATION PHASE

A *software product requirement* is a feature, function, capability, or property that a software product must have. Requirements may be either functional, describing a feature the system will provide, or nonfunctional, describing a constraint under which the system must operate. A *requirements specification document* is a statement of all the requirements for a software product. The goal of the requirements specification phase of the life cycle is to determine software product requirements and state them in a requirements specification document.

The main point in determining and stating requirements is that requirements explain *what* a system is to do and not *how* the system is to do it. This is, however, sometimes difficult. If how the system will do something must be described it should be done at the highest possible level of abstraction. There is a natural tendency, especially for programmers, to stray from stating requirements in favor of specifying design and implementation details. This tendency must be resisted during this phase of the life cycle.

As we discussed for the concept exploration phase, the requirements phase is critically dependent on understanding the needs of potential users. This often requires extensive interaction with potential customers. The Joint Application Design (JAD) methodology for helping with user interactions in the requirements phase is discussed later.

2.2.1 Requirements Specification Document

A requirements specification document serves two major purposes. First, it serves as a guide during the rest of the life cycle. The requirements specification document drives the design and implementation phases because it specifies the essential features of the system. During testing and validation, the requirements serve as the standard against which the finished system is judged for correctness and adequacy. After deployment, the requirements document serves again as a standard for bug fixes, and also as the basis for decisions about changes and enhancements.

Second, the requirements specification document serves as an agreement, or contract, between the developers and clients. The requirements tell the developer what to deliver and tell the client what to expect. As such it is the basis for settling disputes between developers and clients, should any arise, when the system is delivered.

A requirements specification document should contain the following information:

- *Product overview.* Describe the major functions and components of the system in general terms. Summarize the rationale for building the system for readers unfamiliar with the project.

- *Development, operating, and maintenance environments.* Describe the hardware and software resources and tools necessary to build and maintain the product. Specify the target hardware and software environment, including the optimal and minimal configurations for the use of the product.

- *Conceptual model.* Present a conceptual model of the system (a high-level view showing the major services and components of the system and their relationships with each other). Graphical notations are usually preferred for this task, but other mechanisms, such as clear English, decision tables, grammars, and so on, may be used.

- *User interface specifications.* Describe screens, windows, graphics, and other visual aspects of the system. State any special keyboard key bindings. Define any command languages. Specify the interaction or dialogue conventions governing the user interface in complete detail. Because these specifications are often difficult to state on paper, user interface prototypes are sometimes used (see later discussion).

- *Functional requirements.* Describe the services, operations, data transformations, and so forth, provided by the system. This portion of a requirements document is usually the largest, because system functionality must be described fully and precisely. Many formal methods and notations may be employed for this purpose.

- *Nonfunctional requirements.* State the constraints under which the software must operate. Typical nonfunctional requirements deal with efficiency, reliability, robustness, portability, maximum memory size, quality standards, response time, cost, maintainability, and so on.

- *External interfaces and database requirements.* Describe the interfaces to other systems. The logical organization of databases used by the system also should be described.

- *Error handling.* Catalog exceptional conditions and error conditions, and responses to these conditions, as completely as possible.

- *Foreseeable changes and enhancements.* State any foreseeable changes and enhancements for the benefit of the designers and implementers. Such changes generally arise from hardware evolution, changing user needs, the introduction of other systems in the operating environment, and so forth.

- *Design, implementation, and testing hints and guidelines.* Inevitably, design, implementation, and testing insights come to mind during the requirements phase of a project. Such insights should not be lost, even though they do not properly belong in the requirements specification document. This section of the document provides a place for statements of design features, constraints, testing strategies, pitfalls, or other observations.

- *Glossary.* Define all software engineering technical terms for the benefit of customers and all application technical terms for the benefit of software engineers.

- *Index.* Provide a standard alphabetical index. Other kinds of indexes may be provided as well.

Although the initial version of the requirements specification document is completed during the requirements specification phase of the life cycle, it will change and should be placed under version control (see Chapter 9). Unexpected changes in customer needs, funding, personnel, resources, hardware, and so on may lead to changed requirements. Unexpected difficulties during design, implementation, or testing often force changes in requirements.

An example requirements document for **ccount**, our C metrics tool, is included in Appendix A.

2.2.2 Quality Criteria for Requirements Documents

In writing a requirements document every attempt should be made to ensure that it meets the following criteria:

- *Completeness.* All functions, features, capabilities, constraints, and other properties of the target system are described in detail.
- *Testability.* Each requirement is stated so that it can be tested. For example, the statement "the system must respond to queries in a reasonable amount of time" is not testable. A testable equivalent might be, "the system must respond to any query within 10 seconds."
- *Consistency.* Requirements do not conflict with one another. Terms are used consistently.
- *Conciseness.* No extraneous information is included in the requirements document. In practice this means that information about the project history, costs, schedule, and so on appears elsewhere.
- *Readability.* The requirements document is easy to read and understand, and each requirement is stated unambiguously.
- *Traceability.* Means are provided to verify whether the requirements are realized in design and code. Numbering individual requirements and referring to them by number in design documents and the source code can help.
- *Feasibility.* All requirements can be satisfied using the tools, techniques, people, and budget available. Prototyping may be needed to help determine feasibility. Although feasibility should have been considered during the concept exploration phase, the requirements specification phase is a good time to re-evaluate feasibility.
- *Changeability.* The requirements specification document is written so that it is easy to change later in the life cycle.

2.2.3 Requirements Phase Tools and Techniques

Completeness, testability, and consistency are crucial quality attributes of requirements documents that are difficult to achieve and verify using English. Natural language does not lend itself to formal analysis (at least not yet), so it is difficult to ensure these attributes for natural language requirements documents. In an effort to overcome this problem, much work has gone into developing formal requirements specification techniques. Davis[4] provides an excellent overview and comparison of many of these techniques.

Techniques for formal requirements specification include finite state machines, decision tables and trees, and pseudocode languages. Two important criteria that any of these techniques must satisfy is that they be comprehensible to an end user and general enough to express anything the requirements writer needs to say. Because none of the formal techniques completely meet these criteria, requirements are still almost always written in natural language despite the problems mentioned earlier.

Templates that give a consistent structure to requirements documents are useful. A sample requirements document template based on our discussion appears in Appendix C. In addition, our `ccount` example uses this template.

The UNIX system provides little support for the requirements phase of the life cycle, as it provides little support for the concept exploration phase. The powerful text processing and version management tools available in the UNIX environment are good for writing and maintaining requirements specification documents, however, and for writing and maintaining concept exploration documents. The UNIX environment also provides some good prototyping tools. These are discussed in the following sections.

2.3 PROTOTYPING AID IN EARLY PHASES OF LIFE CYCLE

A *prototype* is a partial implementation of a software product that typically has limited functionality, low reliability, poor performance, and a lack of robustness. Prototypes are often developed quickly in high-level languages or special prototyping languages, without much attention to correctness, robustness, and so on. Prototypes have four major purposes: (1) to help in developing requirements when they cannot be determined easily; (2) to validate requirements, especially with customers and potential users; (3) to explore technical issues of feasibility, performance, and so forth; and (4) to serve as stages of development when using a prototype evolution development strategy.

There are two kinds of prototypes. *Throwaway prototypes* are built to help clarify or validate requirements or design, or to show feasibility. Once these goals have been achieved, the prototype is discarded. *Minimal useful system prototypes* are built as initial stages of a final system, which is constructed, at least in part, from the prototype. A minimal useful system may also be used to show feasibility, and to help clarify requirements and design.

The possible advantages of constructing a prototype include the following. Misunderstandings between system developers and system users can be identified and corrected. Features that users find confusing can be identified and corrected. Missing or faulty requirements can be identified. A working prototype may be useful for proving to management that a project is feasible and therefore warrants continued support.

The possible disadvantages of constructing a prototype are as follows. System users or funders may want to use the prototype as the final system. Because most prototypes are not built according to exacting standards, this may create a maintenance nightmare. Prototyping may be expensive—the cost of constructing a prototype may be prohibitive. The use of high-level languages for prototyping can help in this regard. Prototypes may not accurately reflect the operating characteristics of the final system. This may result in an inaccurate evaluation of the prototype, particularly by customers and potential users who may not understand the distinction between the prototype and the final system.

In summary, prototypes offer great advantages for exploring, clarifying, and validating requirements, and for exploring and proving feasibility. Prototypes may be misleading, however, or result in poor decision making in the wrong environments. The decision whether to use prototypes depends on the technical and political environment, and the needs of the developers.

Some good prototyping languages, and the domains for which they are most appropriate, are the following:

- *APL*.[5] APL is a powerful language for prototyping mathematical applications. The language offers high-level operations that can speed development enormously. For example, matrix inversion and full vector and matrix mathematical operations are available as primitive operations in the language. APL, however, gives poor support for structured programming.
- *Prolog*.[6] Prolog is a language based on a subset of first-order logic. It makes sophisticated database operations easy to program. Certain kinds of expert systems can also be constructed easily using Prolog. On the negative side, many versions of Prolog offer poor input and output facilities, and little support for floating point arithmetic.
- *The UNIX Shell Language*.[7] [8] The UNIX Shell Language offers a good prototyping environment for many applications. It is interactive and offers many powerful integrated tools for the manipulation of byte streams. The next section discusses the capabilities of the UNIX shell as a prototyping tool in some detail.

Some methods for generating requirements incorporate prototyping as an integral component. JAD[9] is a technique for requirements definition developed at IBM, used there extensively, and now marketed by IBM as a product. The major idea of JAD is to get all parties interested in a software system to meet and agree on its requirements. Because major problems often arise in system development through misunderstandings between system users and system developers, JAD addresses a serious problem of this phase of the life cycle. A primary focus of JAD is to prototype the user interface for interactive systems. Techniques for rapid screen prototyping must be used. JAD is only applicable to those systems whose users are willing to participate in the process. This often presents problems. It is unlikely, for example, that developers of a completely new category of software system will be able to identify such a user population.

2.3.1 UNIX Shell Language as a Prototyping Tool

The UNIX shell language has several features that make it an attractive prototyping tool. First, the UNIX shell provides a wealth of small tools that *filter* data streams, that is, tools that read data from an input source and write data to an output sink. For example: `cat` lists file contents on the standard output; `grep` finds all lines read from the standard input matching a pattern and lists them on the standard output; `cut` selects columns from lines read from the standard input; `sort` sorts lines read from the standard input.

Along with a wealth of filtering tools, the UNIX environment offers the ability to assemble tools so that the output of one tool becomes the input to another. These connections, called *pipes*, and denoted by the vertical bar "|", enable users to make complicated filters from simple filters. For example, suppose we have a file called **partyfile** containing names and political party affiliations as follows:

```
Collins   Republican
Jones     Democrat
Abbott    Democrat
Wilson    Republican
```

A sorted list of all Democrats in the file can be obtained with the following pipeline:

```
cat partyfile | grep Democrat | cut -f1 | sort
```

The output of this pipeline is:

```
Abbott
Jones
```

This pipeline is started when **cat** produces a data stream containing the contents of **partyfile**. This stream is piped to **grep**, which passes along only the lines containing the string "Democrat"—the two middle lines from **partyfile**. **grep**'s output is piped to **cut**, which removes the first field of each line and passes the data along in turn. At this point, the data stream consists of two lines containing the names in the pipe. **sort** orders these lines to produce the result. Clearly many lines of code in a standard programming language, such as C, would be needed to accomplish the same task.

Finally, the UNIX shell language provides control structures that incorporate UNIX tools and pipes. Among these constructs are **if-then-else**, **while**, **for**, and **case** statements. As a short example, suppose we want a shell program to produce a sorted list of Democrats from all files in a directory like those in the preceding example. The following Korn shell program accomplishes this task:

```
# Program to get sorted lists of Democrats
# From all files in the current directory

for FILE in *
    do
        cat $FILE | grep Democrat | cut -f1 | sort
    done
```

The **for**-loop works by assigning each file in the current directory to the shell variable **FILE** in turn, and executing the loop body.

For some kinds of applications, the speed with which prototypes can be built using the UNIX shell is impressive. We have seen undergraduate students learn the UNIX shell and build a boolean information retrieval system in a few days. The same students often have difficulty building such a system in C in several months.

2.3.2 C Metric Program Prototypes

In concept and design, **ccount** is straightforward (see Appendix A); there is no question of its feasibility, so there is not much need to prototype it. The point of this section is to provide a simple prototyping example, and to show some of the power of the UNIX shell and UNIX tools for prototyping. We present three **ccount** prototypes. The first two are short UNIX shell programs that provide quick and dirty counts. Although simple, these prototypes show some of the usefulness of **ccount**. The third prototype is an **awk** program that meets most of the requirements of **ccount**. Besides demonstrating the power of the **awk** language, it is useful for exploring some of the subtleties of parsing C source code files to generate counts of commentary and noncommentary lines.*

Perhaps the easiest way to estimate the number of noncommentary source lines (NCSL) in a C source file is to count the lines containing semicolons, because a semicolon must be used to terminate many C statements. This will only be a rough estimate because it will miss source code lines containing only curly brackets, many variable declarations, function declaration header lines, and so on. Similarly, commentary source lines (CSL) can be estimated by counting the lines containing comment delimiters. This is also a rough estimate because it misses lines internal to comments. Our first prototype uses these rough means to estimate its counts:

```
#
#     ccount Prototype 1
#
#     This program estimates NCSL and CSL by grepping.
#     NCSL are estimated by grepping on semicolons,
#     and CSL are estimated by grepping on comment
#     delimiters.
#
echo "File        CSL        NCSL        CSL/NCSL"
for FILE do
    NCSL=`grep -c ';' $FILE`
    CSL=`egrep -c '/\*.*\*/' $FILE`
    RATIO=`bc <<-end
        scale=2
        $CSL/$NCSL
        end`
    echo "$FILE    $CSL        $NCSL        $RATIO"
done
```

The first line of this shell program prints a header. The **for**-loop processes each file specified on the command line, assigning each name to the variable **FILE** for one pass through the loop. The body of the loop uses the **grep** and **egrep** programs with the −**c** option (which causes them to count matched lines) to estimate NCSL and CSL.

---

*Our prototypes are written in the Korn shell programming language.[10] All three have been tested on Suns and VAXen. All three are listed in Appendix B.

These estimates are then fed to the calculator program **bc** to compute the comment-to-code ratio. The results are echoed to the standard output.

As a test, Prototype 1 was run on the sample C source file **prog.c** containing 661 NCSL, 433 CSL, and a comment to code ratio of 0.66. Prototype 1 issued the following report:

```
File      CSL    NCSL    CSL/NCSL
prog.c    249    284        .87
```

These estimate are rough. The coding style used in **prog.c** tends to produce many lines of source code without semicolons; **prog.c** also contains many long comments whose internal lines were not counted. A better prototype is clearly desirable.

The next prototype makes use of the C preprocessor to count NCSL accurately. The C preprocessor, besides expanding macros, removes all comments from the source file. It also preserves line breaks, although it adds blank lines. Thus NCSL can be counted by passing a source file through the C preprocessor, then counting the remaining nonblank lines. Counting CSL accurately demands the use of a more powerful tool for text processing than the shell language. We use the UNIX pattern-matching language **awk**[11] in this prototype.

```
#
#    ccount Prototype 2
#
#    This utility counts NCSL using the C preprocessor,
#    counts CSL using awk, and computes the total
#    CSL/NCSL ratio.
#
echo "File        CSL      NCSL     CSL/NCSL"
for FILE do
        sed -e 's/#//g' $FILE > /tmp/ccount.tmp
        NCSL=`/lib/cpp -P < /tmp/ccount.tmp | grep -c '[^    ]'`
        CSL=`awk -f csl.awk $FILE`
        RATIO=`bc <<-end
           scale=2
           $CSL/$NCSL
        end`
        echo "$FILE        $CSL      $NCSL       $RATIO"
done
rm /tmp/ccount.tmp
```

Like Prototype 1, this prototype echoes a header, then loops through each file provided as an argument on the command line. NCSL are counted by passing the input file through the C preprocessor **cpp**, then using **grep** to match on lines containing characters other than blanks and tabs. The **–P** on **cpp** prevents it from adding lines to the file, which would inflate the count. Preliminary processing with **sed** is essential, because the preprocessor imports **#include** files, expands macros, and so on. Removing pound signs from the source file prevents the preprocessor from carrying out its expansions.

The **awk** program **csl.awk** used in this prototype estimates CSL by watching for comment delimiters as the **egrep** estimator did. It also keeps track of whether lines without comment delimiters are inside a comment, however, so it does not fail to count these lines. The **csl.awk** program is the following:

```
#
#        csl.awk
#
#    This awk script counts the commentary source
#    lines in a C source file.
#
BEGIN                  { csl = 0; is_comment = 0 }

                         # skip blank lines
/^[ \t]*$/             { next }
                         # count lines with complete comments
/\/\*.*\*\//           { csl += 1; next }
                         # count lines that open a comment
/\/\*/                 { csl += 1; is_comment = 1; next }
                         # count lines that close a comment
/\*\//                 { csl += 1; is_comment = 0; next }
                         # count lines inside a comment
                       { if ( is_comment ) csl += 1 }

                         # print total csl
END                    { print csl }
```

The output from Prototype 2 is the following:

```
File      CSL    NCSL    CSL/NCSL
prog.c    433    661       .65
```

All the numbers produced by Prototype 2 are correct for **prog.c** (except for a small round-off error in the comment-to-code ratio). This prototype succeeds in producing accurate counts of the total CSL, NCSL, and comment-to-code ratio.

As a basic prototype, Prototype 2 may be enough to show the functionality and explore the usefulness of the tool. Our final prototype is presented to illustrate that powerful programs can be produced using the UNIX shell and UNIX tools like **awk**. Prototype 3 behaves much as specified in the **ccount** requirements. It accepts a −**t** flag, and produces tabbed or nontabbed format reports that display counts and ratios for each function definition, for lines external to any function definition, and for the file as a whole. One major difference between the prototype and the final product is that in the prototype the function delimiter string is fixed as "**Z**," the function start delimiter used in the prototype test program **prog.c**. In **prog.c** the **Z** is **#define**d as nothing and placed before function definitions. Although this is adequate for the prototype, it falls short of the product requirements.

The following shell script drives Prototype 3:

```
#
#   ccount Prototype 3
#
#   This utility counts CSL and NCSL, and computes the
#   CSL/NCSL ratio for each function definition, code
#   external to any function definition, and for the
#   file as a whole.
#
#   It relies on awk to do its counting and most output.
#   The awk program ccount.awk produces reports formatted
#   according to whether the variable F is set to
#   "TABBED" or "NONTABBED".
#
if [ "-t" = $1 ]
    then
    shift
    for FILE do
       echo $FILE
       awk -f ccount.awk F="TABBED" $FILE
    done
else
    for FILE do
       echo
       echo $FILE "          " `date`
       echo
       echo "      Function           CSL    NCSL    CSL/NCSL"
       echo "-------------------------------------------------"
       awk -f ccount.awk F="NONTABBED" $FILE
    done
fi
```

This shell script decides whether a tabbed or nontabbed format report should be produced, prints out headers, and feeds the source files to the **awk** program that does the counting. The **awk** program **ccount.awk** is long; we list it in Appendix B with the other prototypes. The output of Prototype 3 in nontabbed format for **prog.c** satisfies its requirements and produces correct counts for the following example:

```
prog.c    Thu Feb 9 14:41:20 EDT 1989
```

Function	CSL	NCSL	CSL/NCSL
Refresh_Form	23	29	0.79
Build_Form	102	145	0.70
Init_Form_Frames	30	121	0.25
Set_Form_Defaults	42	36	1.17
Ex_Form_Frame	32	44	0.73
Exec_Form	53	61	0.87
external	149	225	0.66
total	433	661	0.66

Prototype 3 behaves like the target system. It might be made more robust, complete, and maintainable, and used as the final system, as suggested in the solution strategy discussion in the Concept Exploration Document. Unfortunately, this prototype is not fast enough. When measured by the UNIX `time` command on a Sun 3/50, Prototype 3 uses almost 9 seconds of CPU time to produce a report for `prog.c`, which is 55,190 bytes long. This clearly does not meet the target of at most 2 seconds of CPU time for files of 40,000 bytes. The final version of `ccount` is able to meet this requirement, taking just over 1 second to process `prog.c`, and under 1 second for files of 40,000 bytes.

2.4 CONCLUSION

The concept exploration and requirements definition phases of the software life cycle are vital for the success of a development project and a software product. They are also the most difficult, the least understood, and the least addressed by proven tools and techniques. The most significant recent technological advance in the concept exploration and requirements phases is the extensive use of prototypes to test feasibility and to refine requirements, particularly user interface requirements. Although the UNIX environment provides powerful prototyping facilities, UNIX tools are best for functional prototyping and usually cannot help to prototype the sophisticated window-based user interfaces that are becoming standard.

REFERENCES

1. Boehm, B., "The Spiral Model of Software Development and Enhancement," *IEEE Computer*, 21, no. 5 (May 1988), 61–72.

2. Henniger, K., J. Kallander, D. Parnas, and J. Shore, *Software Requirements for the A7-E Aircraft*, NRL Memorandum 3876, November 1978.

3. Macdonald, N. H., L. T. Frase, P. S. Gingrich, and S. A. Keenan, "The WRITER'S WORKBENCH: Computer Aids for Text Analysis," *IEEE Transactions on Communications*, 30, no. 1 (January 1982), part 1, 105–110.

4. Davis, A. M., "A Comparison of Techniques for the Specification of External System Behavior," *Comunications of the ACM*, 31, no. 9 (September 1988), 1098–1115.

5. Iverson, K., *A Programming Language*. New York: Wiley, 1962.

6. Clocksin, W. F., and C. S. Mellish, *Programming in Prolog* (3rd ed.). New York: Springer-Verlag, 1986.

7. Kernighan, B. W., and R. Pike, *The UNIX Programming Environment*. Englewood Cliffs, N.J.: Prentice Hall, 1984.

8. Thomas, R., L. R. Rogers, and J. L. Yates, *Advanced Programmer's Guide to UNIX System V*. New York: McGraw-Hill, 1986.

9. Wood, J., *Joint Application Design*. New York: Wiley, 1989.

10. Bolsky, M. I., and D. G. Korn, *The KornShell*. Englewood Cliffs, N.J.: Prentice Hall, 1989.

11. Aho, A., B. Kernighan, and P. Weinberger, *The AWK Programming Language*. Reading, Mass.: Addison-Wesley, 1988.

3

Software Design Process

The design phase focuses on how system requirements are met. During the design phase the structure and processing details of the software product are conceived, documented, and reviewed. A description of a software structure that satisfies software requirements is captured in one or more *design documents* that act as blueprints for the implementation phase, and provide guidance during the testing and maintenance phases. Several important concepts and principles such as abstraction, modularization, cohesion, coupling, and information hiding guide design. We discuss these concepts and principles in the first section.

Software designers also use design methods, notations, and tools. A *design method* is a systematic procedure for producing descriptions of software systems from requirements. Design methods help designers develop a system architecture (a refined conceptual model of the system), define major data elements, and specify high-level processing plans and algorithms. Most design methods include *design notations* for describing system structures, data elements, and processing steps. Design notations include graphs, diagrams, charts, tables, and formal languages, as well as natural language. *Design tools* are programs intended to support the design process by helping to create, analyze, and verify designs. In the second section of the chapter, we discuss four of the most commonly used design methods and their notations. In the third section we review several design tools. In the final section we discuss the contents of a design document—the output of the design process.

3.1 SOFTWARE DESIGN CONCEPTS AND PRINCIPLES

In this section we discuss the design principles of abstraction, cohesion, coupling, modularity, and information hiding.

3.1.1 Abstraction

Abstraction is the suppression of some properties of objects, events, or situations in favor of others. The more properties suppressed, the higher the *level of abstraction*. In software engineering, abstraction usually involves the suppression of details in favor of general properties. This simplifies analysis by ignoring irrelevant differences. For example, a list can be considered at a level of abstraction that ignores insertion and deletion policies. At this level, stacks, queues, dequeues, and general lists are all the same: ordered collections of elements. At a lower level of abstraction, insertion and deletion policies may be considered, but implementation details suppressed. At this level, no distinction is made between stacks implemented using linked lists or arrays. The latter distinction is only made at a third, lower level of abstraction.

The design process can be *bottom-up* or *top-down*. Bottom-up design begins at a low-level of abstraction and works upward to greater generality. Top-down design begins at the highest level of abstraction and works downward toward greater specificity. Strictly top-down or bottom-up approaches are rarely practical, however. The usual approach is to work both top-down and bottom-up, with top-down thinking predominating, and top-down considerations given precedence.

Abstraction is a powerful technique for analysis and design. Levels of abstraction must be carefully and clearly distinguished, and *all* details not appropriate to a particular level of abstraction strictly suppressed. Unfortunately, there are no mechanical procedures for identifying good levels of abstraction, or for sorting out essential from nonessential details.

3.1.2 Modularity

A system is typically decomposed into smaller subsystems. Subsystems are repeatedly decomposed until the resulting parts are intellectually and technically manageable as single units. A *module* is any part or subsystem of a larger system. Modules fall into two classes: those decomposed into other modules—internal modules—and those not further decomposed—leaf modules. Internal modules are used for organizing other modules. Leaf modules do not contain other modules; they contain code and data.

A system is *modular* if it is composed of well-defined, conceptually simple, and independent parts interacting through well-defined interfaces. Modular systems are desirable for several of the following reasons:

- They are easier to understand and explain because they can be approached a piece at a time, and because the pieces have well-defined inter-relationships.
- Because they are easier to understand and explain, they are easier to document.

- They are easier to program because independent groups can work on separate modules with little communication.
- They are easier to test because they can be tested separately, and then integrated and tested together, one module at a time.
- When modules are truly independent, they are easier to maintain. Changes can be made in a few modules without disturbing the rest of the system.

Good modularity is based on principles for decomposing systems into parts, called *modularization criteria*, as follows. Modules should hide implementation decisions that may be subject to change (the principle of information hiding). Modules should implement single logically independent tasks. Modules should minimize module coupling, and maximize module cohesion. Modules should implement abstract data types or distinct logical objects, and should reflect levels of abstraction in the system design. Modules should enhance testability by providing separate, easily testable units. Finally, leaf modules should perform one specific function and should be less than one page.

The first few of these criteria are most important, and we discuss them further later. The least important principles of modularization involve coding and efficiency. This reflects a cardinal rule of modularization: *It is far more important to decompose a system so that it is simple, understandable, and has independent parts, than it is to decompose it so that it is efficient or easy to code.*

3.1.3 Cohesion

Cohesion is the strength of the relationship between module elements. Modules should be as cohesive as possible. Levels of cohesion similar to others in the literature,[1] [2] ranked from highest (best) to lowest (worst), are as follows:

- *Data-type cohesion.* Modules that implement abstract data types have data-type cohesion. An *abstract data type* is a set of data values and operations. An implementation of an abstract data type is a representation of values of the type, along with subprograms for the operations. For example, a module that implements the type **int_stack** would provide a data structure to represent stacks of integers, along with functions for operations like **push**, **pop**, **empty**, and so on.
- *Functional cohesion.* A module has functional cohesion if it contains subprograms and data structures that collectively implement a single function, feature, or operation. For example, a module for displaying a graphic on a terminal exhibits functional cohesion.
- *Logical cohesion.* A module has logical cohesion when its elements form a set of logically related tasks. For example, a module consisting of functions for printing a variety of error and warning messages has logical cohesion. In this example, the functions do not work together or pass data to one another; the functions merely do the same logical task of printing error and warning messages.
- *Sequential cohesion.* A module containing elements that are executed in sequence has sequential cohesion. Data is typically passed along from one routine to the

next, with each routine transforming the data before passing it on. An example of such a module might be one for formatting text. Initial functions might process special parts of the text like tables and equations. Functions later in the pipeline might break the text into lines, then into paragraphs, pages, and sections. The final functions might insert printer control sequences. Another example of sequential cohesion are pipes in a UNIX shell program.

- *Incidental cohesion.* A module has incidental cohesion when there is no significant relationship between its elements.

A study at the National Aeronautics and Space Administration Software Engineering Laboratory[3] showed that highly cohesive modules have a lower fault rate and lower cost than less cohesive modules, and that good programmers tend to write highly cohesive modules.

The level of cohesion in a module should be considered when defining and evaluating the structure of a software system. A module can have several kinds of cohesion. For instance, a module can have both sequential and data-type cohesion if its functions sequentially operate on common data (Table 3.1).

Table 3.1:   Summary of Module Cohesion Levels

Level of Cohesion	Module Characteristic
Data type	Implement an abstract data type
Functional	Elements collectively implement one task
Logical	Elements implement logically related tasks
Sequential	Elements executed in sequence
Incidental	Unrelated elements

3.1.4 Coupling

Coupling is the strength of the linkage between modules based on the amount of communication that takes place between them. Like cohesion, coupling comes in a variety of levels. In general, lower-level coupling is better. Loosely coupled modules are easier to understand, document, code, test, and maintain.

We distinguish five levels of coupling, listed subsequently from lowest (best) to highest (worst):

- *Data definition coupling.* When modules manipulate data of the same type, they have data definition coupling.
- *Data element coupling.* Modules that pass data elements through a disciplined interface, like a parameter list, have data element coupling. Modules coupled only through data elements may be changed independently as long as their interface is unchanged.
- *Control coupling.* Modules have control coupling when one module is able to influence the flow of control within another module by passing control

information as "flags." This form of coupling disperses decision-making code between modules, making the modules more interdependent.

- *Global coupling.* Modules that reference common global variables display global coupling. Because the interface between modules that share global data may be undisciplined, this brand of coupling tends to increase program complexity enormously.

- *Content coupling.* Content coupling occurs when one module alters data or control local to another module. This form of coupling can occur only in languages with weak scope rules or weak type checking, or in languages where code can be altered at run time. In C, content coupling occurs when pointers are used to access supposedly private (i.e., `static`) data local to another module.

Content coupling should never occur. Global coupling should be minimized and controlled as much as possible through the judicious use of scope rules. Control coupling can usually be avoided. Data definition and data element coupling are the preferred intermodule communication mechanisms (Table 3.2).

Table 3.2: Summary of Module Coupling Levels

Level of Coupling	Module Characteristic
Data definition	Modules share a data declaration
Data element	Modules pass data through parameters
Control	A module affects control flow in another
Global	Modules access global data
Content	A module alters private objects of another module

Cohesion and coupling are usually complementary. Highly cohesive modules are generally weakly coupled to other modules, but modules that lack cohesion tend to be tightly coupled to other modules. Unfortunately, it is common for highly cohesive modules to be tightly coupled with other modules because of a tendency to share global data instead of passing data with parameters.

3.1.5 Information Hiding

Information hiding is a decomposition strategy in which each module shields the internal details of its processing from all other modules.[4] [5] [6] All communication between modules takes place through well-defined interfaces. Information about a module thus falls into two categories: private and public information. Private information includes the details of a module's internal data representations, algorithmic operations, internal organization, and the data objects and operations it requires from other modules. This information is also called a module's *secrets*. The information necessary to make use of a module's services are specified in the module's public interface. Interfaces specify the names, properties, and parameters of the data objects and operations provided by the module, their behavior, and their error conditions.

One way to think about modules that reinforces the principle of information hiding is the *producer-consumer model*. In this model, *products* are data objects, like values of abstract data types, or instances of classes in object-oriented programming. *Services* are operations or functions for manipulating data objects, controlling devices, and so forth. A module is a *producer* of those products and services that it supplies to other modules. A module is a *consumer* of products or services supplied by other modules. Information hiding holds for both producers and consumers. The consumer of a product or service has no access to the mechanisms used by the producer to provide its products or services. Likewise, the producer has no access to the mechanisms used by the consumer when it makes use of products or services. The principle of information hiding thus has two aspects applying equally to producers and consumers.

Information hiding takes place at several levels in a software system. The principle that objects always be made as local as possible is the principle of information hiding applied at the block level (e.g., in C all code between curly brackets) and at the compile module level. The packaging of private (in C **static**) functions and data objects in a compile module is a manifestation of this principle at the compile module level.

Information hiding has many advantages. First, information hiding is a species of abstraction. A module's secrets are details suppressed in the specification of a module's interface. Information hiding thus reduces complexity. Second, modules that thoroughly hide their internal details tend to be highly cohesive and loosely coupled. Finally, when design and implementation details are hidden inside modules, they become independent of other modules. This is especially important when implementation details must be changed. Secrets can be changed more easily and reliably because the effects of such changes are restricted to the modules where they are hidden.

Information hiding is a powerful principle that encourages other good modularization practices. Based on our experience, we believe that information hiding is the fundamental principle of modularization.

3.2 SOFTWARE DESIGN METHODS

A *design method* is a systematic procedure or technique for generating software system designs from software product requirements. We discuss four popular design methods: structured design, data structure design, object-oriented design, and dataflow design. The key elements distinguishing these design methods are the mechanisms used to decompose systems into smaller subsystems, and the notations used to express designs. Data structure design relies heavily on data structures as the basis for decomposition, and its notation is a graphical representation for data structures. In contrast, structured design relies on operations as the basis for decomposition, and its notation is a graphical representation of relations between operations. Dataflow design and object-oriented design use both data structures and operations as the basis for decomposition, and incorporate both into their design notations.

Frequently, several complementary methods are used on a project. For example, one may use functional decomposition to do a top-level system decomposition and then use object-oriented design to derive the modules making up the system.

3.2.1 Structured Design

Structured design, also called *functional decomposition* or *top-down design*, is a "divide-and-conquer" approach to problem solving. It was introduced by Wirth[7] [8] in 1971 and is among the first design methods. In structured design one first analyzes requirements to determine a few high-level functional steps that solve the problem or satisfy the requirements. These functional steps are then decomposed into more detailed functional steps. Successive decomposition continues until all functions can be expressed in programming language constructs.

At each decomposition step, care must be taken to ensure that the subfunctions into which a function is decomposed are correct. During decomposition, design decisions are postponed as long as possible so that implementation commitments are driven into the lowest levels of the system, helping to decouple modules. Decoupling is also promoted by making processing steps independent. Functional cohesion is encouraged by the decomposition mechanism itself.

Functional decomposition was formalized by Yourdon and Constantine,[1] and Myers[2] in the mid-1970s. *Structure charts* or *hierarchy charts* can be used to represent designs resulting from functional decomposition. Structure charts are tree diagrams representing the functional hierarchy of a system, like the following example (Figure 3.1) showing the design of a compiler.

Each rectangle represents a module in the system. An arc (*rounded arrow*) represents an iterated calling structure (i.e., repeatedly scan input, then update symbol table, then build parse tree). A black diamond marks a conditional call (e.g., the `insert_new_symbol` module is called by the `update_symbol_table` module only if the `search_for_symbol` module does not return `found`). Arrows show parameter passing between modules, with the name of the passed parameter attached to the arrow. An open-ended arrow marks a data couple, whereas a closed-ended arrow marks a control couple (such as a flag like `found`).

Structured design has been used to solve a broad range of problems. It is a popular, well-known method and fits in well with other design methods, as we will see in the following discussion. The biggest problem with structured design is that it does not have clear principles guiding decomposition. Another difficulty is that structured design focuses on operations, not data. Consequently, structured design does not encourage information hiding. Finally, structured design is a purely top-down approach, so common low-level data representations and operations may be missed, leading to less concise designs.

3.2.2 Data Structure Design

The *data structure design* method is based on the premise that identifying the data structures in a problem leads to a correct solution. This design method was introduced by Jackson[9] in the mid-1970s and has been enhanced into a more comprehensive

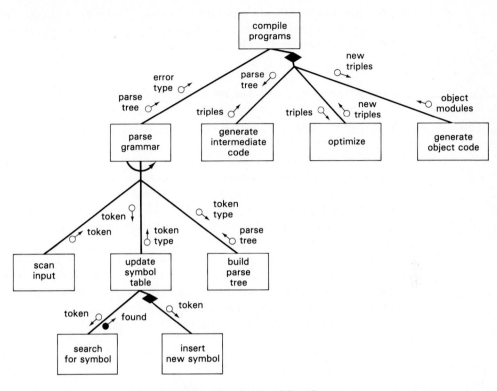

Figure 3.1   Design of Compiler.

development methodology called Jackson System Development (JSD)[10] in the 1980s. We only discuss the basics of Jackson's approach. Readers interested in the nuances of JSD should consult Jackson's books.

The four steps in the data structure design method follow:

1. Identify and graphically describe the input and output data structures.

2. Determine points of correspondence between the input and output data structures and use these correspondences to generate a graphical representation of the program structure.

3. Identify operations required to transform input data values into output data values, and associate these with appropriate portions of the graphical representation of the program structure.

4. Transform the graphical representation of the program structure into procedural representation (in pseudocode) using the operations identified in Step 3 and adding the necessary conditions and procedural details.

Jackson's method uses *data structure diagrams* to represent input and output data structures. Data structure diagrams represent data structures as trees. Each node represents a data element; child nodes represent constituent data elements of their parent. Thus the root of a tree represents an entire data structure, and the other nodes represent its parts. Nodes are drawn as rectangles. Data items are grouped to form larger data structures as follows:

- *Sequencing of data items.* A data structure may be composed of a group of data items; for instance, a data structure may be a sequence of the four fields: name, age, sex, and occupation. Sequences are represented by child nodes corresponding to constituent data items.

- *Repetition of data items.* A data structure may be composed of several occurrences of a particular data structure. For example, a data structure might be composed of zero or more instances of some record. Repetitions are represented by a single child node with an asterisk (*) in the upper right-hand corner of its rectangle. The upper left-hand corner of the rectangle may contain a range limiting the repetition of elements.

- *Selection of data items.* A data structure may be composed of one of several alternative data items (like a **union** in C). For example, a data structure may be an error message or a success message, but not both. This is represented in a data structure diagram with child nodes for the alternatives; each alternative has a small circle in the upper right-hand corner of its rectangle.

An example data structure diagram appears in Figure 3.2. In this example, a **message** can be either an **error_message** or a **success_message**. An **error_ message** can be either a **lexical_error_message** or a **syntax_error_ message**.

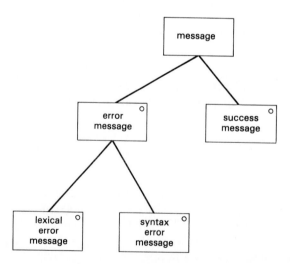

Figure 3.2   Data Structure Diagram.

The graphical representation of program structures derived from data structure diagrams is similar to the data structure diagrams. Nodes are rectangles, but they represent process steps or operations, not data items. Children of operation nodes represent either a sequence of operations, iterated operations, or conditionally executed alternative operations. As in data structure diagrams, conditional alternatives are distinguished by placing small circles in the upper right-hand corners of their rectangles, and iterated operations are shown by placing asterisks in the upper right-hand corners of their rectangles. For example, we could interpret the diagram in Figure 3.2 as a program structure diagram. The message issuing operation `message` consists of the conditionally executed alternative operations `error_message` or `success_message`. The former operation is in turn composed of the conditionally executed alternative operations `lexical_error_message` or `syntax_error_message`.

Data structure design provides more guidance in producing a complete design than do the other methods. This method is popular for designing data structures but is not widely used as a complete design methodology. This may be because data structure design does not encourage important design concepts and principles, such as information hiding. The method is also difficult to use on large projects where data structures may not be known early in the design process.

3.2.3 Dataflow Design

Dataflow design was popularized by DeMarco[11] and Gane and Sarson.[12] It focuses the designer's attention on data and data flow rather than operations and control flow. Another way of looking at dataflow design is as functional decomposition with respect to data flow.

Dataflow design relies on four notational tools: dataflow diagrams, data dictionaries, structure charts, and pseudocode. *Dataflow diagrams* are graphical representations of how data is consumed, transformed, and produced in a system. Four basic symbols used to depict data flow follow:

- Circles represent processes that change data, called *transforms*.
- Open rectangles represent temporary holding places for data such as files, databases, and so on, called *data stores*.
- Arrows, called *dataflows*, represent paths for movement of data through a system.
- Rectangles represent resources outside the system that are originators or receivers of system data, called *sources* or *sinks*, respectively.

Figures 3.3 and 3.4, taken from the design for `ccount`, illustrate the use of dataflow diagrams.

The top-level dataflow diagram represents the entire system structure. There are three data sources: the user, the standard input stream `stdin`, and C source files. These sources supply the command line, and C source code, respectively, to the main data transform `ccount`. A data store holds the delimiter string. The `ccount` process produces error messages and metrics reports consumed by the sinks `stderr` and `stdout`. The decomposed dataflow diagram for the `ccount` transform bubble appears as the second dataflow diagram.

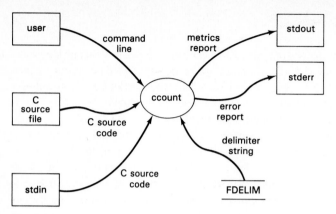

Figure 3.3   Top-Level **ccount** Dataflow Diagram.

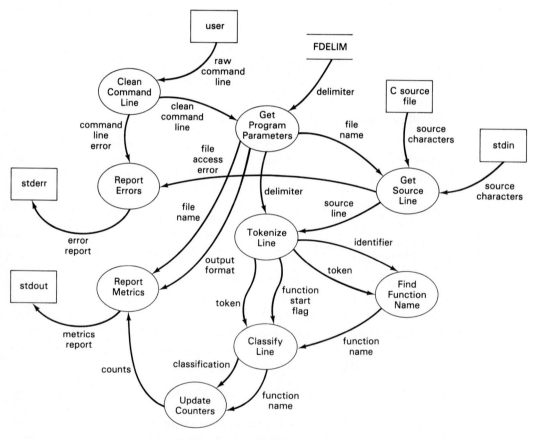

Figure 3.4

A *data dictionary* is a master directory of all the data structures and data elements in a system. It is used to provide information about the definition, structure, and use of each data element. Data element names, descriptions, types, and range of values are examples of information stored in a data dictionary.

Structure charts can be generated from dataflow diagrams to produce a functional hierarchy of subsystems corresponding to the transforms in the dataflow diagrams. Pseudocode or *mini-specs* are used to describe the algorithms implemented in the lowest level transforms. *Pseudocode* is high-level programming language code, such as C code, augmented with English whenever convenient. Pseudocode is a convenient mechanism for informally describing program function without concern for the formal details of a programming language.

Four steps to dataflow design follow:

1. Model the entire system using a high-level dataflow diagram and an initial data dictionary.

2. Decompose the high-level dataflow diagram by forming a hierarchy of dataflow diagrams. Refine the data dictionary by expanding it to reflect the lower-level dataflow diagrams.

3. Following a top-down procedure, map the dataflow diagrams into structure charts forming a functional decomposition of the entire system. This activity is guided by information from the data dictionary, and modularization criteria such as cohesion, coupling, and information hiding.

4. Use the structure charts and the data dictionary as a guide in producing pseudocode for the entire program.

This mechanism has been worked out and documented in great detail.[11][12] Much guidance is given to the designer at various steps in this process, although there are places, such as the analysis of dataflow, and the transformation of dataflow diagrams to structure charts, where skill and experience are important. Dataflow design is supported by strong notation; it has proved to be a powerful aid in analyzing and specifying system structure even outside the dataflow design paradigm. The method also has the advantage of incorporating design heuristics, such as modularization criteria and the top-down approach.

Dataflow design sometimes fails for systems that are algorithmically intense and have little data (e.g., mathematical applications). The method also offers little opportunity to incorporate abstract data types, an important design tool. Another drawback of classic dataflow design is that it is impossible to represent control flow in dataflow diagrams. This makes the approach difficult to use in designing systems, such as real-time systems, where control flow is essential to design. This deficiency has recently been addressed in extensions to the dataflow design approach for real-time systems by Hatley and Pirbhai,[13] and Ward and Mellor.[14] Their extensions of dataflow design notations provide ways of representing control flow and data flow in dataflow diagrams.

3.2.4 Object-Oriented Design

Object-oriented design is based on decomposing a system into an interacting collection of objects.[15] [16] [17] [18] An *object* is an encapsulated collection of data and operations. For example, in a window management system, windows might be objects. A window would encapsulate data such as its location, dimensions, contents, and so on. It would also encapsulate operations such as opening, closing, moving, resizing, and so on. An object is an instance of a *class*, which is a collection of objects with common data and operations. In a window management system, there are typically several active windows. Each such window is a distinct object, but all windows share many properties (data fields) and operations, so they form a class.

Most object-oriented methods involve the definition of classes from which subclasses can be derived. Attributes (data fields) and operations of a class may be *inherited* by its subclasses. Subclasses may have additional attributes and operations, and they may replace some of their inherited operations. For example, the window class may have push buttons as a subclass with additional operations to handle pushing buttons.

Objects or classes are similar to abstract data types. The difference between the two concepts are the entities distinguished by the models, and the entities regarded as active in the models. In an abstract data type, there are two kinds of things: the data values of the type, and the operations that can be applied to the values of the type. In an abstract data type, operations are regarded as active agents that operate on passive data values. In contrast, an object is thought of as a single entity containing both data and operations. The operations are not active, however; they are thought of as capabilities that an object possesses. The active agents in the object model are the objects themselves. Objects are requested to take actions characterized by the operations encapsulated in the object. Thus objects, though formally similar to abstract data types, are conceptually distinct.

Information hiding is a fundamental principle of the object-oriented approach. The internal details of object implementations are shielded from other objects. This is what is meant by encapsulation. Objects communicate through disciplined interfaces that include the object's name, data elements (or *properties*), and operations (or *methods*).

In line with the principle of information hiding, object-oriented design stresses two goals in the definition of objects. First, the ease of making a change should be proportional to the likelihood of the change having to be made. This goal is realized by hiding changeable design or implementation details inside objects as secrets. Details less likely to change may appear as features of an object's interface. Second, a software engineer should be able to understand the activities of an object through its interface without knowing anything about the object's internal details.

Several object-oriented design methods, with accompanying notations, have emerged. Booch,[19] for example, suggests an approach for designing objects by analyzing requirements, and representing objects with a notation called *Booch diagrams*, or *Booch-grams*. In Booch diagrams, objects are represented as rectangles with their data type shown in contained ovals, and their operations listed within contained rectangles. Directed edges between objects show that one object consumes services provided by another object. General Object-Oriented Development (GOOD)[20] uses dataflow diagrams as a basis for identifying and defining objects. Object diagrams are used to show communication among objects. Hierarchical Object-Oriented Design (HOOD)[21] is a method for object-oriented design specifically for Ada programs. Object-Oriented Structured Design (OOSD)[22] enhances structure charts with ideas from Booch diagrams, and additional mechanisms to show exceptions, inheritance, generics, and object visibility relationships. None of these methods and notations has emerged as the method and notation of choice.

Object-oriented design is said to promote reuse because objects can be designed and implemented as independent units useful in a variety of applications. A major advantage of object-oriented design is that it strongly promotes information hiding. It does have weaknesses, however. For large problems, it is sometimes difficult to see how objects might interact to solve the problem. Some applications do not seem to fit well in an object-oriented mold. Often a functional view of a system, or of parts of a system, is more effective. Finally, many designers have a difficult time understanding and applying the object-oriented philosophy, particularly if they have grown used to thinking in terms of functions or data flows.

C++, discussed in Chapter 7, is an object oriented extension to C which has become popular. C++ is more appropriate than C for designing and implementing object oriented systems.

3.3 GRAPHICAL DESIGN TOOLS

Because most design notations are graphical, it has until recently been impractical to provide automated support for these methods in the UNIX system. Although graphical output can be generated in the standard UNIX environment using `troff` with `pic` and `grap`, the awkwardness of these tools, their batch orientation, and the rapidity of design change make them of little value as design support tools. Today, however, graphical tool support for software design in the UNIX/C environment is available from many sources in the growing market of computer-aided software design tools. These tools have powerful graphical editors specially written to support various design notations. They are also able to analyze designs to detect anomalies, inconsistencies, and incompleteness.

Some strong reasons for using such a software design tool follow:

- Manual production of designs, particularly graphics, is error prone and time consuming. Automation of the design process saves time and prevents errors.
- It is difficult to check the correctness and completeness of designs by hand. Sophisticated computerized design tools enhance our ability to check designs for completeness and consistency.
- Graphical design tools enforce a notation. This results in consistent use of notation, which helps communication and avoids errors.
- Some tools can generate pseudocode and data declarations from design representations. This saves time and provides a basis for coding that is guaranteed to be correct and in full agreement with the design.
- Automated tools enable project managers to browse project designs on-line and to do various design analyses.
- Design tools provide a central repository for all design information.

3.3.1 Example of Graphical Design Tool

We now discuss Software Through Pictures (StP), a commercial product from Interactive Development Environments, Incorporated (IDE), to illustrate the capabilities of these new design tools.[23] We have chosen to discuss StP in some detail because it is a popular tool in the UNIX environment, and because it is typical of the broad class of commercially available design tools. We do not endorse StP, or mean to denigrate its many competitors in the Computer Aided Software Engineering (CASE) market.

StP runs on workstations like the Sun and Apollo workstations, and takes advantage of their windowed interfaces and graphics capabilities. StP offers tools supporting numerous software design methods including functional decomposition, data structure design, and dataflow design. StP is a collection of editors for drawing objects like structure charts, data structure diagrams, and dataflow diagrams. The editors can be used jointly to represent the design of a single system. For example, the dataflow editor (DFE) might be used to define the dataflow diagrams for a system, whereas the dataflows might be linked to data structures depicted using the data structure editor (DSE). Each editor produces diagrams stored as UNIX files and in a relational database management system. A closer look at each of the editors follows.

Structure Chart Editor (SCE). The SCE supports the definition of a software architecture—including the input and output parameters for each module in the system—by allowing for the creation, manipulation, and analysis of structure charts. Figure 3.1 was produced using the SCE. The SCE can generate program design language (PDL) skeletons based on a structure chart. The SCE can check consistency between the modules in a structure chart and the processes in a corresponding dataflow diagram. In particular, it checks the consistency between input and output parameters for each node in a structure chart, and the corresponding dataflows in and out of transform bubbles in the dataflow diagram.

Data-Structure Editor (DSE). The DSE supports the hierarchical definition of data structures as defined by Jackson.[9] Figure 3–2 was produced using the DSE. DSE supports the definition of data items including the name, type, and alias of a data object. DSE also generates type and data declarations in C.

Data Flow Editor (DFE). The DFE supports the creation, change, and analysis of dataflow diagrams using either the DeMarco[11] or Gane-Sarson[12] notation. Transforms are automatically numbered to show level and ancestry. DSE has the following graphical analysis capabilities:

- It checks on the decomposition of a diagram against its parent, including checks of the consistency of dataflows between parent dataflow diagrams and their children.
- It checks on data item use, including checks of data in the dataflow diagram against the data dictionary, checks for undefined data in dataflows and data stores,

checks for dataflows that are not part of the right data structures, and checks for parts of a data structure that are not shown as dataflows.

- It checks for invalid diagrams, including checks for unconnected transforms, and for unlabeled dataflows, data stores, and transforms.

Control Flow Editor (CFE).   The CFE supports the creation, change, and analysis of control flow diagrams using the Hatley and Pirbhai notation.[24] Control flow diagrams are used to model the interactions among communicating processes. CFE and DSE are integrated so that data and control flows can be displayed separately or jointly.

Transition Diagram Editor (TDE).   User interface interaction is modeled by state transition diagrams[25] created and changed by the TDE. TDE allows for the description of screen layout, inputs causing transitions to occur, actions associated with transitions, and output prompts and messages. Display information, such as the text to be displayed and the cursor position, is associated with each node. Arcs associate user input with state changes.

TDE automatically generates an executable version of the dialogue represented by the transition diagram that can be used as a prototype. TDE allows input to be passed between C functions, which allows functional prototyping as well. TDE also supports a trace facility animating transition diagram execution.

Entity-Relationship Editor (ERE).   The ERE supports the entity-relationship-attribute (ERA) data modeling approach defined by Chen.[26] The ERE can automatically create a relational database schema based on an entity-relationship diagram.

Picture Editor.   The picture editor is a drawing tool that provides many of the symbols used in business graphics and software design.

Data Dictionary.   Each graphical editor includes operations to generate information for the StP data dictionary. The data dictionary is managed by the graphical editors and is built on a relational database management system.

Graphical Output.   StP can generate graphics from any of its editors in several formats including `pic` format, and Postscript.[27]

3.4 PROGRAM DESIGN LANGUAGES

Many design languages have been proposed in recent years. Most are outgrowths of the original program design language **PDL**.[28] These languages provide software developers with the capabilities of algorithmic specification, automation, and verification. A PDL is a tool that uses the vocabulary of a natural language and much of the syntax of a programming language (e.g., Pascal). A PDL can be thought of as "structured English," a language that allows for the specification of data structures and manipulation logic in a software system. A PDL should be able to express module, control flow, and data structures at an appropriate level of abstraction while minimizing the constraints imposed by a programming language. A more detailed survey of PDLs can be found in Nejmeh and Dunsmore.[29]

3.5 CONTENTS OF A DESIGN DOCUMENT

A design document describes decisions about the structure of a system. It serves at least four of the following purposes:

1. It describes how the system will be structured to satisfy requirements. It must be reviewed to assess its completeness, correctness, and success in satisfying the requirements.

2. It documents the rationale behind design decisions, recording the alternatives that were explored and the reasons for design decisions.

3. It anticipates changes to the system and explains how changes should be made. This makes it easier to evaluate the changeability of the design, and provides system maintainers with valuable information.

4. It serves as a system blueprint for programmers, testers, and maintainers later in the life cycle.

Bad design documents have led to catastrophic problems. Even when design documents are good to start with, they can go bad if they are not kept up to date with design changes. The design document should always accurately reflect system structure and function.

A design document should contain the following information:[30]

- *Design overview.* The overview provides a high-level description of the system's structure with a small collection of top-level modules. The description should identify each module by name, state its purpose, and discuss how it interacts with other modules.

- *Architectural model.* An *architectural model* of a system is a description of the top-level modules, and the data and control flow between them. Graphical notations are preferred for this task, but concise, well-written text may suffice.

- *Module descriptions.* As noted before, a *module* is any part or subsystem of a larger system. A module may itself be decomposed into modules that provide parts of the parent module's functionality and hide some of the parent module's secrets. Certain information must be supplied for every module in a module description, but some information is only needed to document the richer internal structure of leaf modules. Information that should be provided for every module includes the following:

- *Module behavior*. Explanation of a module's behavior includes (1) a catalog of the operations it provides, with descriptions of inputs and outputs and externally visible effects; and (2) a catalog of the data types and objects that the module provides.
- *Assumptions*. A module's assumptions are the conditions that must be satisfied for the module to work correctly. For example, a file processing module might assume that a file passed to it is open and readable.
- *Secrets*. These are the implementation details hidden from other modules inside the module.
- *Constraints and limitations*. The constraints and limitations of a module include performance requirements, maximum memory usage requirements, numerical accuracy requirements, and so on.
- *Error handling*. This category includes errors and exceptional conditions that may be encountered by the module, their causes, and the strategy used to handle them.
- *Expected changes*. Discussion of changes expected by the designers of the module should include ideas about how the changes might be made.
- *Related requirements*. These are the requirements satisfied by the module.

In addition to this information, leaf module descriptions should also include the following:

- *Module packaging*. Packaging information must list all functions provided by the module, with their types, and the types of all their input and output parameters. The externally visible effects of each function should be explained, and any side-effects noted and explained. The salient features of any data types and objects provided by the module should be discussed in detail.
- *Internal structure*. Specification of a module's internal structure should list and explain hidden data types and objects, and internal functions with their types, the types of their parameters, and their effects. If particular sorts of algorithms are supposed to be used in some function, this should be stated and justified. If some algorithm is particularly crucial or tricky, it may be written down in pseudocode.
- *Uses relationships*. Leaf module **A** uses leaf module **B** if **B** must execute correctly for **A** to meet its specification.
- *Rationale*. This section explains design decisions, listing the alternatives explored, and justifying design decisions.
- *Glossary*. As in other development documents, a glossary should be provided so that confusion about technical terms is minimized.

The **ccount** design document is included in Appendix A as an example. Appendix C contains a design document template based on our discussion in this chapter.

REFERENCES

1. Yourdon, E., and L. Constantine, *Structured Design.* Englewood Cliffs, N.J.: Prentice Hall, 1979.

2. Myers, G. L., *Reliable Software Through Composite Design.* New York: Petrocelli/Charter, 1975.

3. Card, D., G. Page, and F. McGarry, "Criteria for Software Modularization," *Proceedings of Eighth International Conference on Software Engineering*, New York: IEEE Computer Society Press, 1985.

4. Parnas, D. L., "On the Criteria to be Used in Decomposing Programs into Modules," *Communications of the ACM*, 15, no. 12 (December 1972), 1053–1058.

5. Parnas, D. L., "Designing Software for Extension and Contraction," *Proceedings of the Third International Conference on Software Engineering* (May 1978), 264–277.

6. Britton, K. H., and D. L. Parnas, *A-7E Software Module Guide*, Naval Research Laboratory, NRL Memorandum Report 4702, December 1981.

7. Wirth, N., "Program Development by Stepwise Refinement," *Communications of the ACM*, 14, no. 4 (April 1971), 221–227.

8. Wirth, N., *Systematic Programming.* Englewood Cliffs, N.J.: Prentice Hall, 1973.

9. Jackson, M. A., *Principles of Program Design.* Orlando, Fla.: Academic Press, 1975.

10. Jackson, M. A., *System Development.* Englewood Cliffs, N.J.: Prentice Hall, 1983.

11. DeMarco, T., *Structured Analysis and System Specification.* Englewood Cliffs, N.J.: Prentice Hall, 1979.

12. Gane, C., and T. Sarson, *Structured Systems Analysis.* Englewood Cliffs, N.J.: Prentice Hall, 1979.

13. Hatley, D., and I. Pirbhai, *Strategies for Real-Time System Specification.* New York: Dorset House, 1987.

14. Ward, P. T., and S. J. Mellor, *Structured Development for Real-Time Systems* (vols. 1–3). Englewood Cliffs, N.J.: Yourdon Press, 1985–1986.

15. Abbott, R. J., "Program Design by Informal Descriptions," *Communications of the ACM*, 26, no. 11 (November 1983), 882–894.

16. Booch, G., "Object-Oriented Development," *IEEE Transactions on Software Engineering*, SE-12, no. 2 (February 1986), 211–221.

17. Cox, B. J., *Object Oriented Programming*. Reading, Mass.: Addison Wesley, 1986.

18. Liskov, B., and J. Guttag, *Abstraction and Specification in Program Development*. Cambridge, Mass.: M.I.T. Press, 1986.

19. Booch, G., *Software Components with Ada*. Reading, Mass.: Benjamin/Cummings, 1987.

20. Seidowitz, E., and M. Stark, *General Object-Oriented Software Development*, Report SEL-86–002, NASA Goddard Space Flight Center, 1986.

21. Heitz, M., *HOOD: Hierarchical Object-Oriented Design for Development of Large Technical and Real-Time Software*, CISI Ingenierie, Direction Midi Pyrennes, November 1987.

22. Wasserman, A., P. Pircher, and B. Muller, "An Object-Oriented Structured Design Method for Code Generation," *ACM SIGSoft Software Engineering Notes*, 14, no. 1 (January 1989), 32–55.

23. Wasserman, A. I., and P. A. Pircher, "A Graphical, Extensible Integrated Environment for Software Development," *Proceedings of Practical Software Development Environments Conference* (December 1986), 131–142.

24. Hatley, D., and I. Pirbhai, *Strategies for Real-Time System Specifications*. New York: Dorset House, 1987.

25. Wasserman, A. I., "Extending State Transition Diagrams for the Specification of Human-Computer Interaction," *IEEE Transactions on Software Engineering*, SE-11, no. 8 (August 1985), 699–713.

26. Chen, P. P., "The Entity-Relationship Model—Toward a Unified View of Data," *IEEE Transactions on Software Engineering*, SE-1, no. 3 (March 1976), 9–36.

27. Adobe Systems Incorporated, *Postscript Language Reference Manual*. Reading, Mass.: Addison-Wesley, 1985.

28. Caine, S. H., and E. K. Gordon, "PDL—A Tool for Software Design," *Proceedings of AFIPS Conference*, 33 (October 1975), 271–276.

29. Nejmeh, B. A., and H. Dunsmore, "A Survey of Program Design Languages," *Proceedings of IEEE COMPSAC '86* (October 1986), 447–455.

30. Parnas, D. L. and P. C. Clements, "A Rational Design Process: How and Why to Fake It," *IEEE Transactions on Software Engineering*, SE-12, no. 2 (February 1986), 251–257.

4

Program Readability

This chapter is the first of three discussing *good programming practices*: programming techniques that help make source code more readable, portable, reliable, and robust. These chapters do not try to teach you how to program in C—we assume that you already know how to do that. Their goal is to provide rules of thumb, hints, and tricks, that you can use to avoid errors and improve the quality of your C code.

Good programming practices are important for writing high-quality code in any language.[1] [2] They are especially important in C programming, however, because C offers so many subtle opportunities for error, as we will see later. Most C tutorials teach the language without mentioning many of the programming practices so important for writing good C programs. Programmers learn C programming lore from more senior peers, experience, the few books that discuss the topic, or not at all. We hope to make this learning process faster and easier by discussing good C programming practice in depth.

This chapter is about source code readability. Chapter 5 discusses practices for writing expressions, statements, and functions. Chapter 6 discusses practices for modularization and information hiding at the compile module level. Although we cover many C programming practices in these chapters, we do not exhaust the topic. Further recommendations can be found, for example, in Harbison and Steele's[3] excellent C reference manual, and in Koenig's[4] book about C programming problems and how to avoid them.

Some experienced C programmers may object to some (or all) of our recommendations. Programming practices seem to inspire the same religious zeal as operating systems, design methodologies, and programming languages. Because reason is insufficient to settle disputes in these areas, tolerance of opposing views is required. Even those who disagree about details, however, admit that good programming practices are important, and that learning and consistently applying some set of programming principles is better than having none at all.

This chapter discusses principles of good programming practice for one of the most important properties of source code: readability. By "readability" we mean the degree to which a reader can quickly and easily understand source code. When code is readable, it should be easy to see what the programmer is trying to do, and how he or she is trying to do it. Readability is important because every production program is read again and again during its creation, inspection, testing, debugging, and maintenance.

The need for readability can be met in two ways: by providing special help to human readers *internally*, in the source code, or by making supporting material available *externally*, as documents or files outside the source code. The first half of this chapter discusses internal program documentation; the second half discusses external program documentation.

4.1 INTERNAL DOCUMENTATION

Internal program documentation takes two forms: *Self-documenting code* is source code that incorporates aids for a human reader; and *comments* are supplementary text, tables, or graphs interspersed with source code. Self-documenting code is better than code that relies on comments. Self-documenting code requires less reading because there are fewer comments. Comments often become outdated when programmers forget (or do not bother) to update them. This cannot occur with self-documenting code. Unfortunately, programming language technology has not advanced to the point that programs can be completely self-documenting. Nevertheless, there is much that programmers can do to make their code more self-documenting. There are also rules and guidelines for writing good comments. In the sections that follow we discuss techniques for making code more self-documenting, then we present a strategy for writing good comments to supplement mostly self-documenting code. Our discussion closes with a brief look at internal documentation metrics and guidelines.

4.1.1 Self-Documenting Code

Use of Good Names.   The best way to make code more self-documenting is to use good names for variables, functions, types, constants, macros, and so on. The main job of any name is to provide a handle for referring to something. Good names can and should do more than this, however. Names should express pertinent information about the named object. A well-chosen name can reveal things like the type of the object named, the origin of the object (a function library, for example), and the role the object plays in the system, program, function, or statement where it appears.

A program object's *role* is the part the object plays in a program. For example, in a routine for computing the average of an array of values, some variable is used to accumulate the sum of the values. The role of the variable is to store the accumulated sum. Expressing the role of a program object is an especially useful and important job for a name to do. To illustrate, consider the following code.

```
int f( a, b, c, d )
   int a,b,c,*d;
   {
   int e;

   do
      {
      e = (b+c) / 2;
      if (a < d[e])
          c = e-1;
      else
          b = e+1;
      }
   while ((a != d[e]) && (b <= c));

   return ((a == d[e]) ? e : -1);
   }
```

You will probably recognize this function as a binary search after studying it for a minute or two. Now consider the following code, which is identical to the first function except for the names.

```
int Binary_Search( key, lo, hi, list )
   int key,lo,hi,*list;
   {
   int mid;

   do
      {
      mid = (lo + hi) / 2;
      if ( key < list[mid] )
          hi = mid-1;
      else
          lo = mid+1;
      }
   while ((key != list[mid]) && (lo <= hi));

   return ((key == list[mid]) ? mid : NOT_FOUND);
   }
```

Anyone can see at a glance that the second function is a binary search. Furthermore, the names of the parameters document the roles of each, as does the name of the local variable. In the first function, the constant −1 appears mysteriously. In the second, this value is named NOT_FOUND, showing that a special value (that happens to be −1) is returned to indicate an unsuccessful search.

This example shows that even a simple and well-known algorithm can be difficult to recognize when poor names are used. Conversely, when good names reflecting the roles of program objects are used, the algorithm becomes clearer, and the details of the implementation are easier to decipher.

Naming is so important in self-documenting code that many naming conventions have been established. Some of these conventions are unwritten but rarely violated. For example, C programmers typically use names containing only uppercase characters for macros. Although naming conventions differ, the following list covers the most common conventions in the UNIX/C community:

- Lowercase letters should not occur in macro names. Sometimes this rule also covers type names introduced by **typedef** statements.

- Uppercase letters should rarely or never occur in names that are not names of macros or **typedef**'ed types. This convention is sometimes modified by some of the others listed subsequently.

- All names should differ in their first 8 characters, and the names of external objects should differ in their first 6 characters. Furthermore, names should never be distinguished solely by the case of their characters. These rules help avoid name clashes because (1) some older compilers only distinguish identifiers that differ over their first eight characters; (2) some linkers only distinguish identifiers that differ over their first six characters; and (3) many linkers, and most people, are not careful of case distinctions.

- Application programmers should never begin names with underscores because the names of system internal objects conventionally begin with an underscore.

- Different words in a multiple word name should be separated by underscores (**max_array_element**), by capitalizing the first letter of each word (**MaxArrayElement**), or both (**Max_Array_Element**).

- Functions or global objects may be distinguished from other objects by capitalizing the first letters of their names (**Get_Token** or **Max_Integer**).

- Prefixes or suffixes may be used to encode information in an object's name. For example, the suffixes **_ptr**, **_int**, **_str**, and so on, can be appended to an object's name to show that it is of type pointer, integer, or string, respectively. Prefixes are commonly used to show that an object is from a particular library. For example, the standard C string manipulation functions, like **strcpy** and **strcmp**, all begin with the prefix **str**.

- Special names can be reserved for commonly named objects. For example, **i**, **j**, and **k** might be reserved for loop control variables, **s** for a string temporary variable, and **n** and **m** for counters. Some programmers use names like **ix**, **sx**, and **nx** to make searching easier.

Whatever naming conventions are adopted, they should encourage programmers to use long, informative, and consistent names.

A final recommendation is that there never be any hesitation about introducing informative names for program objects, even when C does not encourage you to do so.

To illustrate, consider the merits of naming complex types using **typedef**'s. C never requires that a **typedef** be used, but does allow **typedef**'s for any data type or storage class in the language. When should **typedef**'s be used? We think that simple types, like **int** or **double**, should not be aliased with a **typedef**. Doing so burdens the reader with something else to remember, usually without improving clarity. Exceptions are **typedef**'s used to increase portability, to introduce a boolean type, or to correct deficiencies in the compiler. In contrast, we recommend that **typedef**'s always be used to introduce names for **struct**, **union**, or enumeration types (that occur more than once), and to factor complex declarations to improve their readability. For example, consider the following declarations:

```
int (*f)[]();

typedef int (*int_func_ptr)();
typedef int_func_ptr func_array[];
func_array g;
```

The first declaration makes **f** an array of pointers to functions returning integers. This declaration is difficult to decipher. The **typedef** statements introduce two intermediate types, factoring the declaration into intermediate steps. Although **g** is the same type as **f**, its declaration is much easier to read.

Defining types for complex data structures, and using intermediate types to factor complex declarations, has two advantages. First, the type name can help tell program readers about the type under examination. Second, introducing complex types, and declaring functions or variables in two steps divides the job of understanding the code into simpler parts, reducing cognitive load and simplifying things for the reader.

In summary, it pays to be profligate with names. Most program objects should have names, and the names themselves should be long, state the role of the program object, and conform to naming conventions.

Use of Right Types. A *type* is a collection of values and a set of operations that can be performed on the values.[5] In a *typed language* variables and functions are bound to types by declarations, and they can only assume or return values of their bound type. Besides its name, the feature of a variable or function in a typed language that tells a reader the most about it is its type. The type of a variable or a function tells us about the values that a variable can have, or that a function can return, the type conversions that can be applied, and the operations that can be used. This information can be crucial for understanding how a program works.

Careful use of types is a fundamental programming principle in any typed language, but it is especially important in a language like C that is both type-rich and not strongly typed. A *type-rich* language has many built-in types and mechanisms for creating new types. Learning to use types properly in a type-rich language is difficult because there are many types, and the differences between types may be subtle. A language is *strongly typed* if all operations are checked for type validity before program execution. Type errors in programs in a weakly typed language may go undetected for a long time. Programmers can be careless with types, planting time bombs in their programs and making them harder to understand. For example, C programmers are often careless with pointer types, declaring variables with arbitrary types and converting between them arbitrarily. This is confusing, and leads to obscure bugs and nonportable code. Disciplined declaration and use of pointer types avoids these difficulties.

Besides being type-rich and weakly typed, C does many automatic type conversions, and has a default typing mechanism. This provides more error opportunities. For example, automatic type conversion of function arguments is a common source of C errors.

Some principles guiding the selection and use of types depend on portability and performance rather than readability. These are discussed in the next chapter. There are several ways to use types to improve readability, however. For example, C lacks a boolean data type; the integral types are used in boolean expressions. Some programmers routinely **typedef** the **short** or **int** type as **boolean**. Declaring an object **boolean** clarifies the role of the object. Newer versions of C have the **void** type for functions. When a function returns **void**, readers know that it behaves as a procedure and does not return a value. All functions that do not return a value should be declared **void**.

If a programmer does not specify a function's type, or the types of some of its parameters, the compiler defaults the type to **int**. This defaulting mechanism should never be used. When a type specification is missing, there is no way to tell whether it has been left out on purpose or by mistake. Also, parameter declarations should always have a comment explaining the goal or purpose of the parameter (we discuss this further later). If a parameter is not declared, the comment will not appear.

Newer versions of C offer enumeration types that can improve readability. Consider, fcr example, the following declarations:

```
typedef enum { ATLAS, BOOK, INDEX, JOURNAL, MAGAZINE } document_type;
document_type current_document;
```

The variable **current_document** can assume values of the enumeration type **document_type**, namely **ATLAS, BOOK, INDEX, JOURNAL,** and **MAGAZINE**. The enumeration type shows the values making up the logically cohesive group picked out by the type; the names of the values describe what they represent. Declaring a variable to have an enumeration type helps explain its role and limits the values the variable can assume.

Many of our rules have exceptions because of implementation restrictions, memory or efficiency constraints, or the need for portability. For example, older compilers may not recognize the **void** type. If not, it is better to use it, and to **typedef** **void** as **int** in a global header file. This breaks our rule against **typedef**ing simple types, but is recommended anyway because of its documentary value.

Use of Right Control Structures.   A reader can be enlightened by appropriate control structures, or completely confused by inappropriate control structures. Empirical research confirms that good control structures enhance readability.[6] As a simple illustration, consider the following code fragment:

```
i = 0;
while ( TRUE ) {
    Process(i);
    i++;
    if ( MAX == i ) break;
    }
```

The loop counts from 0 to **MAX-1**, so it ought to be a standard **for** loop:

```
for ( i = 0; i < MAX; i++ ) Process(i);
```

It takes a while to figure out from the first fragment exactly what is going on, but it is obvious (to a C programmer) how control flows in the second fragment.

The following guidelines should be used in choosing control structures to maximize code readability:

- Use a **do-while** loop when the loop body is always executed at least once; otherwise use a **while** loop or a **for** loop.

- Use a **switch** statement only when the **switch** will contain more than two alternatives. Otherwise use an **if-then-else** statement.

- Avoid the **goto** statement. An appropriate use of the **goto** statement in C is rare.

- Avoid the **continue** statement. The problem with the **continue** statement (as with other variants of the **goto** statement) is that it alters the flow of control without having its affect mirrored in the static layout of the code. Readers are left without the aids of grouping, indentation, and block delimiters to help in tracing the flow of control. An **if** statement and an extra level of indentation achieve the same effect as the **continue** statement more clearly.

- Avoid breaking out of loops and early function returns. These practices, like the use of the **continue** statement, usually impair readability. Doing without them, however, usually requires extra boolean variables and tests, and deeper nesting levels. This may complicate code so much that its readability declines.

These rules may be broken to achieve other goals, especially efficiency. Eliminating a **continue**, a **break**, or an early function return often requires that a few extra tests be made. If these tests occur in the inner loop of an expensive algorithm, it may not be acceptable to introduce them.

Display of Program Structure.   People often figure out code by tracing execution paths and relating the outcomes of the paths to the goals of the code. Anything that helps trace execution paths is likely to increase program readability. Formatting code so that indentation and white space show functional groupings and subsidiary relationships is the main way to show program structure. The usual formatting rules follow:

- Indent statements at the same block level to the same column.
- Indent substatements with respect to their main statement. An **if-then-else** statement, for example, should be formatted as follows:

```
if ( test )
    statement 1;
else
    statement 2;
```

- Use vertical white space to separate statements into groups that each do part of a task carried out in a block.
- Use horizontal white space to reflect precedence in expressions as in the following examples:

```
a * b + c * d
a*b + c*d
```

The second example helps readers see how the expression is evaluated.

There has been a continuous controversy over the placement of braces around the statements in subsidiary blocks in C code. The four contenders are illustrated schematically as follows:

Pascal Style

```
while ( test )
    {
    statements;
    }
```

Modified Pascal Style

```
while ( test )
{
    statements;
}
```

Kernighan and Ritchie Style

```
while ( test ) {
    statements;
}
```

Modified Kernighan and Ritchie Style

```
while ( test ) {
    statements;
    }
```

Proponents of these alternatives argue that their preference is more readable, less error prone, and nicer looking. In the absence of empirical evidence one way or the other, the choice is left to the reader, with consistency of format the only requirement.

There are several places in C where slight omissions affect program behavior. Such omissions should be marked with comments so that readers will see them. The three most common examples of this are missing **for** loop parameters, missing loop bodies, and missing breaks in **switch** statements. We discuss each in turn.

It is common practice to leave parameters out of **for** loop headers. This should always be marked with a comment, as in the following example:

```
for ( /* current value of i */; i < MAX; i++ ) ...
```

The comment directs a reader's attention to the omission, and shows that it was intentional. A better comment might say why the parameter was left out. A common C programming practice we think ought to be discouraged on grounds of poor readability is to leave out *all* **for** loop parameters to force an infinite loop:

```
for ( ; ; ) ...
```

A more obvious construct is the following:

```
while ( TRUE ) ...
```

Both of these constructs should be rare, because there is no call for infinite loops in most programs, and termination conditions should not be buried in loop bodies.

C has a null statement that can be the body of a loop. It is easy to overlook null loop bodies, or to think that a null loop body is the incorrect result of a wandering semicolon. Marking null loop bodies with comments as in the following eliminates these problems.

```
while ( *dest_ptr++ = *src_ptr++ )
    /* null loop body */ ;
```

In a **switch** statement, control can flow from one case to the next by leaving out a **break** statement. Forgotten **break** statements are a common program bug, but intentionally omitted **break** statements are a common control strategy. Readers have to wonder about missing **break** statements unless the omission is marked as intentional, as in the following example:

```
        ...
case x : case_x_statements;
           /* no break! -- common x and y processing */

case y : case_y_statements;
           break;
        ...
```

4.1.2 Comments

Code is never completely self-documenting; there are always things about a program that are not clear from the code alone. Research has shown that programs are more readable when they contain good comments.[7] [8] Unfortunately, many programmers do not write good comments. This is partly because there are no clear and widely accepted guidelines indicating where comments should go and what they should say. In this section we suggest guidelines for writing good comments. Our discussion is based on a distinction between program goals, plans, roles, and purposes (these distinctions are loosely based on Letovsky and Soloway[9]).

Goals.   A *program goal* is a target action or state for a program or program segment. Programs or program segments are executed to achieve program goals. For example, a program segment goal might be to save data by spilling a buffer to a file whenever the buffer is full. Another might be to present sorted data to a user on request.

Plans.   A *plan* is an outline of processing steps for achieving program goals. Plans are more abstract than algorithms, but they show how program goals are achieved. For instance, the following plan for adding data to a buffer achieves the goal of saving the data by spilling the buffer to a file when the buffer is full:

1. Add a single data item to the buffer.
2. If the buffer is full, spill it to the file.

The next plan achieves the goal of presenting sorted data to a user on request:

1. Sort the data list.
2. Clear the output device (say, a display screen).
3. Write a header to the output device.
4. Write the data from the sorted list to the output device.

Roles.   The *role* of a program object is the part the object plays in a program. Details about an object's role usually depend on what sort of thing the object is. For example, the role of a variable is to store a particular data value, say a count of bytes in a buffer, or the sum of values encountered so far. The role of a function is to do a particular computation, like sorting a list or computing a statistic.

Purposes.   A *purpose* of a program object is a reason the object plays the role that it does. An object's purposes are usually explained by the way it serves plans for achieving program goals. For example, the purpose of a byte counter might be to keep track of when a buffer should be spilled. This purpose serves a plan calling for a test of whether the buffer is full, to reach the goal of spilling a full buffer to a file. The purpose of a sorting function might be to order a list before presenting it to a user. This purpose serves a plan to provide sorted data, to reach the program goal of presenting sorted output to a user. These definitions of program goals and plans, and program object roles and purposes, are summed up in Table 4.1.

Table 4.1:   Program Goals and Plans, and Object Roles and Purposes

Program goal	A target program action or state
Program plan	An outline of steps for achieving a goal
Object role	A part played by a program object
Object purpose	The reason an object plays the role it does

Our commenting technique involves documenting goals, plans, roles, and purposes. Self-documenting code shows *what* processing a program does but usually not *why* it does it. Understanding source code demands understanding why code does what it does. Explaining why code does what it does starts by stating the ends to be achieved by the code (program goals), then explaining in broad terms how these ends are achieved (program plans), and then explaining how the pieces of code that play various parts (object roles) work together to execute the plans (object purposes). Good comments supplement self-documenting code by providing this information about why code does what it does.

Statement of Program Goals.   Program goals can be broad, such as the goal that a program never lose data under error conditions, or narrow, such as the goal that a file be opened for output. Statements about narrow goals are generally not helpful, because they are usually obvious from the code itself. Goal statements should be general and made at a high-level of abstraction. Broad program goals are usually realized by large code segments, so goal statements are most often found in comments that apply to big chunks of code, like the following:

- *Function header comments.* An explanation of a function's purpose in its header comment is often a statement of the function's goals as well.
- *Banner comments.* A goal may be achieved through the joint efforts of several functions. The functions should appear together with a *banner comment* (stretching across a page and occupying several lines) stating the common goal of that bunch of functions.
- *Module header comments.* A compile module is usually intended to achieve a few broad goals. These should be stated in the module's header comment.

The code in Appendix B has many examples of function and module header comments; header comment templates may be found in the **ccount** coding standards document in Appendix A.

Statement of Program Plans.   A plan is an outline of processing steps for achieving program goals. Plans summarize code, divide code into small, understandable units, and help connect goals with code segments. Plans are worked into programs in two places: function header comments and function bodies. The plan for the processing done in a function should be placed in a special location in a function's header comment. The plan should be a short, numbered list of process steps. The list should then be repeated in the body of the function immediately preceding the code for that process step. The following schema illustrates this idea:

```
/***********************************************************

                --- Function Header Comment ---

        Plan:   Part 1:  First process step
                Part 2:  Second process step
                 ...
                Part k: K-th process step

***/

void function_name( argument )
   {

            /* Part 1:  First process step */

            < code for the first process step >

            /* Part 2:  Second process step */

            < code for the second process step >


                     ...

            /* Part k:  K-th process step */

            < code for the k-th process step >

   } /* end function definition */
```

The **ccount** code in Appendix B has many examples of this technique.

   This approach to documenting program plans has several advantages. First, the plan explains (in outline) how a function accomplishes its goals. Second, the plan in the function header gives an overview of the code in the function body. Third, the comments outlining the plan in the function body break the code into smaller fragments, and help the reader grasp the point of each fragment and its relationship to the rest of the function. Finally, the plan in the function header acts like a "table of contents" for the function, with links provided by the comments in the function body.

Statement of Program Object Roles and Purposes. A program object's role is the part it plays in the program. Code is easier to understand if program objects have only one role. Names should indicate roles, and usually names provide adequate role information. In contrast, a program object's purpose is rarely obvious from its name alone—a comment is usually needed to explain it. Definitions and declarations are good places to put role and purpose information. Program objects have to be defined or declared before they are used. Like the compiler, a human reader may not understand an object's use without information about its type, role, and purposes. If role and purpose information is placed with definitions and declarations, readers are sure to see it before the object is used. Furthermore, because all program objects should be defined or declared, definitions and declarations provide an obvious location for conventionally placing role and purpose information.

More specific recommendations for comments about roles and purposes depend on what kind of object is being documented:

- **#define**'d *constants*. Explain why a particular constant value is used in the program. For example:

  ```
  #define BUF1_SIZE    512              /* size of 1 disk block */
  #define BUF2_SIZE   2 * BUF1_SIZE     /* algorithm requires that  */
                                        /* buffer2 be twice buffer1 */
  ```

- *Macros*. Because of their side-effects, macros should only be used instead of functions when efficiency is an issue (more on this later). Focus macro purpose statements on the reason for creating the macro. For example:

  ```
  /* ABS_DBL 5 -- Absolute values of doubles      */
  /* must be computed in the inner loops of the   */
  /* abc and xyz functions.  These loops must be  */
  /* optimized to achieve adequate response times */

  #define ABS_DBL(x)    (((x) >= 0.0) ? (x) : -(x))
  ```

- *Functions*. Function goals and purposes often coincide, so function goal statements generally explain function purposes as well. State these in the function header comment.

- *Variables*. Focus on what the data stored in the variable is used for, and explain *all* the reasons the data is important. Try to say not only *what* data is stored in a variable but *why* the data is being stored in the variable. For example:

```
char input_buf[BUF_SIZE];  /* source for line scanning      */
short buffered_bytes;      /* count of input_buf contents:  */
                           /*  - tracks unprocessed data    */
                           /*  - force buffer refill when 0 */
char line_buf[MAX_LINE];   /* sink for line scanning result */
short line_length;         /* count of line_buf contents:   */
                           /*  - test for line_buf overflow */
                           /*  - used to attach EOS         */
```

- *Parameters.* Provide role and purpose information as for any other variable but also say whether a parameter is (1) an *in* parameter used to send data into a function from the calling environment; (2) an *out* parameter used to send data back from a function to the calling environment; or (3) an *in-out* parameter used both to send data into a function and to send data back from a function.

Explanation of Non-Role-Based Operations.   Program object roles are reflected by names in self-documenting code, so they need not be explained in comments. Similarly, *role-based operations*—operations consonant with an object's role— do not usually need to be explained in comments. For example, consider the following code fragment:

```
sum = 0.0;
sum_of_squares = 0.0;
for ( i = 0; i < array_size; i++ )
    {
    sum += array[i];
    sum_of_squares += array[i] * array[i];
    }
```

The roles of the variables **sum** and **sum_of_squares** are to accumulate the sum of the array elements and of the squares of the array elements, respectively. All operations on these variables are role-based, and comments about these operations (such as "increment the sum_of_squares accumulator") would not provide additional information. In contrast, operations that are not (apparently) in accord with object roles must be explained in comments. For example, consider the following slightly altered version of the previous code fragment:

```
sum = 0.0;
sum_of_squares = 0.0;
for ( i = 0; i < ARRAY_SIZE; i++ )
    {
    sum += array[i];
        /* optimization: avoid expensive multiplication */
        /* by skipping increment when value near 0      */
    if ( (array[i] < -EPSILON) || (array[i] > EPSILON) )
        sum_of_squares += array[i] * array[i];
    }
```

The second statement in the loop body has an operation that does not seem to match the roles of the variables: it does not increment the **`sum_of_squares`** accumulator for certain array elements. Without the comment, this non-role-based operation would puzzle most readers. The comment shows that the operation is intended to achieve a program goal of optimization, however.

Side-Effect Information. A *side-effect* of a program segment (a function, macro, expression, and so on), is a change of state of a resource or object not local to the segment. For example, a function that changes the value of a global variable has the change as a side-effect. Code with side-effects is always puzzling, often buggy, and usually difficult to maintain. Side-effects should be avoided, but if they cannot be (usually for reasons of efficiency) they must be documented. Four pieces of information should be supplied about side-effects: (1) the object or resource affected; (2) the code segment where the side-effect occurs; (3) the consequences of the side-effect; and (4) why the side-effect occurs. Side-effects should be documented in the following three places:

- Comments should flag code segments with side-effects. For example, function header comments should document function side-effects.
- Comments should be added at the point of definition or declaration of objects affected by side-effects. For example, if a global variable is changed as a side-effect of several functions, this should be noted in a comment at the variable declaration or definition.
- Comments should warn of side-effects at the point of invocation of program segments with side-effects. For example, if a function alters a variable as a side-effect, this should be noted when the function is called.

It is difficult and time consuming to document side-effects, but failing to do so can lead to hours of frustration during program testing and maintenance. Again, it is best to avoid side-effects! Techniques for avoiding side-effects are discussed subsequently.

Function and Module Header Comments. Begin each compile module with a banner comment called a *module header comment*. The module header comment should discuss the module's goals and explain how the module fits with the rest of the system. The module header comment should also explain why the module contains the code that it does—for example, to satisfy the principles of information hiding and cohesion (see Chapter 3). Example function and module header comment templates are in the **`ccount`** coding guidelines document in Appendix A.

Each function definition should have a banner comment, called a *function header comment*, immediately preceding its definition. Function header comments should include at least the following information:

- *Function purpose.* Typically, the purpose of a function is to achieve some program goal.

- *Function return value type and purpose*. The return value and the function often have different purposes. For example, the purpose of the return value may be to report an error from the function.

- *Plans*. As discussed earlier, a plan for the processing carried out in a function should appear in a function's header comment, coordinated with comments reiterating the plan in the function body.

- *Notes*. Any information that might help the reader should be included as notes in the function header comment. Examples are references to publications from which code is taken, or where algorithms or data structures are discussed, and references to requirements and design documents.

An example function header comment template incorporating these recommendations appears in the **ccount** coding guidelines document in Appendix A.

Summary.   Commenting strategy is rarely discussed adequately; perhaps that is why programmers so often write poor comments. That is why we have covered the topic in detail. Our commenting strategy is summarized in Table 4.2.

Table 4.2: Commenting Strategy

Items Documented	Where Placed	Contents
Program Goals	Function and module headers, banner comments for large code segments	Target computational state or tasks achieved by a large code segment
Program plans	Function headers and bodies	Outline of how code achieves its goals
Object roles	Points of object definition and declaration	State the parts played by the objects in a program
Object purposes	Points of object definition and declaration	Explain why objects play the parts they do
Non-role-based operations	Where the operation is performed	Explain why the apparently odd operation is done
Side-effect information	Point of object definition and declaration; where the side-effect occurs	Explain side-effects

The **ccount** program is documented using the commenting strategy discussed here. Appendix B contains **ccount** source code and illustrates our approach.

4.1.3 Internal Documentation Metrics

The practices we suggest should produce code measurably different from code produced according to other standards. For instance, we have advised that names be used freely, and that they be long and descriptive. Code written according to our guidelines should have more and longer names. You might expect that tools for producing these kinds of metrics about source code (called *internal documentation metrics*) would be widely available, and that empirical research would have established which coding practices are best. This is not so. There are few tools for generating internal documentation metrics, and little empirical research validating coding practices. Exceptions are metrics based on counts of source lines of code—metrics like those produced by our example program `ccount`. Our discussion of source code metrics is therefore restricted to the small bits of wisdom that have accumulated about counts of source lines of code.

A *noncommentary source line, or NCSL,* is a (syntactically correct) source file line containing at least one token outside a comment; that is, a NCSL contains at least one token processed by the compiler as part of a declaration, definition, or statement during program translation. Counts of NCSL are sensitive to formatting conventions, but otherwise they are a simple and reasonably precise measure of the "size" of a segment of C source code. A *commentary source line*, or *CSL*, is a line of a (syntactically correct) source file that contains at least one printable character inside a comment (including the comment delimiters). Note that some source file lines count as both NCSL and CSL because they contain both program code and commentary. Under these definitions, blanks lines are neither NCSL nor CSL. The *comment-to-code ratio* for a segment of code is the count of CSL in the code segment divided by the count of NCSL in the code segment. The comment-to-code ratio is a simple and intuitive measure of comment density.

Readability is compromised by long functions, although there is no firm answer to the question: How long is too long? Functions of several hundred lines are usually too long, whereas functions of twenty or thirty lines are usually OK. In our own development work we have found a target maximum function length of 60 NCSLs to be satisfactory. Similar remarks apply to comment density as measured by comment-to-code ratio. Although a comment-to-code ratio less than about 0.3 is characteristic of code with too few comments, and code with a ratio above 1.0 is usually OK, there is no obvious ideal value. We have been successful with a target minimum comment-to-code ratio of about 0.8, however.

4.2.4 Internal Documentation Guidelines

Project coding standards should specify internal documentation guidelines. Such guidelines list rules for improving code readability, so they should include naming and formatting conventions, practices in the use of types and control structures, practices and templates for writing comments, and targets for code size and comment density.

An example coding standards document for `ccount` is included in Appendix A. It incorporates most of the internal documentation guidelines we have discussed. In addition, Appendix D lists most of the coding practices that we recommend, including many of those discussed in this chapter.

4.2 EXTERNAL DOCUMENTATION

External documentation is material about source code external to the source code file. Besides helping readers understand code, external documentation can provide an implementation tracking mechanism, a mechanism for tracing the satisfaction of requirements, and helpful summaries of the testing, debugging, and change history of code segments. We first discuss a form of external documentation called the *program unit notebook*, which serves all these purposes. We close this chapter with a discussion of a less ambitious form of external documentation called *implementation notes*.

4.2.1 Program Unit Notebooks

A *program unit* is a code fragment that forms a logical element written by a single programmer. A C program unit is typically a compile module, although it may be as small as a single function or as large as an entire multimodule subsystem. A *program unit notebook* is a diary of the life of a program unit, written by the unit's programmer. A program unit notebook should contain the following information:

- A synopsis of the requirements satisfied by the program unit.
- A review of the program unit's design.
- Discussion of difficult, unusual, or tricky aspects of the implementation.
- Implementation milestones and completion dates for the program unit.
- The program unit test plan.
- The modification history for the program unit.

Program unit notebooks help program readers, serve as a strong link tying development phases together and enhancing traceability, and help track progress during implementation. Program unit notebook maintenance is expensive and difficult, however, and notebooks tend to get out of date when programmers neglect to record changes. The latter problem in particular tends to plague even the most conscientious programmers. The solution seems to be either to abandon program unit notebooks in favor of less ambitious external documentation, or to provide computational support for maintaining the notebooks. The latter is a current research topic; the former is our next topic of discussion.

4.2.2 Implementation Notes

The main point of external program documentation is to improve program readability. Program unit notebooks achieve this goal, and several others as well, but at great expense and with a likelihood of error. An alternative approach is to abandon all but the most essential external documentation, providing it only when necessary as a supplement to internal documentation. We call such external documents *implementation notes*.

Implementation notes usually discuss difficult or subtle algorithms and data structures, include graphs, drawings, charts, and other representations difficult to reproduce in source code listings, and contain photocopies of portions of books or articles relevant to the design or implementation. Because well-written code is usually understandable on its own, only selected portions of a system need to be supplemented with implementation notes. Furthermore, implementation notes may not be written until the code is frozen and unit tested so that effort is minimized and documentation is up to date.

4.3 CONCLUSION

We have discussed how to make C programs more readable with self-documenting code supplemented by comments. This requires a careful strategy of explaining program goals and plans, stating program object roles and purposes, and documenting unexpected and noteworthy items. We have also suggested the use of source code metrics and coding standards and guidelines. Finally, we sketched the use of external documentation such as program unit notebooks and implementation notes.

Appendix A contains an example coding guidelines document for **ccount**, our C source code metrics tool. Appendix D contains a list of C coding practices from this and the next two chapters.

REFERENCES

1. Kernighan, B. W., and P. J. Plauger, *The Elements of Programming Style*. New York: McGraw-Hill, 1978.

2. Ledgard, H., *Programming Practice*. Reading, Mass.: Addison-Wesley, 1987.

3. Harbison, S., and G. Steele Jr., *C: A Reference Manual* (2nd ed.). Englewood Cliffs, N.J.: Prentice Hall, 1987.

4. Koenig, A., *C Traps and Pitfalls*. Reading, Mass.: Addison-Wesley, 1989.

5. Marcotty, M., and H. Ledgard, *Programming Language Landscape* (2nd ed.). Chicago: Science Research Associates, 1986.

6. Sheppard, S. B., M. A. Borst, B. Curtis, and T. Love, *Predicting Programmers' Ability to Modify Software*, TR 78–388100–3, General Electric Company, May 1978.

7. Woodfield, S. N., H. E. Dunsmore, and V. Y. Shen, "The Effect of Modularization and Comments on Program Comprehension," *Proceedings of the Fifth International Conference on Software Engineering* (March 1981), 215–223.

8. Dunsmore, H. E., "The Effect of Comments, Mnemonic Names, and Modularity: Some University Experiment Results," in *Empirical Foundations of Information and Software Science*, pp. 189–196, ed. J. C. Agrawal and P. Zunde. New York: Plenum Press, 1985.

9. Letovsky, S., and E. Soloway, "Delocalized Plans and Program Comprehension," *IEEE Software*, 3, no. 3 (May 1986), 41–49.

5

Low-Level Programming

Low-level programming is programming at the level of expressions, statements, and functions. In contrast, *high-level programming* is at the compile module and system level. This chapter continues our discussion of C programming practice, concentrating on low-level programming; the next chapter is about high-level programming.

5.1 PARAMETERIZATION

Programs depend on values like filenames, search strings, table sizes, fonts, and so forth. Such values can be hard coded into programs, or they can be passed to programs as *parameters*. Parameterization has big advantages: Parameterized code is more maintainable, portable, and reusable because you can enhance and adapt it by changing parameters. Its disadvantages are that it requires more effort initially, and it may have performance problems. It requires more effort to select parameters for algorithms and data structures, and then put them into code. There may be performance problems when extra computation is required to get or generate parameterized values. Parameterization is worthwhile; although it is more work at first, much effort may be avoided later in the life cycle, and performance penalties are usually small.

5.1.1 What to Parameterize

Programming language designers sometimes say that the only numbers that should appear in a language design are 0, 1, and infinity.[1] Much the same can be said of source code, where ideally the only numbers used should be 0 and 1 (and even 0 and 1 should be avoided in favor of more readable names like **NULL, TRUE**, and **FALSE**). Unfortunately, source code often bristles with "magic numbers" reflecting features of the environment, the application, or the implementation. Common magic numbers in C programs include the following:

- *Application-specific values.* These include color codes, field sizes, maximum and minimum allowable values, and so forth.

- *Environment-specific values.* These include word sizes, type sizes, file block sizes, and other values that depend on a particular machine or compiler.

- *Tuning values.* These include buffer sizes, block sizes, table loading factors, and so on.

- *Data type limits.* These include −32768 and 32767 as the minimum and maximum values of the **short** type, for example.

- *Data structure limits.* These include string, array, and table sizes.

- *Internal codes.* These are used to represent special objects or states peculiar to the implementation. Examples of internal codes include values for menu choices, token types returned by parsers, and function return codes. These values are especially magical because they have no meaning outside the program where they appear.

- *Bit masks.* These are used to manipulate bit strings.

- *Offsets.* These are locations of fields in files, buffers, tables, or structures.

Magic numbers are candidates for parameterization. Application-specific values should be made into parameters to ease maintenance. Some magic numbers guaranteed not to change, such as codes for ASCII characters, output display locations, and so on, may not need to be parameterized (although it is difficult to guarantee that values will not change). You should always make parameters out of environment-specific values, data-structure limits, offsets, and other values that tend to change when programs are moved. Bit masks, internal codes, data-type limits, and other values that might puzzle program readers should be parameterized for readability.

It is always a good idea to parameterize data types. UNIX and C are available on diverse machines, from microcomputers to supercomputers. Data types often must be changed to fit these environments. For example, a program for a microcomputer with limited memory and an 8-bit bus might need its integer variables declared **unsigned char** instead of **short** or **int** to make the program fast and small. On a bigger machine, some of the variables might need to be **short** or **int** to solve larger problems.

Operations can be parameterized too. A system can use a computationally expensive algorithm if a floating point accelerator is available, or a less precise but cheaper algorithm if one is not. A choice between the two should be coded as a parameter. Similarly, operations for user interfaces, optimization, problem size, data format, and so on, can all be parameterized.

5.1.2 Ways to Parameterize

C has many ways to parameterize. The most common is function arguments, which are nevertheless underused. For instance, it is common to find sorts or searches with hard-coded data structure limits, user message functions with hard-coded display locations, formats, and color codes, data analysis functions with hard-coded analysis operations, and so on.

Function arguments are good for parameterizing application-specific values, data-type and data-structure limits, and operations. Operations in particular are overlooked because so few programmers are familiar with passing functions as arguments, a powerful mechanism. For example, an array sort can be generalized by passing the comparison operation and the array element size as arguments. The result is a sort that works on any kind of array, and sorts in any order. Consider the following general purpose insertion sort:

```
void Insertion_Sort( array, element_size, array_size, comp_func )
   char *array;          /* in/out: pointer to an arbitrary array */
   int element_size,     /* in: bytes used to make up an element */
       array_size;       /* in: elements in the array */
   int (*comp_func)();   /* in: TRUE iff arg1 bears order relation to arg2 */
   {
   char *tmp;            /* buffer for swapping array elements */
   register int i,j;     /* loop variables: i walks forward, j walks back */

                   /* Part 1: Allocate a swap buffer */
   tmp = malloc( (unsigned)element_size );

        /* Part 2: Swap the smallest value into first place */
   for ( i = element_size, j = 0;
       i < (array_size*element_size);
       i += element_size )
     if ( (*comp_func)(array+i, array+j) ) j = i;

   if ( 0 < j )
     {
     memcpy( tmp,      array,   element_size );
     memcpy( array,    array+j, element_size );
     memcpy( array+j, tmp,      element_size );
     }

        /* Part 3: Insert array elements starting from the third */
   for ( i = (2*element_size);
       i < (array_size*element_size);
       i += element_size )
     {
     memcpy( tmp, array+i, element_size );
     j = i;
```

```
    while ( (*comp_func)(tmp, array+j-element_size) )
      {
      memcpy( array+j, array+j-element_size, element_size );
      j -= element_size;
      }
    memcpy( array+j, tmp, element_size );
    }

              /* Part 4: Deallocate the swap buffer */
  free( tmp );

  } /* Insertion_Sort */
```

The comparison function encapsulates information about the array elements and determines how to order them. Because the sort does not need to know these details, it works fine with the result returned by the comparison function. We tested this sort on our system and found it to be about four times slower than a nongeneric version. The slowdown is from the function call overhead in comparisons and data moves. However, when insertion sort is appropriate (arrays with no more than about 30 elements), this loss of efficiency would probably not be important, or even noticeable. The time to rewrite the sort for different data types would be noticeable, however.

C macros are another important parameterization mechanism, especially for making code more portable. Macros for environment- and application-specific values, tuning values, bit masks, offsets, and other nonportable magic numbers can be put in header files. Then when ports, fixes, changes, or enhancements require a change, it is easy to change the macro definitions and recompile. Sometimes macros are used for internal codes or flags naming data values or internal states. For example, in a compiler, token types returned by the lexical analyzer might be assigned special codes. Token codes can be defined as the following macros:

```
            #define IDENTIFIER       0
            #define SEMI_COLON       1
            #define LEFT_BRACE       2
            #define RIGHT_BRACE      3
            #define INTEGER_LITERAL  4
            #define REAL_LITERAL     5
            etc.
```

Although this is acceptable, it is better to use the following enumeration data type:

```
        enum token_type { IDENTIFIER,
                          SEMI_COLON,
                          LEFT_BRACE,
                          RIGHT_BRACE,
                          INTEGER_LITERAL,
                          REAL_LITERAL,
                          etc.
                        };
```

An enumeration type has two advantages: You don't have to reassign code numbers when the list changes, and the compiler can do better type checking.

Type definitions are another C parameterization mechanism. Like macros, type definitions can be put in a few header files, changed when necessary, and the system recompiled. You should always use a type definition rather than a macro when parameterizing types. Consider the following example:

```
#define CHAR_PTR        char *
CHAR_PTR p, q;
```

When the macro is expanded, the declaration reads:

```
char *p, q;
```

This declares **p** as a pointer to a **char**, but **q** as a **char**. Using a **typedef** for **CHAR_PTR** solves this problem.

Table 5.1 summarizes our discussion of parameterization:

Table 5.1:   C Parameterization

Candidate	Mechanism
Application-specific values	Function arguments, macros
Environment-specific values	Macros
Tuning values	Macros
Data-type and -structure limits	Function arguments
Bit masks	Macros
Offsets	Macros
Internal codes	Enumerations
Operations	Function arguments
Types	Type definitions

5.2 C PREPROCESSOR

The C preprocessor is a macro processor run on C source code as the first stage of compilation. The preprocessor pulls the contents of other files into the source file according to **#include** directives, expands macros, and conditionally retains or removes portions of the source file. We have already discussed how parameterless macros increase portability and maintainability. This section provides further guidelines for using the preprocessor.

One abuse of the C preprocessor is using it to disguise C as another language. Suppose, for example, that the following preprocessor definitions are made:

```
#define IF          if (
#define THEN        )
#define REPEAT      do {
#define UNTIL( b )  } while (! (b) )
```

Using these macros, consider the following code fragment before preprocessing:

```
REPEAT
    ch = getch();
    IF ch < BLANK THEN ch = ESC;
UNTIL ( ch == BLANK );
```

This code is transformed by the preprocessor into the following:

```
do {
    ch = getch();
    if ( ch < BLANK ) ch = ESC;
} while (! (ch == BLANK) );
```

The first fragment looks like Pascal, except for the assignment and equality operators. The second fragment is C code. A recent article[2] provides complete instructions for disguising C as Pascal.

At first, the idea of disguising C may not seem so bad—there is a certain cleverness and elegance to it, it costs little in compiler performance, and it may provide a crutch for new C programmers who know some other language. Disguising C is a bad idea for several reasons, however. First, no matter how cleverly C is dressed up as some other language, the disguise is never perfect. Constructs from the other language are always missing, and C idioms and operations peek out everywhere. For example, there is no way to mimic Pascal's set type operations using the C preprocessor because there is no way to make the operators "+", "−", "*", and "=" behave the way they do in Pascal. As a result, disguised code is a confusing hash of two languages that is idiosyncratic, undocumented, and unsupported. Second, disguising C for novice C programmers turns out to be more of a hindrance than a help. Because the novice does not know C, he or she cannot tell C from its disguise. So on top of learning C, the novice programmer must also sort out C language features from those of the disguise, and "unlearn" parts of the disguise mistaken as C. Third, C can be disguised when it is written, but the disguise is stripped away during compilation: The program executed is a C program. During debugging, you have to know exactly what your program is doing, so you must penetrate any disguise to see the C program actually executed. This makes the job harder, not easier. Finally, disguising C programs makes them difficult to read. There are no standard disguises for C. When C programmers read disguised programs, they are forced to decipher a disguise in addition to figuring out someone else's code.

Other problems can be traced to misunderstanding the differences between macros and functions. Macros are not program objects in their own right but abbreviations for code fragments. Once the preprocessor is done with a source file, all macros disappear in favor of their definitions. In contrast, functions remain throughout program translation and exist as separate entities in the object code. This makes a big difference. Function arguments are evaluated during execution and the result passed to the function, but macro arguments are substituted textually during preprocessing. Macros can interact with surrounding code in ways that functions cannot, often to the surprise of the programmer. For example, suppose the following macro is used to compute geometric means:

```
#define G_MEAN(a, b)  sqrt(a * b)
```

The expansion of **G_MEAN(x+4, y+2)** is **sqrt(x+4 * y+2)**. This expression does not compute the geometric mean and is probably not what was intended. The problem is easily fixed. Place parentheses in the macro definition as follows:

```
#define G_MEAN(a,b)  (sqrt((a) * (b)))
```

As a rule, macros and their parameters should be isolated by parentheses in their definitions.

Other problems may arise from differences between macro and function arguments. Consider the following definition for the maximum of two values:

```
#define MAX(a, b)   (((a) > (b)) ? (a) : (b))
```

This definition looks fine, but consider **MAX(i++, j++)**. You would expect **i** and **j** to be incremented, and the value of the expression to be the greater of the original values of **i** and **j**. Look at the following expanded code, however:

```
(((i++) > (j++)) ? (i++) : (j++))
```

This expression increments one of **i** or **j** *twice*, and its value is the greater of the two *plus 1*. The side-effects that cause these surprises cannot occur with function parameters. Side-effect problems plague many macros; avoid them by using functions instead of macros if possible.

Macros with large definitions can cause yet another problem—unexpectedly large object code. This problem does not occur for functions because only one copy of a function body exists no matter how many times the function is called.

The only good reason for using a macro in place of a function is speed: Because macros are expanded where they occur and have no local context, they do not have the call and return overhead that functions do. In most C implementations, function call and return overhead is small, but sometimes replacing functions with macros is necessary to speed up code enough to satisfy requirements. If so, develop and debug the program with functions, and replace the functions with macros before final unit testing.

5.3 C FUNCTION LIBRARIES

Unlike many other languages, C has no built-in operations for input and output, string manipulation, and some common arithmetic operations, like exponentiation. Consequently almost every C program must use C function libraries. Many of the function libraries are highly standardized, especially now that there is an ANSI C standard, but others are less standardized, or are only available in certain environments. C function libraries typically include the following:

- *Input and output functions.* These are for opening and closing text files, checking file status, seeking and rewinding files, and reading and writing files. All implementations of C provide the core functions in the standard I/O library, often augmented by others tailored to particular environments.
- *String manipulation functions.* These are for copying, concatenating, comparing, searching, and finding the lengths of strings. These functions are highly standardized and widely available.
- *Memory allocation and manipulation functions.* These are for allocating and freeing memory from a heap of free storage and are standard. Most implementations also provide routines for copying and initializing memory, testing the free memory remaining, and so on.
- *Mathematical functions.* These are a surprisingly varied collection of mathematical functions. There does not seem to be much standardization in this category beyond functions for square roots, logarithms, and exponentials.
- *Data conversion functions.* These are for transforming numeric data between character and binary representations. There is little uniformity in such libraries.
- *Operating system service functions.* These provide access to low-level input and output, peripheral device control, process control, and date, time, and system status information. The routines are standardized in UNIX environments but vary widely in others.

Some programmers shun library functions in favor of home-grown functions. This is poor practice. The standard portions of the C function libraries, particularly input-output functions, are recognized by all experienced C programmers. Code that uses them is more readable because it contains familiar elements. Library functions are documented by compiler suppliers and supported along with the compiler. Part of program documentation and maintenance is borne by the compiler supplier when a program makes use of library functions. The C function libraries provide common high-level services that help insulate a program from its environment. Programs that do not take advantage of this insulation are less portable. C library functions are tested extensively, so they are more reliable than functions programmers write for their own use. Furthermore, library functions have been crafted for robustness and efficiency, often by experienced specialists using assembly language to achieve optimal performance. Finally, using C library functions increases programmer productivity. There is no reason to write, document, test, debug, enhance, and maintain tens, hundreds, or thousands of lines of C code when the same (or better) functionality is already available in libraries supplied with C compilers.

Besides the C function libraries that come with the compiler, there are other function libraries that you should exploit. There is a substantial market in specialized C function libraries, particularly for microcomputers. Many of these products are first rate. Of special importance are libraries that conform to standards, like Graphics Kernel System (GKS),[3] a national graphics standard. Libraries that conform to standards are well planned and well documented, and are replaceable by other libraries that conform to the standard.

5.4 EXPRESSIONS

Because expressions are used more in C than in other similar languages, and C expressions are complex, expressions are a source of problems in C programming.

Parenthesization.   C has 1 ternary operator, 34 binary operators, and 9 unary operators arranged in a 15-level precedence hierarchy. Although some of these operators are rarely used, and the precedence levels are like those in other languages, order of evaluation in complex expressions can still cause confusion and errors. The best way to avoid confusion and guarantee that expressions are evaluated as intended is liberal use of parentheses. Extra parentheses cost nothing in compilation and run-time efficiency, but increase readability and reliability.

Side-Effects.   C has several operators with side-effects: the increment and decrement operators, and the assignment operators. Many C programmers regard expression side-effects as among the strongest features of the C language; we regard it as among the weakest. Although source code can be shortened with expression side-effects, readability usually declines and error proneness increases. We recommend that expression side-effects be used sparingly.

Bitwise Operations.   Reflecting its pedigree as a systems programming language, C offers a rich variety of operations for manipulating bits. Some programmers cannot resist the temptation to twiddle bits even when there is no need to do so, using shifts for integer multiplication and division, storing multiple flags or counters in single words, and so on. Except when the application or performance requirements demand it, these practices should be avoided.

Complex Boolean Expressions.   Most people, even programmers, are easily confused by complex boolean expressions. Readability, robustness, reliability, and maintainability tend to increase when boolean expressions are simplified. A method for simplifying boolean expressions is based on DeMorgan's Laws as follows:

```
! ( A && B )   is equivalent to   ( !A || !B )
! ( A || B )   is equivalent to   ( !A && !B )
```

Consider, for example, the boolean expression `! ( (4<=A) && (A<=6) )`. This expression reads: true when it is not the case that both **A** is at least 4 and **A** is not more than 6. Applying DeMorgan's Law we get **((A<4) || (6<A))**, which reads simply: True when **A** is less than 4 or greater than 6. In general, boolean expressions are easier to understand when DeMorgan's Laws are used to drive negations inside expressions—nested negations tend to be confusing.

Other mechanisms useful in simplifying complex boolean expressions (and in formulating them correctly in the first place), are decision tables,[4] Karnough maps,[5] decision trees,[6] and Marquand diagrams.[7] These tools are also helpful in figuring out complex nested conditionals.

Complex boolean expressions are a frequent source of side-effect bugs. C's boolean operators are short-circuit operators, so expression evaluation stops as soon as possible. Hence if **A** is less than 4, then evaluation of the boolean expression **(A<4) || (6<A)** stops after the first relation is evaluated (because then the entire expression must be true). This works fine as long as there are no side-effects. But if, for example, this expression were **(i<4) || (6<i++)**, then **i** would be incremented only if it started off being 4 or greater. These problems are avoided if complex boolean expressions do not have side-effects.

Relational Expressions.   Despite their simplicity, relational expressions can be confusing. Some people think about numerical relations spatially, imagining values in their relative positions on the number line. When confronted with a relation like **(X >= Y)**, these people mentally "flip" the relation to **(Y <= X)**. Doing mental gymnastics while keeping track of what is going on in a program is too difficult. Avoiding the relational operators **>** and **>=** in favor of the operators **<** and **<=** solves this problem by removing any need to flip relations, and conforms more closely to standard mathematical notation as well.

Many experienced C programmers cite one particularly annoying bug as their nemesis: mistyping the equality operator **==** as the assignment operator **=** in relational expressions. Programs with this bug behave strangely, but the source code looks correct—you tend to read past the error, seeing the assignment operator as the equality operator. One simple practice reduces the frequency of this bug (and increases code readability as well): Whenever equality comparisons are made with a constant, place the constant on the left. Because a constant cannot be assigned a value, the compiler will catch an equality operator mistyped as an assignment operator.

Loop Termination Expressions.   A *loop termination expression* is tested to determine whether a loop should terminate. The boolean expression in the header of a **while** loop is a loop termination expression, for example. A common loop termination expression tests whether a loop control variable has reached some value. For example:

```
for ( i = START_VALUE; i != STOP_VALUE; i++ )
   { ... loop body ... }
```

This achieves the programmer's intention and is readable, but is less robust than it might be. There is no guarantee that **i** is not altered in the body of the loop to jump past **STOP_VALUE**, causing an infinite loop. Better is the following:

```
for ( i = START_VALUE; i <= STOP_VALUE; i++ )
    { ... loop body ... }
```

This loop will stop on any value of **i** at least as large as **STOP_VALUE**, whether the exact value is reached or not. This gain in robustness is achieved by giving the loop termination expression the greatest possible opportunity to fail, that is, by making it as weak as possible. This suggests another rule of practice: Make loop termination expressions as weak as possible.

Loop termination expressions should also be complete, in the sense that all (nonexceptional) tests for loop termination should occur in the loop expression, not in the body of the loop. Loops are easier to understand when all their termination conditions are displayed together, and the conventional place to do this is the loop termination expression.

5.5 TYPES IN C

Poor use of data types causes confusion, bugs, and portability problems in C programs. There are several sources of problems: As noted in Chapter 4, C is type-rich, not strongly typed, and does many automatic type conversions. Second, C provides low-level access to the computer, leading to type portability problems. Third, the C language definition leaves certain key features (such as the data type sizes) to the implementation, again leading to portability problems. We consider all these problems in surveying practices in the use of types in C programming.

C has several integral types differing in their range of values. The choice among these types depends on the memory required to store values of the type, the execution speed of operations applied to values of the type, the robustness and portability of code employing the type, and the range of values allowed by the type. The most important of these is the last, particularly because the range of values allowed by a type conveys the most information to a program reader about the role of a program object. The following rules help make the choice between integral types in C:

- Use signed types instead of unsigned types. C cannot provide good error checking support for unsigned types: Negative values can creep into unsigned contexts, be interpreted as unsigned quantities, and cause errors. If variables or functions are declared with a signed type, even when their values are supposed to be unsigned, checks for negative values can be inserted by the programmer, and other indications (such as negative output) are more likely to expose errors. Exceptions to this rule are made only when using bit strings, or when the range of values requires it.

- Use the **char** type exclusively for character data. It is confusing to declare variables or functions as **char** when the data involved is not really character data. In the interest of readability, the **char** type should only be used when the data is character data (unless space requirements dictate otherwise).

- If the required values can be represented in no more than 16 bits, use the **int** type, otherwise use the **long** type. It turns out that **int** values are almost always represented in at least 16 bits, and **long** values are almost always represented in more than 16 bits. Thus switching from **int** to **long** at 16 bits is more likely to avoid porting problems.

- Do not use the **short** type unless memory limitations demand it. Values of **short** type are converted to **int** values in integer expressions involving **int** data, and in function arguments. These conversions are not always handled properly by compilers.

Another way to deal with portability problems of the integral types is to use a standard-type defining header file in which integral types are given special names reflecting their properties and sizes. When the system is ported to a new environment, only the **typedef**'s in the header file need to be changed. For example, such a header file might contain **typedef**'s like the following:

```
typedef S_INT_8  char;            /* signed 8 bit integer     */
typedef U_INT_8  unsigned char;   /* unsigned 8 bit integer   */

typedef S_INT_16 short;           /* signed 16 bit integer    */
typedef U_INT_16 unsigned short;  /* unsigned 16 bit integer  */

typedef S_INT_32 int;             /* signed 32 bit integer    */
typedef U_INT_32 unsigned;        /* unsigned 32 bit integer  */

typedef S_INT_64 long;            /* signed 64 bit integer    */
typedef U_INT_64 unsigned long;   /* unsigned 64 bit integer  */
```

The difficulty with this solution is that some types may not be available, so the portability problem may resurface.

C provides two floating point types: **float** and **double**, but all floating point operations, and all floating point values passed as parameters, use **double** values. A **float** variable occupies less space than a **double**, but its value is always converted to **double** before it is used. The code needed to convert **float** to **double** takes time to execute, and often uses more space than is saved by declaring a few variables **float** instead of **double**. Consequently, all floating point functions and variables should be declared **double**.

Because C has weak type checking, pointer types can be converted freely, pointers can point at data of any type, and pointers may be converted to integral types and vice versa. All these practices are error prone, make code harder to understand, and cause serious portability problems. Conversion between pointer types, and especially between pointer and integral types, should hardly ever occur in good C code. When it does occur, it should be marked by an explicit cast operator.

Another source of subtle type bugs is function arguments. Function arguments have two classes of type bugs. The first class occurs because C compilers (traditionally) do not check function argument types. The best guard against these bugs is to use function prototypes, which are the proposed ANSI C function type checking mechanism. The next best weapon against them is **lint**, a powerful C syntax checking tool (see Chapter 7).

The second class of function argument type bugs arises from conversions applied to function arguments when functions are called. Function arguments are converted according to the "usual arithmetic conversions" at the point of call: **char** and **short** values are converted to **int**, and **float** values are converted to **double**. Subtle bugs sometimes occur when function parameters have types other than the targets of the usual arithmetic conversions. Usually these bugs are the fault of the compiler (we have encountered them in several compilers). The best way to avoid these bugs is not to declare function parameters with types that are not targets of the usual arithmetic conversions. In particular, function parameters should not be declared as **char**, **short**, or **float**.

5.6 IMPROVEMENT OF EFFICIENCY

Programs often have performance constraints in their specifications, so programmers must make their code efficient as well as correct, robust, reliable, and maintainable. *Optimization* is the activity of altering a system to make it faster or smaller. Part of the reason for C's popularity is that it provides facilities that make code optimization easier. Optimization is difficult. Misguided attempts often cause serious problems. In this section we explain some of the difficulties of C code optimization and suggest ways to avoid them.

The first rule of program optimization is avoid optimization if possible. Code written for efficiency is usually less readable, less robust, less portable, and less maintainable than it would otherwise be; readability, robustness, portability, and maintainability are usually more important than speed. Optimization is time consuming and error prone. Usually, programs turn out to be fast enough as written. If there are performance problems, consider alternatives to optimization. One alternative is to upgrade the hardware or the operating system. Adding memory chips or a floating point coprocessor may improve performance by orders of magnitude. Later releases of operating systems often display great improvements in system throughput. Another alternative is to upgrade your compiler. New versions of compilers, or optimizing compilers, may be able to generate smaller and faster code.

If easy gains from improved hardware or software tools are not available, then you may have to use optimization techniques. The largest gains come from improving a system's algorithms and data structures. This topic, which is a core area of computer science with a large literature, is outside the scope of our discussion. When a system incorporating good data structures and algorithms still fails to meet performance objectives, improvements can be made using techniques that Bentley,[8] in his excellent book about optimization, calls *writing efficient code*. These techniques rearrange source code so that it is translated into more efficient object code. Good practices are crucial when applying these optimization techniques. Empirical studies[9] have shown that in typical programs, most of the time is spent executing a small part of the code. Therefore, overall performance is improved only if the right parts of a system (the bottlenecks) are optimized. Unfortunately, programmers are notoriously bad at guessing what parts of a system are bottlenecks. Much effort may be wasted optimizing the wrong parts of the system. Furthermore, programmers are also bad at estimating the efficiency of alternative program constructs—sometimes code is slower after programmers have "improved" it.

In light of this, we recommend the approach discussed by Bentley.[8] First build the system using good software engineering techniques without trying to optimize code, putting the focus of development where it belongs: on achieving readability, correctness, reliability, and so on. Once the system is finished, measure its performance. If it fails to meet requirements, then study the system to find its bottlenecks. Because programmers are not good at guessing where bottlenecks are, system performance must be measured using performance analysis tools, or *profilers*. Several UNIX profiling tools are discussed in Chapter 7. Attack program bottlenecks systematically, making changes one at a time. Measure the system after each change to verify that changes are really improvements. Because optimizations often introduce bugs as well, the system must also be regression tested after each change (see Chapter 8). Once the system's performance has been improved enough to meet its requirements, *stop optimizing*. Any substantial program can be improved forever, but the *useful* improvements are generally made early.

Bentley[8] discusses many optimization techniques. The following are some of the possibilities:

- Store precomputed results to reduce the cost of recomputing an expensive function.
- Cache frequently needed data to reduce search and access time.
- Do lazy evaluation whenever possible. *Lazy evaluation* is the policy of not computing a result until it is needed.
- Code motion out of loops. Place calculations that need not be redone at each loop iteration outside the loop, avoiding recomputation of known values.
- Unroll loops. Instead of using a loop, write out the statements that the loop would have executed, avoiding the overhead of loop control.
- Fuse loops. If two loops are near each other and range over the same data, combine them to avoid an extra loop.

These code optimization techniques are programming language independent. Techniques especially useful for C include the following:

- Compile without the debugger, profiler, and path checking flags. This should substantially reduce both execution time and program size.
- Declare frequently accessed variables, like loop control variables, with the **register** storage class.

- Use macros in place of short bottleneck functions. This will generally improve execution time but can also be dangerous (see earlier).
- Replace array indexing operations with pointer operations, avoiding loop indexing arithmetic.

These optimization techniques can achieve dramatic results. Bentley gives many examples where speedups ranged from a factor of 2 to 200.

5.7 CONCLUSION

As this chapter shows, there are endless details to be mastered about C programming practice, particularly at the statement, expression, and macro level. Although we have not mentioned all of them by any means, we surveyed the most important. The list in Appendix D collects most of those we have discussed.

REFERENCES

1. MacLennan, B. J., *Principles of Programming Languages: Design, Evaluation, and Implementation.* New York: Holt, Rinehart and Winston, 1986.

2. Orlin, P., and J. Heath, "Easy C," *Byte*, 11, no. 5 (May 1986), 137–148.

3. Hopgood, F. R., D. A. Duce, J. R. Gallop, and D. C. Sutcliffe, *Introduction to the Graphical Kernel System (GKS).* New York: Academic Press, 1983.

4. Hurley, R. B., *Decision Tables in Software Engineering.* New York: Van Nostrand Reinhold, 1983.

5. Kolman, B., and R. C. Busby, *Discrete Mathematical Structures for Computer Science.* Englewood Cliffs, N.J.: Prentice Hall, 1984.

6. Stanat, D. F., and D. F. McAllister, *Discrete Mathematics in Computer Science.* Englewood Cliffs, N.J.: Prentice Hall, 1977.

7. Gardner, M., *Logic Machines and Diagrams.* Chicago: University of Chicago Press, 1982.

8. Bentley, J. L., *Writing Efficient Programs.* Englewood Cliffs, N.J.: Prentice Hall, 1982.

9. Knuth, D. E., "An Empirical Study of FORTRAN Programs," *Software Practice and Experience*, 1, no. 2 (April-June 1971), 105–133.

6

High-Level Programming

High-level programming is programming at the level of systems, subsystems, and major system components. At this level, the programmer's goal is to realize a system's design in program parts that fit together cleanly, are self-contained, and are logically independent. The first section discusses rules for writing C program modules to achieve good modularization. These principles are illustrated with a large example in the next section. The last section discusses module size and complexity standards.

6.1 IMPLEMENTATION OF MODULES IN C

High-level design, or architecture, drives high-level programming. A high-level design specifies the *design structure* of a program. The modules making up a program, along with their organization, constitute the *implementation structure* of the program. Implementation structure should closely reflect design structure; ideally, design and implementation structures are the same. Implementation structure may differ from design structure for several reasons, however. First, a design structure may not contain as much detail as an implementation structure. This is particularly true of system parts that are "standard," such as a lexical analyzer, or modules implementing various common abstract data types like stacks or queues. Second, an implementation structure may contain several modules that correspond to a single module in a design structure. Part of a system that logically forms a unit may be implemented in several modules to control size and complexity, improve testability, and so on. When implementation structure is forced away from design structure the design should be reworked to make simpler, smaller modules. Nevertheless, practical details often force implementation structure to differ slightly from design structures in many systems.

You should create implementation modules using the same modularization criteria governing system design including the principles of cohesion, coupling, and information hiding (see Chapter 3). In addition, implementation modules are constrained by size and complexity limits. Implementation modules should contain no more than some maximum number of NCSL and should not exceed some maximum complexity. We discuss size and complexity standards later.

In C programs, implementation modules are compilable files. Because they have extensions of ".c" on UNIX and many other systems, they are called *dot-c files*. They are also called *compile modules*. C functions can be thought of as modules at a different level of abstraction. Although this is legitimate, we reserve the term *module* for compile modules.

6.1.1 Program Object Access Control

Information hiding and module decoupling depend on controlling access to functions, variables, and data types. Early programming languages like FORTRAN and COBOL have few mechanisms for program object access control; modern languages like Modula and Ada have rich mechanisms for access control. The C programming language is intermediate between these extremes: C has several access control mechanisms but neither requires nor encourages programmers to use them. It is up to you to learn how to control access to program objects in C and to have the self-discipline to do so.

Control of access to program objects is based on scope rules and techniques for using external names, header files, and function parameters. We discuss these in turn.

Scope Rules. C scope rules resemble scope rules of other block structured languages, but they are more complex because of the preprocessor and the way scope is defined for names declared outside functions. The most important C scope rules are the following:

- Preprocessor macro definitions have scope extending from their **#define** to the end of the compile module, or to the first **#undef** that cancels the definition. For example, the scope of a macro definition of **MAX_ARRAY_SIZE** at line 40 of a source file extends from line 40 to the end of the file.
- Nonpreprocessor names declared outside functions are said to have *nonlocal scope*. Nonlocal scope extends from the point of declaration of the name to the end of the compile module. For example, if **buffer_size** is declared outside a function at line 25 of a file, then the scope of this declaration extends from line 25 to the end of the file. Names with nonlocal scope may be visible outside the compile module where they are declared—we discuss this in detail later.
- Nonpreprocessor names declared as formal parameters, or at the start of a block, are said to have *local scope*. Local scope extends from the point of declaration of the name to the end of the function or block in which the declaration occurs. For instance if **buffer_size** is a function parameter, then the scope of

buffer_size extends from its declaration to the closing curly bracket at the end of the function.

A declaration is *visible* at some point in its scope if the binding established by the declaration is in force at that point. Declarations may be *hidden* by other declarations of the same name between the original declaration and the point of use of the name. This is the same as in other block structured languages.

Scope provides a way to block access to program objects. Because access to program objects should be allowed only when necessary, declarations should have the smallest possible scope. In practice, this means that you should avoid nonlocal declarations (that is, declarations outside any function) in favor of local declarations. You can even declare names in the innermost blocks in which they appear, declaring variables in inner-nested blocks. Although this is common in other block structured languages, many programmers do not even know you can do this in C, and few programmers make it a practice. Because it is so rare, it may not be worth the confusion to declare variables local to blocks.

Because nonlocal scope and the scope of preprocessor macro definitions extend from the point of declaration or definition to the end of the source file, nonlocal declarations and macro definitions can occur as far into the file as possible to limit their scope. Again, this is a good practice but unusual in the C community; most C programmers use the convention that macro definitions and top-level declarations appear near the beginning of C source files. A decision to adopt this convention should take this into account.

You should also avoid hiding a declaration with an intervening declaration of the same name. Readers are likely to be confused when the same name is used for two things in the same compile module.

External Names.   The scope of C identifiers is limited to the compile module in which they are declared. A name of a function or variable may be made an *external name*, however. External names in two or more compile modules are linked, so they refer to the same thing in each compile module. This effectively extends the scope of a declaration beyond compile module boundaries and is the way global variables are created in C. Names are explicitly made external by being declared **extern**, and nonlocal variable and function names are external by default. The default mechanism can be halted, and names made private to their compile module, by declaring them **static**. Names of functions and nonlocal variables should always be declared **static** unless they must be available outside the module. Functions often have to be externally accessible; nonlocal variables rarely need to be, so ought to be declared **static** as a matter of course.

External names have several declarations (one in each of several compile modules), but only one *defining declaration*. The compiler, linker, and human program readers must be able to tell which declaration is the defining declaration. This problem is especially acute for external variables, because there is no standard way to distinguish defining declarations for variables (see Harbison and Steele[1] for a discussion of the alternatives employed by various compilers). The best practice for most compilers and people is the following: In a defining declaration, omit the **`extern`** keyword from the declaration. For variables, it is also a good idea to provide an initializer, because the presence of an initializer is used by some compilers to identify defining declarations. In a nondefining declaration, always use the **`extern`** keyword.

These rules provide a tidy mechanism for controlling access to nonlocal functions and variables in C. Nonlocal private names are declared **`static`**; names linked to public nonlocal objects are declared **`extern`**; names of public locally defined objects are not declared either **`static`** or **`extern`**. Table 6.1 summarizes this mechanism:

Table 6.1:   Access Control for Nonlocal Variables and Functions

Storage Class	Public or Private	Where Defined
`static`	Private	Current file
`extern`	Public	Elsewhere

Header Files.   So far we have discussed ways of *restricting* access to program objects; C header files are a powerful way of *providing* access to program objects to several source code files. A C *header file* is a source code file, conventionally having the extension ".h," and often called a *dot-h file*, incorporated into C compile modules using preprocessor **`#include`** directives. Header files have two advantages for sharing information among compile modules. First, they ensure that source files get exactly the same information. For example, if macro and type definitions and **`extern`** declarations appear in common header files rather than separately in each source code file, there is no chance that the source files will use inconsistent definitions or declarations. Second, putting common definitions and declarations in header files makes development, maintenance, and porting easier and less error prone because you only need to make changes in one place.

Function Values and Parameters.   The final way to control object access in C is with function parameters and return values. Function parameters and return values are a better alternative to external variables—that is, instead of passing data in external variables, data should be passed in function parameters or by return values. This is true even when parameters are merely passed through a function to another. Data structures can be hidden better when values are passed as function parameters. This helps decouple modules and hide information. Access is more disciplined when controlled through functions. External variables can be read or changed at any time by any program component. If access is controlled through functions, variables can only be read or changed by special functions that can check these operations. Finally, code that restricts data communication to function values and parameters is more robust and reliable because side-effects are avoided. When programming in an object-oriented style, access to even simple values may be wholly restricted to functions. Special *access functions* are used to set and retrieve values of private variables. We present an example of this approach subsequently.

6.1.2 Module Contents and Organization

Compile modules contain C functions and data structures. The source code for an entire C program can be in a single compile module, if the compiler can handle it. For small programs—say a few hundred lines—this practice is OK. Most real programs are much too large to place entirely in a single compile module, however; even if they were, doing so would not be good practice. Distributing source code in several modules hides information, decouples modules, and makes program structure clear. Furthermore, if a program is in several source files, then only parts of the program must be recompiled when changes are made. Testing is easier when programs can be tested in parts, which is encouraged when code is placed in separate modules. Finally, reuse is encouraged because self-contained modules can be used more readily in other applications.

Some programmers take the practice of dividing code into several files to an extreme, placing every function in a separate source file. This is a bad programming practice too. Compile modules should group code according to principles of modularization that reflect the program's design structure and help readers understand the program's implementation structure. You cannot do this when every function is in a separate file. Also, when every function is in a separate file, it is not possible to have private functions and variables, which severely limits opportunities to control access to program objects and to hide information. Finally, even a medium-sized program can become a file management problem when every function is in its own source file.

Decisions about what code to place in what module (i.e., about the implementation structure) must be based on the system design structure, on modularization principles like information hiding, cohesion, and coupling, and on pragmatic principles about maximum module size and complexity.

We can divide the contents of compile modules into six broad categories:

- Header files included in the compile module by preprocessor **#include** directives.
- Declarations of imported public variables and functions defined in some other compile module, but accessed in the current compile module.
- Declarations of private program objects. This category includes macro definitions, type definitions, **static** variables, and nondefining **static** function declarations.
- Defining declarations of private **static** functions.
- Declarations of public exported variables.
- Defining declarations of public exported functions.

Conventionally, included header files are listed first in compile modules. Declarations of public variables and functions imported from other modules are next, followed by declarations of public and private program objects. It does not matter whether public objects or private program objects come first, as long as the grouping is consistent. Defining function declarations come last, grouped together as public or private. Function ordering reflects preference for top-down or bottom-up presentation. Because private functions can only be accessed from within the compile module, they are generally called by the public functions instead of the other way around, so they are closer to the bottom of the function hierarchy. The bottom-up or top-down approach should also be reflected in the ordering of the functions within each group.

Nondefining declarations of private functions should appear near the top of the compile module to give the reader a catalog of coming function definitions, and to tell the compiler about function return types and arguments (if function prototypes are supported) so that it can do type checking and data conversions properly.

6.2 C MODULARIZATION EXAMPLE

In this section we present an example illustrating good high-level programming. The example is an implementation of an abstract data type from **ccount**. This example is similar to many others in various books[1] [2] [3] that discuss techniques for implementing abstract data types. Our example is an implementation of an abstract data type called a *count list*. Count lists record function names and counts of CSL and NCSL for functions analyzed by **ccount**. As an abstract data type, count lists are ordered sets of triples consisting of a character string and two long values.

The interface for the count list data type consists of a data type name and four functions. The count list data type is called **count_list**. The four functions in the data type are as follows:

- **Create_List**—a **void** function that takes a pointer to a count list variable and assigns it a new, empty count list.
- **Is_Empty_List**—an **int** function that takes a count list as its only argument, and returns **TRUE** (1) if the list is empty, and **FALSE** (0) if the list is not empty.
- **Append_Element**—a **void** function that adds elements to the end of a count list. This function takes four arguments: a pointer to a count list, a string, and two **long** values. The function forms a list element from the triple consisting of the string and the two numbers, and appends it to the count list. The list element contains its own copy of the string.
- **Delete_Element**—a **void** function that removes elements from the head of a count list. This function takes four arguments: a pointer to a count list, a string buffer, and two pointers to **long** variables. The function removes the triple at the head of the list, copies the string portion of the triple into the string buffer argument, and places the **long** values from the triple into the **long** arguments. If the count list is empty, the function returns without altering its arguments.

Many other functions, such as a list destruction function, other list insertion and deletion routines, a list length routine, and so on could be added to this data type, but they were not needed for our implementation of **ccount**.

The header file for the count list module, called **list.h**, is included in files where count lists are used. It contains a declaration of the count list data type `count_list`, and external declarations for the four functions discussed earlier. The following is an abbreviated version of this file (see Appendix B for the full source code):

```
/********************************   list.h   ********************************

     Purpose:  Header for count list abstract data type module.

**/

/*************************   Public Data Type   *************************/

typedef struct count_struct *count_list;  /* pointer to linked list of counts */

/*************************   Public Routines   *************************/

#ifdef __STDC__

extern int Is_Empty_List( count_list list );
extern void Create_List( count_list *list );
extern void Append_Element( count_list *list, char *name, long CSL, long NCSL );
extern void Delete_Element( count_list *list, char *name, long *CSL,long *NCSL);

#else

extern int Is_Empty_List();       /* check whether a count list is empty */
extern void Create_List();        /* create a new count list */
extern void Append_Element();     /* add an element to the tail of a list */
extern void Delete_Element();     /* remove an element from the head of a list */

#endif
```

There are several notable points about this header file. First note that **count_list** is type defined as a pointer to a structure. The structure definition is hidden in **list.c**, the file where the abstract data type is implemented.

It may appear odd that there are two sets of function declarations. The requirements of **ccount** state that the software has to be ported to and tested on at least three systems. We used a Sun workstation running SunOS,®* a VAX running UNIX System V, and a PC compatible microcomputer running DOS as our three systems. The compiler on the PC is ANSI C compatible, but the compilers on the other systems are not. Because we had to port the system anyway, we built porting mechanisms into the implementation. ANSI C function prototypes are included as well as older declarations, and the preprocessor is used to choose between them, depending whether the symbol **__STDC__** is defined. The latter is defined with a nonzero value in ANSI compilers.

---

*SunOS is a registered trademark of Sun Microsystems, Inc.

This header file shows how to make an abstract data type available to other portions of a program. When a client of the count list module wants to use its services, it need only include this header file to obtain the necessary data type definitions and function declarations. Had other constants or macros been required, these could also have been written into the header file.

Most of the implementation of the count list data type is contained in the compile module **list.c**. This file is too long to list here (it is listed in Appendix B), but the following portion illustrates our discussion (many comments have been deleted to save space):

```
/*******************************    list.c    *******************************

        Purpose:  Provide count list manipulation routines.

**/

#include <stdio.h>
#include <malloc.h>
#include <string.h>

#ifdef __STDC__
#   include <stdlib.h>
#endif

#include "ccount.h"                    /* program-wide definitions */
#include "list.h"                      /* header for this module */
#include "error.h"                     /* error functions and messages */

/******************   Private Definitions and Declarations   ***************/

struct count_struct {          /* an element of a count list */
        char *name;                    /* function whose lines are counted */
        long CSL,                      /* commentary source lines counter */
            NCSL;                      / noncommentary source lines counter /
        count_list next;               /* link to next count struct */
        };

/***********************   Declared Functions   ***********************/

#ifdef __STDC_

static count_list Create_Node( char *name, long CSL, long NCSL );
static void Destroy_Node( count_list ptr );

#else

static count_list Create_Node( /* char *name, long CSL, long NCSL */ );
static void Destroy_Node( /* count_list ptr */ );
```

```
#endif

/*************************     Private Routines    **************************/

/*FN**********************************************************************


        Destroy_Node( ptr )


   Returns: void


   Purpose: Free the space for an unneeded list node.
**/

static void
Destroy_Node( ptr )
   count_list ptr;    /* in: node to be deleted */
   {

        /* Free the space for the name field and the node itself */
   if ( NULL != ptr )
      {
      if ( NULL != ptr->name ) free( ptr->name );
      ptr->next = NULL;
      free( (char *)ptr );
      }

   } /* Destroy_Node */



/*************************     Public Routines    **************************/

/*FN**********************************************************************


        Is_Empty_List( list )


   Returns: int -- TRUE if the list is empty, FALSE otherwise.


   Purpose: See if a count list is empty.
**/

int
Is_Empty_List( list )
   count_list list;    /* in: linked list of counts to check */
   {

   return( NULL == list );

   } /* Is_Empty_List */
```

Included files are listed first in this module. The program-wide header file, **ccount.h**, and header file for the current file, **list.h**, are included. The header file for the error reporting module **error.h** is included because error messages may be reported by this module. Private definitions and declarations are listed next, then nondefining declarations of private functions. Private and public functions are defined next, following a bottom-up presentation style. Access to the private function **Destroy_Node** is restricted to the containing module by declaring it **static**. Although the public function **Is_Empty_List** is declared **extern** in **list.h**, it is declared without the **extern** keyword when it is defined, showing which function declaration is the defining declaration.

6.3 MODULE SIZE AND COMPLEXITY STANDARDS

As noted, modules should not be too large or complex. Unfortunately, good upper limits for module size or complexity are not known. We have found that modules tend to become awkward once they grow beyond five or six hundred NCSLs, so we recommend 500 NCSLs as a target maximum compile module size.[4] Sometimes this goal must be changed to hide information, increase cohesion, or decrease coupling. Usually this goal is easy to meet in a well-designed and properly modularized system.

Functions should be much smaller than modules, of course. Some people argue that functions should fit entirely on a single page of printer output so that you do not have to flip pages. Including the usual comments, this means that functions should contain no more than 20 or 30 NCSLs. We prefer a target maximum function size of 60 NCSLs in our coding practice, which accords with other recommendations in the literature.[5]

Complexity measures, such as McCabe's[6] cyclomatic complexity metric, are used by some C programmers to monitor their code complexity. Others rely on rules of thumb like the following:

- Do not nest blocks more than 7 deep.
- Do not use boolean expressions with more than 4 components.
- Do not nest conditional expressions more than 2 deep.
- Avoid pointers to pointers.
- Factor complex declarators using type definitions.

Although these rules are helpful, the primary determinant of complexity seems to be sheer program size, so probably the best way to curb complexity is simply to restrict size.

Our example software product **ccount** provides size counts that can be used to monitor conformance to module and function size standards. For example, a run of **ccount** on the count list module discussed in the previous section yields the following output:

```
list.c  Thu Aug 11 16:39:46 1988

    Function          CSL   NCSL   CSL/NCSL
--------------------------------------------
   Create_Node         21    17     1.24
  Destroy_Node         11    11     1.00
  Is_Empty_List         9     6     1.50
    Create_List         9     6     1.50
 Append_Element        15    17     0.88
 Delete_Element        20    16     1.25
       external        31    22     1.41
          total       116    95     1.22
```

These functions are well below the target maximum of 60 NCSLs, and at 116 NCSLs, this module is well below the target maximum module size of 500 NCSLs. Had the module been over 500 NCSLs, we might have remodularized to form several smaller modules. Had any of the functions been over 60 NCSLs, we would have looked at them to see whether they could be split into smaller functions.

6.4 CONCLUSION

This and the previous two chapters have discussed many rules of good C programming practice. Most of the rules of coding practice discussed in this and the previous two chapters are listed in Appendix D.

   To be effective, rules of practice need to be codified and followed by the project team. Consequently it is helpful to adopt a coding standard for development and maintenance. As an example and a summary of our discussion, we have written a coding standards document to govern the coding phase of our implementation of **ccount**. This standard is included in Appendix A.

REFERENCES

1. Harbison, S., and G. Steele, *C: A Reference Manual* (2nd ed.). Englewood Cliffs, N.J.: Prentice Hall, 1987.

2. Booch, G., *Software Engineering with Ada* (2nd ed.). Reading, Mass.: Benjamin/Cummings, 1983.

3. Weiner, R., and R. Sincovec, *Software Engineering with Modula-2 and Ada.* New York: Wiley, 1984.

4. Frakes, W. B., "A Software Engineering Methodology for the UNIX/C Environment," *Proceedings of the AT&T Bell Laboratories Software Quality Symposium*, Holmdel, New Jersey, 1985.

5. Potier, D., "Experiments with Computer Software Complexity and Reliability," *Proceedings of the 6th International Conference on Software Engineering* (October 1982), 92–102.

6. McCabe, T., "A Complexity Measure," *IEEE Transactions on Software Engineering*, SE-2, no. 4 (April 1976), 308–320.

7

UNIX Tools for Coding Phase of Life Cycle

One reason for the popularity of the UNIX/C environment is the wealth of software engineering tools it provides. In this chapter we describe tools for the coding portion of the software life cycle. Software engineers and software managers need to be aware of tools to make informed decisions about them when creating project methodologies because not all tools are appropriate for every project.

The tool descriptions given here are brief. They are meant to show what a tool is for rather than to give details about its use. There are many books and articles explaining how to use standard UNIX tools in detail. These are referenced throughout the chapter.

Some of the tools described in this chapter are not generally available. As stated in the preface, we decided to discuss the best tools we know of for UNIX/C development regardless of their availability. These tools demonstrate technologies to solve important problems; a reader familiar with a technique for solving a problem can build the tool if necessary. We hope that all these tools will become generally available.

We have divided the tools into the three following categories for purposes of discussion:

- *Program generation tools*. These are used to write, compile, and interpret code.
- *Static analysis tools*. These are used to analyze code before execution.
- *Dynamic analysis tools*. These are used to monitor the runtime behavior and performance of code.

7.1 PROGRAM GENERATION TOOLS

7.1.1 Editors and Browsers

Many text editors are currently available to C programmers; the best known are **ed**, **vi**, and **emacs**. Which of these is used will depend on availability, what programmers already know and are comfortable with, and personal preference. Our purpose here is to provide a brief description of each of these editors, with special attention to the programming support that they provide. We also discuss newer developments such as syntax directed editors.

A simple line editor is **ed**. It is normally not used for writing C code if **vi** or **emacs** is available, though its variant **sed** (stream editor) is frequently used as a filter in shell programs. Screen-oriented editors, such as **vi** and **emacs**, are usually preferred for programming because they allow you to see the context of work, and require fewer keystrokes. A detailed discussion of **ed** and **sed** can be found in Kernighan and Pike.[1]

Developed at U.C. Berkeley, **vi**[2] [3] is probably the editor most used by UNIX/C programmers, though **emacs** is rapidly gaining in popularity. Especially for program development, **vi** has several helpful features. For example, the *autoindent* feature causes **vi** to begin a new line in the same column as the first nonwhite space character in the previous line. This is useful for code indentation. Another useful feature is *showmatch*, which allows a search for matching braces and parentheses; a laborious task without this aid. **vi** will number the lines in the file, helping to locate the lines referred to by the compiler or **lint**. **vi** also allows shell commands to be issued from within the editor. This allows code to be edited, compiled, and executed without leaving the editor.

Originally developed by Stallman,[4] **emacs** has spawned numerous imitations. It is more powerful, and consequently more complicated, than **vi**. **emacs** users claim that learning to use just the functions of **emacs** that are equivalent to **vi** can be done quickly, and more advanced features can be learned as needed. **emacs** has an extensive macro facility that allows programmers to adapt the editor to their specific needs. Its features make it easy to interact with the shell environment. One can, for example, import the output of a shell process directly into the editor. **emacs**'s split screen facility makes it easy to examine such output, or multiple files, simultaneously.

Most versions of **emacs** have some of the facilities of a syntax directed editor (discussed later). For example, if a "**{**" is entered, **emacs** will insert correct spacing for good readability. **emacs** also keeps track of braces, parentheses, and brackets to ensure that they match. Like **vi**, **emacs** will search for matching braces, parentheses, and unlike **vi**, will do the same for square brackets.

One problem frequently encountered in working with C software systems is that changes made in one compile module may affect code in other compile modules. If an external function in one compile module, for example, is changed by adding an argument to its parameter list, each instance of the function call in other compile modules has to be changed. A tool capable of coordinating the editing of several compile modules simultaneously is desirable. **cscope**[5] interacts with a text editor to help you browse and change multiple C source files. When first invoked, **cscope** builds a symbol cross-reference updated as files are changed.   **cscope**'s menu provides an idea of its capabilities as follows:

```
$ cscope infeng.c

Cscope version 7.5                      Press the ? key for help

List references to this C symbol:
Edit this function or #define:
List functions called by this function:
List functions calling this function:
List lines containing this text string:
Change this text string:
List file names containing this text string:
Edit this file:
List files #including this file:
```

In the following example, we use **cscope** to locate all references in the file **infeng.c** to the function **userprmt**. We have typed **userprmt** in response to a request from **cscope** for a C symbol.

```
Searching symbol: userprmt
File      Function   Line
1 infeng.c infeng     85    int pushgoal(), popgoal(), userprmt(), factvalue(),
                            foundrule(),
2 infeng.c infeng    146    if (userprmt(kb, &goalhead, lp) == FAIL) {
3 infeng.c userprmt 219    static userprmt(kb, goalhead, lp)


List references to this C symbol: userprmt
Edit this function or #define:
List functions called by this function:
List functions calling this function:
List lines containing this text string:
Change this text string:
List file names containing this text string:
Edit this file:
List files #including this file:
```

cscope will work with any UNIX editor.

Syntax-directed editors[6] [7] [8] use information about the syntax of a programming language. Syntax-directed editors provide instant feedback on syntax errors, provide templates for language constructs, and incrementally compile code. There are several common criticisms of syntax-directed editors. One is that they inhibit novices from learning a language well, because the novices come to depend on the editor rather than their own knowledge of the language. Many expert users find them constricting. The value of syntax-directed editors is unknown and must await better experimentation, or at least wider use.

Syntax-directed editors exist for C but are not in general use. **syned** is a syntax-directed editor for C developed at Bell Labs and Bellcore.[9] It attempts to address the expert user problem by allowing the syntax-directed features to be turned off. **syned** is not generally available. Nor do we know of any other syntax-directed editors for C that are available.

7.1.2 Tools for Searching and Printing Code

As we discussed in Chapter 4, code readability is important. There are several tools for formatting and printing C code. These tools are particularly useful for printing readable copies of code for code reviews, testing and debugging, and maintenance activities. **cb** (C beautifier) reformats C code to improve its readability by spacing and indenting to display program structure. The effect of **cb** on a poorly formatted program can be seen in the following examples. Following is a code fragment before running **cb**:

```
/* GETTOK : gets a token from stream fp and puts it in
     token. Returns 0 for EOF, 1 for EOL, 2 for token. */

#include "infeng.h"

gettok(fp, token)

FILE *fp;
char *token;
{

int state, i, x;

for(state = 0, i=0, x = getc(fp); ; x = getc(fp)){
switch(state){
case 0: if(x == ' ' || x == ' ') {
state = 0;
break;
}
if( x == '\n' )
return(1);
if( x == EOF ) {
return(EOF);
}
else { /* x is a char */
token[i] = x;
++i;
state= 1;
break;
}


}
```

The following is the code fragment after running **cb**:

```
/* GETTOK : gets a token from stream fp and puts it in
   token. Returns 0 for EOF, 1 for EOL, 2 for token. */

#include "infeng.h"

gettok(fp, token)

FILE *fp;
char *token;
{

    int state, i, x;

    for(state = 0, i=0, x = getc(fp); ; x = getc(fp)){
        switch(state){
        case 0:
          if(x == ' ' || x == ' ') {
              state = 0;
              break;
          }
          if( x == '\n' )
              return(1);
          if( x == EOF ) {
              return(EOF);
          }
          else { /* x is a char */
              token[i] = x;
              ++i;
              state= 1;
              break;
          }
        }
    }
}
```

Indent is a tool similar to **cb** available with 4.xBSD. It has many options to tailor formatting to specific needs.

Why worry about writing readable code when tools like **cb** and **indent** can clean it up later? Because writing readable code from the beginning helps programmers to write good code. Code must be read as it is being written, because parentheses and braces must be matched, control structures deciphered, and so on. Furthermore, programmers can always format better than tools like **cb**, because they understand the intent of the code. Thus, our view is that tools like **cb** and **indent** are for making unreadable code more readable during maintenance rather than for making one's own code more readable during development.

On projects with large numbers of modules and functions, a clear indexed listing of them is important. **cpr** is a tool for printing source listings. It produces a list, with page numbers, of the functions in compile modules, and a source listing with the beginnings of functions highlighted in bold type. Comments are in italics. **cpr**'s output can be tailored to a specific printer by setting such parameters as page width, and length. **cpr** is not generally available. A condensed example of **cpr** header output follows:

```
Tue Dec 16 17:51:13 1986

aparser.c ........................... 1
          aparser ...................... 1

checkobj.c ..........................  7
          main ........................  7
```

A list of all files with page numbers and functions

```
avien.mk ............................ 53

Tue Dec 16 17:51:13 1986

aparser ...................... 1
atvalmenu .................... 33
clearfacts ................... 8
```

A list of all functions with page numbers

```
setvalue ..................... 35
stradd ....................... 15
stradd ....................... 42
writefact .................... 50
```

A software system's function hierarchy is useful in development, testing, and maintenance. **cf** and **cflow** produce C system function hierarchies. **cf** and **cflow** provide nearly the same information but format it differently. The following example shows the output of **cf** for a parsing program:

```
cf fparser.c

main() not found

Uninvoked function in fparser.c:
[fparser:  16]    1       1    fparser(2)
                  2       2    |  fopen(2)
                  3       2  2 |  printf(2, 1)
                  4       2    |  gettok(2)
[fparser:  58]    5       2    |  state0(3)   (Static)
```

```
                              6        3     |  |   calloc(2)
                              7        3     |  |   sprintf(3)
        [fparser:    77]      8        2     |   state1(4)   (Static)
                              9        3     |  |   printf(1)
                             10        3     |  |   strcmp(2)
                             11        3     |  |   hashadd(4)
                             12        3   2 |  |   strcat(2)
        [fparser: 100]       13        2     |   state2(3)   (Static)
                             14        3     |  |   printf(1)
                             15        3     |  |   sprintf(3)
        [fparser: 115]       16        2     |   state3(3)   (Static)
                             17        3   2 |  |   strcat(2)


Number of declared functions = 5
```

This output shows that the function **fparser** calls, among other functions, **state0**, which in turn calls **calloc**. It also shows that the program used seventeen total function calls, and that a total of five functions were declared. Other columns show the levels of nesting, and how many times calls are made in functions.

Programmers often need to search for strings in files. UNIX has a family of tools, called **grep** tools, used to search for patterns in files. Consider, for example, a file called **tst.c** that contains the following small C program:

```
#include <stdio.h>

extern char yytext[];
main()
{
    int type;

    while (type = yylex())
        printf("%s                    %d\n",yytext,type);
    printf("%d\n",type);


}
```

The shell command **grep yylex tst.c** selects the line **while (type = yylex())** from **tst.c**.

A useful related tool is **diff**, which compares two files and displays line by line differences. Say for example that I change the variable **type** to **token** in the preceding example. If I then run **diff** on the files containing the two variants of the program, I get the following output:

```
6c6
<      int token;
---
>      int type;
```

```
8,10c8,10
<     while (token = yylex())
<         printf("%s                    %d\n",yytext,token);
<     printf("%d\n",token);
---
>     while (type = yylex())
>         printf("%s                    %d\n",yytext,type);
>     printf("%d\n",type);
```

This says that the first difference occurred on line 6 of the two files. Each version of line 6 is given. The output also shows that lines eight through ten also differ. **diff** is often used to locate changes that have been made to source files. If I have an old version of the program in one file and a newer version in another file I can use **diff** to find the differences between them.

7.1.3 Compilers and Interpreters

C compilers translate C source code into machine code, sometimes producing assembly code as an intermediate step. There are C compilers for machines from micros to mainframes. The versions of C they support vary somewhat in syntax and functionality, though the ANSI standard for C should help eliminate these differences.

UNIX system C compilers (usually called **cc**), do not check syntax completely, and generally provide poor diagnostic error messages, sacrificing safety for speed of compilation. UNIX system C compiler error messages tend to be terse and cryptic. Many syntax errors, for example, elicit the unhelpful error message "syntax error," perhaps with a line number where the error is detected. This lack of error diagnosis is a shortcoming when using C as an application development language. For example, C compilers do not complain when integer values are assigned to pointer variables, though this violates type constraints and is usually an error. The poor compile time checking done by the C compiler is the reason for using a sophisticated syntax checker like **lint** (discussed later). The C compiler does not generate many runtime checks either, again sacrificing error checking for speed. For example, the C compiler does not generate code to check array bounds violations. Assignments beyond an array boundary can overwrite other data or even program instructions on some computers. This can result in difficult bugs.

Compilers translate source code into assembler or object code in several steps. C differs from many languages because its compiler's first step uses a preprocessor to expand macros, include files, and handle conditional compilation. These capabilities provide many features for making C code more readable and understandable (see Chapters 4 to 6). Following preprocessing, the compiler breaks the source code into tokens in a lexical analysis phase, parses the program, and produces an intermediate representation. This intermediate representation is used to generate assembler or machine code. Optimization procedures may be applied at several points in this process.

Because of the complexity of compiler construction,[10] tools have been developed to aid in the process. **lex**[11] reads files that associate regular expressions with actions expressed as C code. **lex** then generates C code implementing a finite state machine that takes action when it changes state. Thus, **lex** can be used to generate lexical analyzers and other functions that use finite state machines. **yacc**[12] (short for "yet another compiler compiler") generates parsers from context free grammars. **yacc** input is a file with a grammar for the language to be parsed. Actions, expressed as C code, are associated with grammar productions. **yacc** generates C code that parses input and takes actions when productions are applied in the parsing process.

Interpreters are programs that translate and execute a program piece by piece, instead of first translating it all, then executing it, like a compiler does. They are useful because they shorten the edit, execute, and debug cycle. Many popular languages were designed to be interpreted, including BASIC, APL, Lisp, and Prolog. Lisp interpreters in particular have led the way in showing how a powerful, interactive, unified programming environment can increase programmer productivity.[13] The drawback of interpreters and interpreted code is their performance. Interpreting code is usually much slower than executing compiled code. You can get an interpreter's advantages without its drawbacks by allowing compiled modules to be linked with interpreted modules. Program development can then proceed using the interpreter, but the system can be compiled to create an efficient program for delivery.

C interpreters and other unified C programming environments are common on microcomputers. Such environments typically provide several integrated tools including a screen editor, a file manager, the compiler and linker, and a make utility.[14] UNIX system C interpreters are rare, though they do exist.   **cin** is a C interpreter developed at AT&T Bell Laboratories.[15] **cin** has no built-in editor, though it can be used with other editors, like **emacs**, that can pipe data to other programs.   **cin** implements full ANSI C, supports multiple compile modules, and generates executable files. It does extensive error checking on its input and provides good error messages. For example, **cin** would catch the array bound errors discussed earlier. **cin** also provides descriptive error messages.

cin also has many features of a debugger, such as the ability to set and remove break points, examine and change the values of variables during execution, and display the execution stack. C interpreters are interesting and potentially useful tools; it is unfortunate that UNIX system C interpreters like **cin** are not in wider use.   **cin** is not available outside AT&T.

7.1.4 C++

C++[16] [17] is an extension of C created by Bjarne Stroustrup at Bell Laboratories. C++ is mostly upwardly compatible with C. That is, a C program can be compiled under C++. Consequently, C programmers are free to use as many or as few of C++'s new features as they wish. C++ was developed to add object-oriented programming constructs to C. The major new features of C++ are class declaration and inheritance mechanisms, stronger typing and type checking, and operator and function overloading.

In Chapter 3 we defined a class as a collection of objects with common data and operations. C++ allows a programmer to specify a class and provides a mechanism for controlling access to class members. For example, consider the following C++

declaration for the class **document** (C++ recognizes a double slash as a left comment delimiter; the comment extends to the end of the line):

```
class document {

    // private implementation details
    int keynumber;
    char title[MAXFIELD];
    char author[MAXFIELD];

public:
    // these functions provide the only access to a document

    // constructor function to create a document
    document(int keynumber, char* title, char* author);

    // destructor function to destroy a document
    ~document();

    // add a document to the database
    void add_document(int keynumber, char* title, char* author);

    // delete a document from the database
    void delete_document(int keynumber);

    // search for a document in the database
    int find_document(char* query);
};
```

The internal data in a document is hidden from the rest of the system by the class declaration. The only way that another system object can access a document is via the public constructor and destructor functions, and **add_document**, **delete_document**, and **find_document**. Constructor and destructor functions are also a new feature. Constructor functions create and initialize instances of a class; destructor functions destroy instances. These new constructs help programmers control access to program objects, and encourage programmers to use abstract data types, hide information, and make highly cohesive, loosely coupled modules.

Inheritance is a technique that allows a class to acquire (inherit) features of another class. Inheritance is important because it simplifies the definition of new classes. This reduces the programmer's work, and encourages the formation of class hierarchies. In C++, for example, one could declare a new class called **library_document** that would inherit all the data and operations of a **document**, and would also add others such as a library call number and a function to sort documents by call number.

C++ allows any operator to be assigned additional functional capabilities. For example the + operator could be assigned the string concatenation function, along with integer and floating point addition. This technique is called *operator overloading*.

Function overloading is similar, with function names assigned different function bodies. This allows a single name (e.g., **sort**), to name functions to sort integers, reals, complex numbers, strings, and so on. In both cases of overloading, the correct operation or function is determined by the compiler based on argument types supplied to the operator or function. Overloading is important because it simplifies module interfaces and, if used properly, might make systems more maintainable and reusable. If an operator or name is overloaded with all the operations or functions that do some task for all types, then arguments can be changed without having to change functions or operations. Furthermore, new types can be added to a system with minimal code changes. See Cox[18] for an excellent discussion of the advantages of object-oriented programming and operator and function overloading.

C++ provides many of the type checking advantages of ANSI C. In particular, C++ provides the same function prototyping as ANSI C, so both function return types and arguments can be checked by the compiler. C++ is a software engineering advance over C because it provides better support for many sound software engineering principles such as strong type checking, information hiding, data abstraction, and modularity. Object-oriented programming in general, and C++ in particular, are also said to give better support for software reuse. Whether C++ will improve software quality and productivity is still debated. Many C software engineers are enthusiastic C++ supporters, whereas others think that it will have little effect on software engineering problems. Only time (and ideally empirical data) will tell.

7.1.5 Make

As we discussed earlier (in Chapter 6), C programs are usually divided into several compile modules and one or more header files. This structure makes systems more modular, supports information hiding, makes files smaller and therefore easier to edit, and makes it possible to recompile only those compile modules that have been changed rather than the entire system. The management of these files, however, can be troublesome. This is because it is necessary to know the following:

- The files needed to produce the entire system.
- The files needed to produce components of the system.
- The files that have been changed since the last time the system was created.

An important tool that automates these tasks is **make**.[19] [20] A *makefile* contains a list of the files that are needed to build a system and information about how those files depend on each other. In the **ccount** makefile in Appendix B, for example, are the following lines:

```
ccount: $(OBJECTS)
        $(CC) $(CFLAGS) $(OBJECTS) -o ccount
```

The first line gives **ccount**'s dependencies. It says that **ccount** is dependent on the objects specified by the variable **OBJECTS**. These objects are specified in a line in the makefile that reads:

OBJECTS = ccount.o params.o counter.o classify.o report.o list.o error.o

The second line of the **ccount** definition specifies how to build the program out of its components. With all its variables expanded, the line would read as follows:

cc ccount.o params.o counter.o classify.o report.o list.o error.o -o ccount

This command links all the .o files to produce **ccount**.

All the .o files themselves have dependencies that are specified in the makefile. **make** has built-in information about how to create .o files from .c and .h files.

If a source file is changed after **ccount** is created, and the makefile is executed, **make** will determine that all .o files that depend on the changed source file will need to be recreated. This frees the software engineer from having to keep track of this information.

Besides building systems and system components, **make** has other uses. The last lines of the **ccount** makefile, for example, specify how to build a cpio file for the **ccount** system. **cpio** is a UNIX tool that is used to package collections of files so that they can be stored and moved as a single unit. It is commonly used to package C based software systems for distribution. Makefiles often contain commands for printing system files, running diagnostic tools such as **lint**, and many others. **make** is also commonly used to manage project documentation.

7.1.6 **ar** (archive) Command

The **ar**[21] command is used to bundle object files into a library file with a single name. The link editor **ld** combines library functions with object files in the system being built to create an executable program. Say, for example, that I have C functions in two compile modules **x.c** and **y.c** , and I would like to use **ar** to put them into an archive library file. First, they will typically be compiled into **x.o** and **y.o**. Then the archive command could be used as follows:

```
ar r mylib.a x.o y.o
```

mylib.a can now be linked into a system as follows:

```
cc -o system mainmodule.c mylib.a
```

ar is an important tool for promoting function level reuse for the C language. In the **avien** system,[22] for example, we implemented an inference engine as a set of C functions. With the use of a generic driver program, we created a tool level version of **avien** for end users. We used the **ar** command to bundle **avien**'s functions, and made them available as a library. This allowed their incorporation at any point in a C application. **super**, a hardware reliability estimation system written in C, for example, used **avien**'s functions with an appropriate knowledge base to help users determine whether **super** was the right tool for their problem and, if so, which of its analysis methods to use.[23]

7.2 STATIC ANALYSIS TOOLS

Static analysis tools analyze code before execution, and provide information about program structure and attributes. Some of the tools already discussed, such as **cscope**, also provide static analysis information in addition to their role as program generation tools.

The most valuable static analysis tool in the C environment is **lint**. Because of the meager error checking done by most C compilers, **lint** was developed as a supplemental diagnostic tool. **lint** is extremely important for helping to ensure the quality of C code in environments where the compilers do not provide thorough checking.

Among the useful things **lint** reports are the following:

- The syntax errors the compiler would have found.
- Functions without return value checks.
- Function declarations and calls with incorrect numbers or types of arguments.
- Variables declared but not used.
- Unreachable program statements.
- Inadvisable automatic type conversions.

Software methodologies for C development projects should stipulate that all code be run through **lint**, and the causes of all errors and warnings be removed or precisely explained. An example of this can be found in the **ccount** coding standards document in Appendix A.

Another useful static analysis tool is **cia**,[24] a tool that extracts from C source code information about functions, files, data-type macros, and global variables, and stores this information in a relational database. This information can then be accessed via **cia**'s reporting tools, by **awk**, or by other database tools. One type of information, for example, that **cia** captures is the calling relationship among functions. **cia**'s reporting tools can then be used, with other graphics tools, to generate a graph like the one in Figure 7.1. Such a graph should prove useful to anyone needing to understand a software system, such as a tester, reviewer, or maintenance programmer.

cia's authors point out many potential uses of **cia**. Among these are the following:

- *Software metrics.* **cia** can be used to compute many software metrics. Because C program objects are explicitly stored, it is obviously possible to count them. More sophisticated metrics can also be generated. A measure of the coupling between two functions can be calculated, for example, by counting the number of program objects jointly referenced by the two functions.
- *Program version comparisons.* Two versions of a program can be compared by looking at differences in the **cia** databases for the versions. This comparison can reveal declarations created, deleted, or modified, and changes in relationships

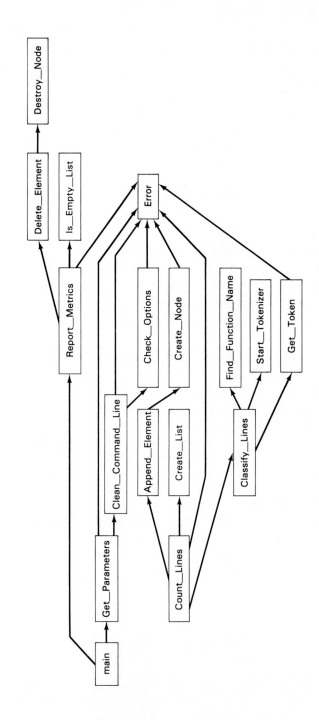

Figure 7.1 Sample Graph from Static Analysis Tool.

among program objects. This is more useful than the UNIX system **diff** command that only compares lines.

- *Reuse*. The information **cia** produces about which functions are most used by other functions could be used to identify reusable components. In the **ccount** graph in Figure 7–1, for example, the **Error** function seems like a good candidate for reuse because it is used by seven other functions.

cia is currently unavailable outside AT&T.

7.2.1 Software Metrics

Software metrics are quantitative measures of software life-cycle products or processes. Many metrics for life cycle products and processes have been proposed (see Conte et al.[25] for a good review), but their utility is the subject of debate among software engineers. Metrics are used in an attempt to monitor software quality and productivity, and to predict such things as resource needs and software errors. Process metrics that measure the tools and methods used to develop the product, such as design technique, programming language, and so on are needed for use in effort estimation models such as COCOMO.[26]

Common software product metrics are those for code complexity, measured as counts of lines, statements, tokens, logical execution paths, and so on. Many tools have been developed for calculating product metrics for C code. **ccount** is a simple version of such a product metrics tool. A more sophisticated C metrics tool is **CMET**.[27] **CMET** computes complexity metrics for each function in a preprocessed C file. The preprocessed C file can be created from a .c file via the **cc –P** command or the **cc –I** command. **CMET** reports values for the following metrics:

    NCSL   (noncommentary source lines)
    STMTS   (count of statements)
    TOKENS   (count of tokens)
    V   (count of logical conditions plus one)
    FCALLS   (count of function calls)
    NSP   (count of structure pointers)
    NPATH   (count of acyclic execution paths)

For example, **cmet** was run on the following simple C program:

```
#include <stdio.h>

main()
{
        /* prints hello on standard out */
    printf("hello\n");
}
```

The following report was produced:

```
CMET RELEASE 1.0


CMET Output for Module hello.c 03/25/89 11:52:01 PM


Function          NCSL    STMTS    Tokens   V     FCALL NSP    NPATH
--------          ----    -----    ------   -     ----- ---    -----
main              4       2        9        1     1     0      1
```

The **CMET** report for **list.c** (part of **ccount**) was the following:

```
CMET RELEASE 1.0


CMET Output for Module list.i 03/26/89 12:00:58 AM


Function          NCSL    STMTS    Tokens   V     FCALL NSP    NPATH
--------          ----    -----    ------   -     ----- ---    -----
Create_Node       16      15       110      3     6     6      4
Destroy_Node      10      7        44       3     2     3      3
Is_Empty_List     5       3        16       1     0     0      1
Create_List       5       3        15       1     0     0      1
Append_Element    16      11       82       3     2     3      3
Delete_Element    15      13       81       2     2     4      2
```

Software complexity measurement tools such as **CMET** are often used to determine parts of code that should receive the most testing effort. The assumption is that more complex code will contain more errors than will less complex code. Complexity metrics are also sometimes used to identify code modules that are considered too complex, and should thus be redesigned, partitioned, or otherwise rewritten. **CMET** is currently unavailable outside AT&T.

Static metrics tools, such as **ccount** and **CMET**, are not the only ones available for C code. Dynamic tools such as **nvcc**, **prof**, and **lprof** are discussed later.

7.3 DYNAMIC ANALYSIS TOOLS

Dynamic analysis tools are used to investigate the runtime behavior of software. They are used to find and remove bugs, and measure the execution speed of programs and program components.

7.3.1 Debuggers

Debugging is the process of finding and correcting errors in programs. It is often a frustrating and difficult task, and is yet another place that good programming techniques will help. For example, if code is well structured and modular, then isolating the location and cause of an error will be a much easier task.

In the early days of computing, debugging was often done by examining octal or hex program dumps. This is a poor debugging method because it gives only a static snapshot of a program's execution and is difficult for people to read. An improvement is the technique of using print statements to display variable values during program execution. This technique allows some of the information about the dynamics of a program to be seen, but the process is slow and the output may be overwhelming.

Dynamic debuggers attempt to overcome some of these problems by allowing a user to do the following:

- Examine source code during execution.
- Insert breakpoints (i.e., points in the program where execution will pause).
- Examine variable values at any point during program execution.
- Change a variable's value.
- Examine the function calling stack at any point during program execution.
- Execute a program line by line (single step).

If a C program fails, debuggers can also report on error locations.   **sdb**,[3] perhaps the best-known debugger for C on UNIX system V, provides these services. **sdb** can be used if the −**g** flag is used during compilation. The following presents an example of the use of **sdb**. In the example, the file **loops.c** is compiled using the −**g** option, **sdb** is invoked, and some of its features are illustrated.

```
cc -g loops.c

sdb a.out

No core image        <-- this means that there is no core file available
                         if the program had dumped core, there would be one.
* z                  <-- I ask for a print of at most 10 lines from the program

6: {
7:
8:     int i;
9:
10:    for (i = 0; i < MAXNUM; ++i)
11:        printf("%d\n",i);
12: }
*11b                         <-- I set a break point at line 11, the program execution
                                 will now pause at this statement.
```

```
main:11 b              <-- SDB verifies that the breakpoint has been set.
*r                     <-- I tell SDB to execute the program.
a.out
Breakpoint at
main:11:  printf("%d\n",i);    <-- program halts at break statement.
*i/                    <-- I ask for the value of variable i at this point.
0                      <-- The value of i is currently 0.
*q                     <-- Quit command to exit SDB.
```

Another popular UNIX system C debugger is **dbx**.[28] It has roughly the same functionality as **sdb**. **dbxtool**, a window based version of **dbx** for the Sun workstation, is a better debugging tool than either **sdb** or plain **dbx**. The gain here is from the quality of a user interface that takes advantage of the Sun's windowing, menu, and mouse environment.

7.3.2 Tracing Tools

ctrace inserts print statements into a C program. These statements allow program statements and variable values to be displayed during program execution. Consider the following simple C program:

```
#include <stdio.h>
#define MAXNUM 5

main()

{
    int i;

    for (i = 0; i < MAXNUM; ++i)
        printf("%d\n",i);
}
```

To run **ctrace** on this code, which is in a file called **loop.c**, we issue the following command:

```
ctrace loop.c > traceloop.c
```

ctrace will insert the appropriate code into our file, and write the result to **stdout**. We have redirected this output to a file called **traceloop.c**. As this file is large, and not particularly readable, we will not show it here. We now compile **traceloop.c** as usual, and execute it. Our program trace output is as follows:

```
4 main()
10    for (i = 0; i < MAXNUM; ++i)
```

```
          /* i == 0 */
          /* MAXNUM == 5 */
   11         printf("%d\n",i);
          /* i == 0 */
    0

   10     for (i = 0; i < MAXNUM; ++i)
          /* i == 1 */
          /* MAXNUM == 5 */
   11         printf("%d\n",i);
          /* i == 1 */
    1

       /* repeating */
    2
    3
    4

       /* repeated 3 times */
   10     for (i = 0; i < MAXNUM; ++i)
          /* i == 5 */
          /* MAXNUM == 5 */
       /* return */
```

The output consists not only of the program results (the integers 0 to 4) but also a program trace together with the appropriate variable values. Although such output can be helpful in debugging, the output from **ctrace** can become overwhelming for large programs. Because of this, **ctrace** is typically used only when other debugging methods have failed.

7.3.3 Debugging Advisers

As we noted earlier, the messages produced by C compilers and **lint** are often extremely cryptic. Fortunately, tools are available to help with this problem. **chelp**, an internal AT&T tool, provides interpretations of messages from the C compiler and **lint**, and run time error messages, identifying possible causes of the problem that led to the diagnostic message. For example, we ran **lint** on a compile module containing the variable **howrule**, and **lint** produced the following message:

```
warning: howrule may be used before set
```

We then ran **chelp** on the message and received the following analysis:

> This local variable is not given a value before it is used. Note that global and static variables are guaranteed to be 0 if not initialized, but local variables have the value of whatever happens to be in memory at that stack location.

Although **chelp** is useful for certain messages, we found that it would often fail for common error messages such as bus error, because there were too many possible causes. What is needed is a tool, probably using expert system technology, capable of doing finer analyses of these messages.

7.3.4 Performance Monitoring Tools

Once code is written, it is often necessary to measure its execution speed. Such measurement is used to see if the system meets requirements or if parts of the system need to be optimized. Several tools are available in the UNIX/C environment for measuring execution speed.

 time reports on program CPU usage. For example the command "**time who**" produces the following output:

```
            real     0m2.91s
            user     0m0.25s
            sys      0m0.30s
```

This information shows that 2.91 seconds of elapsed clock time took place during execution of the **who** command, 0.25 seconds of time was spent in the **who** program, and it took 0.30 seconds for the kernel to execute the command.

 By compiling C code with the **−p** flag, the **prof** utility can be used to measure the time each function in the system takes to execute. When code is compiled in this way, a file called **mon.out** is generated during execution. This file contains data correlated with the object file and used by **prof** to produce a report of the time consumed by individual functions in the program. When run on an example program, **prof** produced the following report:

```
%Time Seconds Cumsecs  #Calls   msec/call  Name
 50.0   0.02    0.02       1       17.      _read
 50.0   0.02    0.03       8        2.      _write
  0.0   0.00    0.03       2        0.      _monitor
  0.0   0.00    0.03       1        0.      _creat
```

This report shows that the function **read** was called once, and this call took 17 milliseconds, about 50 percent of the total execution time for the program. The functions **monitor** and **creat** show zero execution times because they used amounts of time too small for **prof** to measure.

 As with any measuring device, there are limits on the accuracy of **prof**. Measuring very small times can give relatively large measurement errors, for example. Results can also vary widely if measurements are done on a heavily loaded system. For a clear view of execution times it is usually necessary to use averages derived from multiple measurements collected on dedicated or lightly loaded machines.

 Another dynamic analysis tool is **lprof** (which must be used with a special version of the C compiler called **lcc**) that provides execution counts for each line in a program. This is useful for determining the most heavily used parts of a program. For example, the following is the output of **lprof** for a lexical analysis program. There are two kinds of useful information in this output. First, it is easy to see the lines of code that have been executed. This is important for testing. Second, it is easy to see which lines are most heavily used. Examination of the following output showed that execution time may be saved by declaring **state**, **i**, and **x** as register variables:

```
              #include "infeng.h"
              /* Gets a token from stream fp and puts it in token.
                 Returns 0 for EOF, 1 for EOL, 2 for token. */
              gettok(fp, token)

              FILE *fp;
              char *token;
   492 [1]    {

              int state, i;
              int x;

   492 [6]    for(state = 0, i=0, x = getc(fp); ; x = getc(fp)){
  2491 [7]        switch(state){
   520 [8]          case 0: if(x == ' ' || x == ' ') {
    28 [9]                      state = 0;
                               break;
                          }
   492 [12]                if( x == '\n' )
    75 [13]                    return(1);
   417 [14]                if( x == EOF ) {

     1 [16]                    return(0);
                          }
                          else { /* x is a char */
   416 [19]                    token[i] = x;
   416 [20]                    ++i;
   416 [21]                    state= 1;
                              break;
                          }
  1971 [24]         case 1: if(x == ' ' || x == ' ') {
   354 [25]                    token[i] = ' ';
   354 [26]                    return(2);
                          }
  1617 [28]                if( x == '\n' ) {
    62 [29]                    token[i] = ' ';
    62 [30]                    ungetc(x, fp);
    62 [31]                    return(2);
                          }
  1555 [33]                if( x == EOF ){
     0 [34]                    token[i] = ' ';
```

```
     0 [35]                          ungetc(x);
     0 [36]                          return(2);
                                   }
                                   else { /* x is a char */
  1555 [39]                          token[i] = x;
  1555 [40]                          ++i;
  1555 [41]                          state= 1;
                                     break;
                                   }
                              }
  1999 [45]               }
     0 [46]       }
```

lprof is not available outside AT&T.   **tcov**[28], however, is a 4.xBSD tool that provides this type of information.

7.4 CONCLUSION

In this chapter we have described C based support tools for the coding phase of the software life cycle. These tools are used to write, compile, and interpret code, and to analyze code statically and dynamically. These tools as a group provide one of the most powerful programming environments available, but could be augmented and integrated to provide an even better environment. These issues are discussed in Chapter 10.

REFERENCES

1. Kernighan, B., and R. Pike, *The UNIX Programming Environment*. Englewood Cliffs, N.J.: Prentice Hall, 1984.

2. Bolsky, M. I., *VI User's Handbook*. Piscataway, N.J.: AT&T Bell Laboratories, 1984.

3. AT&T Bell Laboratories, *UNIX System V: User Reference Manual*. Murray Hill, N.J.: AT&T Bell Laboratories, 1983.

4. Stallman, R., *GNU Emacs Manual*. Cambridge, Mass.: Free Software Foundation, 1987.

5. Steffen, J. L., "Interactive Examination of a C Program with Cscope," *Proceedings of the USENIX Winter Conference* (1985), 170–175.

6. Teitelbaum, T. and T. Reps, "The Cornell Program Synthesizer: A Syntax-Directed Programming Environment," *Communications of the ACM*, 24, no. 9 (September 1981), 563–573.

7. Horgan, J., and D. Moore, "Techniques for Improving Language Based Editors," *Proceedings of the ACM SIGSoft/SIGPlan Software Engineering Symposium on Practical Software Development Environments* (April 1984).

8. Rajani, P. "Syntax Directed Editors," *The C Journal*, 2. no. 2 (Summer 1986).

9. Gansner, E., et al., "Syned: A Language Based Editor for an Interactive Programming Environment," *COMPCON Proceedings* (March 1983).

10. Aho, A., R. Sethi, and J. Ullman, *Compilers: Principles, Techniques, and Tools*. Reading, Mass.: Addison-Wesley, 1986.

11. Lesk, M. E., *Lex—A Lexical Analyzer Generator*. Computing Science Technical Report 39, AT&T Bell Laboratories, Murray Hill, N.J., 1975.

12. Johnson, S. C., *Yacc: Yet Another Compiler Compiler*. Computing Science Technical Report 32, AT&T Bell Laboratories, Murray Hill, N.J., 1975.

13. Tichy, W. R., "What Can Software Engineers Learn From Artificial Intelligence," *IEEE Computer*, 20, no. 11 (November 1987), 43–54.

14. Borland, *Turbo C User's Guide*. Scotts Valley, Cal.: Borland International, 1987.

15. Belanger, D., G. Bergland, and M. Wish, "Some Research Directions for Large-Scale Software Development," *AT&T Technical Journal*, 67, no. 4 (July-August 1988), 77–92.

16. Stroustrup, B., *The C++ Reference Manual*. Reading, Mass.: Addison-Wesley, 1986.

17. Berry, J., *C++ Programming*. New York: Howard Sams and Company, 1988.

18. Cox, B., *Object Oriented Programming*. Reading, Mass.: Addison-Wesley, 1986.

19. Feldman, S. I., "Make—A Program for Maintaining Computer Programs," *Software Practice and Experience*, 9, no. 4 (April 1979), 255–265.

20. Thomas, R., L. R. Rogers, and J. L. Yates, *Advanced Programmer's Guide to UNIX System V*. New York: McGraw-Hill, 1986.

21. Earhart, S. (ed), *The UNIX Programmers Manual* (vol. 1). New York: Holt, Rinehart and Winston, 1986.

22. Frakes, W. B. and Fox, C. J., "CEST: An Expert System Subroutine Library for the UNIX/C Environment," *The AT&T Technical Journal*, 67, no. 2 (March-April 1988), 95–106.

23. Frakes, W. B., Myers, D. M., "Using Expert Systems Components to Add Intelligent Help and Guidance to Software Tools," *Information and Software Technology*, 31, no. 7 (September 1989), 366–370.

24. Chen, Y., N. Nishimoto, and C. Ramamoorthy, "The C Information Abstraction System," *IEEE Transactions on Software Engineering*, SE-16, no. 3 (March 1990), 325–334.

25. Conte, S. D., H. E. Dunsmore, and V. Y. Shen, *Software Engineering Metrics and Models*. Reading, Mass.: Benjamin/Cummings, 1986.

26. Boehm, B. W., *Software Engineering Economics*. Englewood Cliffs, N.J.: Prentice Hall, 1981.

27. Nejmeh, B. A., "NPATH: A Measure of Execution Path Complexity and its Application," *Communications of the ACM*, 31, no. 2 (February 1988), 188–200.

28. Sun Microsystems, *Commands Reference Manual*. Mountain View, Cal.: Sun Microsystems, 1986.

8

Software Testing
and Quality Assurance

The first half of the chapter discusses software quality assurance. We begin by explaining the importance of establishing a quality system covering the entire life cycle and making use of techniques shown to be effective. We then discuss major quality assurance techniques including reviews, inspections, and process audits.

The second half of this chapter discusses one of the most difficult and poorly executed phases of the software life cycle: the testing phase. After an overview of the testing process, we discuss who should do testing, and the importance and difficulty of effective testing. Then we discuss stages in the testing process, and testing techniques, strategies, and tools. We end our discussion of testing by illustrating the testing procedure we used on the **ccount** source code metrics tool.

8.1 SOFTWARE QUALITY ASSURANCE

Software quality is a major problem for both software engineering practitioners and researchers. Effective procedures, methods, notations, tools, and practices for promoting software quality are essential to success in the software industry. Software quality has been defined in several ways including the absence of errors, conformance to requirements, fitness for use, and customer satisfaction. Our preferred definition of quality is *fitness for use*.[1] This definition of quality includes many attributes that other definitions omit. In general, products fit for use are affordable, reliable, meet customer expectations, include the features desired by customers, are easy to install, operate, fix, and maintain, and are well documented.

Software quality, and quality in general, is the job of the requirements writer, designer, developer, tester, and so on—that is, quality is everybody's job. Because quality is everybody's job, practices that promote quality must be applied throughout the development process. If quality is fitness for use, then all project work products should be fit for use. For example, if the requirements document is incomplete, inaccurate, or inconsistent, then it is not fit for use by the designers, testers, and others who must rely on it. Similarly, if the design and implementation are full of errors, they are not fit for use by the testers.

Quality affects productivity. Increasing quality increases productivity (in the long run) because it eliminates rework. The opposite, however, is not necessarily true: increasing productivity may not increase quality; an increase in productivity may decrease quality if increased productivity results from poor programming practices, omission of documents, and so forth.

Our approach emphasizes improving the quality of the software development process to improve the software products created by the process. Development process quality improvement is achieved by a *quality system*, a collection of techniques whose application results in continuous process quality improvement. Elements of the quality system include reviews, inspections, and process audits.

A quality system should address two different aspects of quality: process quality and product quality. *Process quality* is the fitness of the development process for producing a product. *Product quality* is the fitness for use of the product resulting from some process. As discussed in Chapter 1, there are many attributes that a quality system should foster in the work products created during the life cycle, including clarity, completeness, conciseness, consistency, correctness, simplicity, conformance to standards, implementability, maintainability, and nonredundancy. The following sections discuss leading methods for achieving high quality processes yielding high quality software work products.

8.2 REVIEWS

One of the most important, but often neglected, methods in software quality assurance is reviews. A *review* is an objective evaluation of a software engineering product or process. Reviews can be formal or informal. Informal reviews typically lack a systematic procedure and structure. Formal reviews use a systematic and focused approach. We advocate a formal review process heavily based on the work of Parnas and Weiss[2] on active reviews.

8.2.1 Problems with Traditional Review Process

The traditional review process involves the review of a large volume of detailed documentation by customers, users, programmers, and consultants. Reviewers are told to read as much documentation as possible, locate errors, and make suggestions. This approach is often unsuccessful for the following reasons:

- Reviewers are overwhelmed with unnecessary information.

- Reviewers are not familiar with the goals, scope, and constraints of the document under review.

- Reviewers do not clearly understand which parts of the document they should focus on because they are told to do a general review of the document.

- Reviewers are not rewarded for uncovering errors in the document.

- Reviewers and the members of the team that wrote the document rarely meet for individual discussion. Typically reviewers and writers meet in large groups, so issues cannot be discussed in detail.

- Reviewers do not have the right skills because they are chosen for their availability.

- Reviewers often believe that their work is not taken seriously, so they do not do a thorough job.

- Reviewers do not use systematic procedures. Discussion is not guided by a prepared set of questions or key points. Typically, this results in a cursory review.

For these reasons, reviews resulting from the traditional process are not effective at uncovering errors. The result is an increase in costs with no increase in quality.

8.2.2 Active Review Process

As part of the SCR A-7 project, Parnas and Weiss[2] devised a review method known as *active reviews*. The following points characterize the active review process:

- Different reviewers should focus on different points. That is, one reviewer may focus on consistency, whereas another may concentrate on completeness. This helps ensure that every important aspect of the document is considered.

- Each reviewer should have a focus consistent with his knowledge and skills.

- In addition to focused reviewers, a few reviewers should do an overall review. This helps guard against overlooking global issues.

- Each reviewer should be provided with a systematic set of questions to be answered in writing.

- Reviewers should meet with the document team in small groups to discuss the review.

- If follow-ups are necessary, the goals of the follow-up should be documented.

- No one should review his or her own work.

8.2.3 Review Readiness

Reviews are costly, so reviewing documents that are not ready to be reviewed is wasteful. A review readiness check should be made when the document team requests a review. Sometimes, reviews are scheduled when materials are not ready. This typically occurs when customers want product reviews at regular intervals.

In general, the best way to assess review readiness is to have someone outside the project review the document, checking to see that all sections are complete, and spot checking some sections in detail. If the document is ready for review, then the review begins with a start-up meeting.

8.2.4 Review Start-Up Meeting

The purpose of the review start-up meeting is to make sure that people understand the review process, to communicate roles to reviewers, and to provide an overview of the product under review. The meeting opens with a description of the review process by a member of the quality or methodology team. This helps ensure that all reviewers and document producers understand the review process. Then, a member of the document team summarizes the product under review. Each reviewer is assigned a focus, and given a list of questions. Time is allowed for reviewers to ask questions of producers, and review discussion sessions are scheduled.

8.2.5 Performance of Review

Focus questions guide the active review process. Answering these questions should require careful examination of the document and force reviewers to take an active part in the review process. For example, active questions such as: Which assumptions convince you that the operation behaves as described? are preferable to passive questions such as: Is there an assumption that justifies the description of the operation?

Areas of focus for reviews include the following:

- *Assumption validity*. The focus is whether assumptions made in the document are correct. Typical questions are: Which assumptions in the document are not valid and why? What other assumptions can be made in the document, and why can they be made?

- *Operation assumption consistency*. The focus is whether assumptions are consistent with the operations that depend on them. Typical questions include: Which operations do you think cannot be implemented with the assumptions provided and why? For each operation, what assumptions convince you that the operation can be implemented as described?

- *Adequacy of operations*. The focus is whether the product meets user needs. Typical questions include: Are there operations users would like that the product will not allow? If so, please explain. Are there operations that you think will take an unacceptably long time to accomplish? If so, please explain. Are there unneeded operations? If so, please explain.

- *Error conditions*. The focus is whether all error conditions have been anticipated and documented. Typical questions include: Are there any undetectable error conditions? Are there any error conditions that cannot occur? Are there any error conditions that can occur but are not documented?

8.2.6 Review Completion Criteria

A review is complete when the reviewer has answered all questions assigned and has provided the appropriate document team member a copy of the answers.

8.2.7 Review Meetings

After the document team reads and studies the answers to the review questions, they meet individually or in small groups with reviewers to discuss any questions they may have. Meetings should continue until producers and reviewers understand the issues.

8.2.8 Reporting of Review Results

On completion of all reviewer-producer meetings, the producers should provide a list of all issues raised during the review and their resolutions. Reviewers should confirm that all issues were cataloged, addressed, and resolved.

8.3 CODE INSPECTIONS

Software inspections use procedures and techniques for detecting errors in source code. Inspections are group source code readings in which members of the group play specific roles. The goal of inspections is finding as many errors in the source code as possible. Most discussions of inspections focus on inspection procedures and forms. We briefly discuss such matters. We then discuss a review checklist for C source code. This checklist appears in Appendix E. Readers interested in a more detailed discussion of inspections should see articles by Fagan[3] [4] and Freedman and Weinberg.[5]

Four people are typically involved in an inspection. The *moderator* manages the inspection. The moderator schedules meetings, ensures that everyone has the proper materials, reports inspection results, and monitors any follow-up activity. He or she must be a competent developer, but independent of the project. The *implementer* is the programmer who wrote the source code under inspection. The other inspection team members are usually the *designer* of the source code under inspection and the *tester* of the source code.

The inspection process consists of six tasks: inspection readiness, overview, preparation, inspection, rework, and follow-up.

8.3.1 Inspection Readiness

Inspection readiness is a check by an independent party to determine whether the code is ready for full inspection. The checker should make a cursory check that the source code implements the design, compiles cleanly, and is properly commented. If the readiness inspector decides that the source code is ready, the inspection begins. Otherwise, he or she reports problems to the implementer. The implementer and readiness inspector then work together to improve the code until it is ready for inspection.

8.3.2 Inspection Overview

The *inspection overview* is a meeting of the entire inspection team. Its purpose is to educate the team about the source code to be inspected. At the inspection overview, the implementer describes the source code being inspected, its purpose, and the design. The source code, its design documentation, and `lint` output, are distributed to inspection team members. In addition, each team member is given an error checklist that guides the review. The checklist helps inspectors (particularly novice inspectors) identify errors.

8.3.3 Inspection Preparation

Each member of the inspection team prepares for the inspection by familiarizing himself or herself with the details of the source code. Inspectors search for errors guided by the error checklist.

8.3.4 Team Inspection

The objective of the *team inspection* is to find errors in the source code. An error is defined as any discrepancy between the design and the source code, or deviations from coding standards established for the project. During the inspection, the implementer reads the source code aloud and describes the intent of each statement. As the implementer discusses the source code, questions are raised and pursued until either they are satisfactorily answered or an error is identified and understood by the implementer. The error is documented by the moderator who records a description of the error, who located the error, the location of the error (e.g., line number), the type of error (e.g., data declaration, data reference, control flow, interface), and the severity of the error. If the solution to the error is obvious, it is noted; otherwise the inspection continues. The goal of the inspection process is to find errors, not to correct them. Within a day after the inspection, the moderator should provide a written report of the inspection results to all inspection team members.

8.3.5 Rework

Rework is correcting errors discovered during the inspection process.

8.3.6 Follow-Up

Follow-up is the process of ensuring that the rework done by the implementer resolves the errors discovered during the inspection process. The moderator is responsible for ensuring that all errors have been resolved. The moderator may reconvene the inspection team to reinspect reworked code. Typically, reinspections are done when many errors were found or serious errors were found.

Software inspections have been used for several years. Experience has suggested several of the following useful guidelines:[6]

- Inspectors should attend no more than one meeting per day.
- Inspections should last no longer than two hours.
- On average, an inspection overview can be done at the rate of 500 noncommentary statements per hour.
- On average, inspection preparation can be done at the rate of 125 noncommentary statements per hour.
- On average, team inspections can be done at the rate of 90 noncommentary statements per hour. The maximum effective team inspection rate is 125 noncommentary statements per hour.

Inspection results should never be used for personnel evaluation because this could greatly reduce the effectiveness of inspections.

8.3.7 Error Checklist for C

Appendix E contains an example of an error checklist for guiding an inspection of C source code. The checklist is not meant to be exhaustive, but representative and illustrative. **lint** finds many of the errors mentioned in the checklist. Therefore, the output of **lint** should be used as input to the inspection process. Many of the ideas for the error checklist have come from Bentley,[7] Myers,[8] and Dunn.[9]

The error checklist has the following categories:

- *Data declaration errors* arise from incorrect use of C data types, or from incorrectly initializing or naming data structures.
- *Data reference errors* arise from misuse of data in a function. Invalid array or pointer references are the most typical data reference errors.
- *Computation errors* are miscomputations. Examples include errors from mixed-mode arithmetic, overflow, and underflow.
- *Comparison errors* occur when comparisons are done incorrectly. Examples of comparison errors include incorrect comparison conditions and undesired side-effects of comparison operations.
- *Control-flow errors* occur when there is incorrect control flow. Unreachable code and nonterminating loops are examples of control-flow errors.
- *Input-output errors* occur when there is incorrect input or output to peripherals. Examples of such errors include improper attributes on an open statement (e.g., opening a file for reading when the function attempts to write to the file) and forgetting to close a file.
- *Comment errors* are incorrect or incomplete comments.

- *Modularity errors* are related to the improper structuring of modules. An example of a modularity error is grouping unrelated functions in a module.

- *Language usage errors* are abuses of a programming language. For example, using a series of **if-else** statements instead of a **switch** statement is a language error.

- *Storage usage errors* are errors related to the improper use of storage. Not allocating enough memory or not freeing memory are examples of storage usage errors.

- *Performance errors* contribute to the function not executing within acceptable bounds. Examples of such errors include recomputing a function whose value never changes and unnecessary logical tests within a loop.

- *Maintenance errors* reduce program maintainability. Examples of such errors include poorly documented code and code that does not conform to the coding standards established for the project.

- *Traceability errors* occur when requirements or design specifications are not met. For example, if a program is required to verify the range of user input, but does not do so, it contains a traceability error.

8.4 PROCESS AUDITS

The primary objective of a process audit is to help a development team improve its productivity and quality through independent evaluations of the development process and associated development work products. This section is based on work discussed in Crawford and Fallah.[10] The process audit consists of five tasks: definition and plan of the audit, education of auditors about the project, characterization of the development process, formulation and communication of audit team findings, and implementation of audit team recommendations.

8.4.1 Definition and Plan of Audit

When an audit is begun, several things should be defined and planned including the following:

- A definition of the goals and objectives of the audit based on project goals.

- The formation of an audit team based on the goals and objectives of the audit, as well as the domain of the project. The audit team should not include project members.

- The development of an audit plan stating what will be audited, the goals and objectives of the audit, who the auditors are, what the audit tasks will be, when the tasks will be done, and how and when the results of the audit will be reported.

8.4.2 Education of Auditors

Auditors must understand the goals and organization of the project. Project personnel should provide this. The audit team should read project descriptions and review organization charts to understand functional areas of responsibility.

8.4.3 Characterization of Development Process

The audit team should analyze the documented development methodology, as well as the methodology used in practice. This is done by analyzing the development methodology documents, interviewing development project personnel, attending project meetings (including reviews and inspections), and reviewing selected development work products. A primary reason for interviewing people, attending meetings, and reviewing work products is to understand the methodology used in practice (as opposed to the documented development methodology).

8.4.4 Formulation and Communication of Audit Findings

When done, the audit team should meet to discuss, combine, and document their findings in an audit report. When discussing audit results, the team should identify project strengths and weaknesses. The team should identify major and minor problems, and provide evidence of such problems. The audit team should recommend solutions to problems, such as training and education, new technology (hardware and software), and so forth. In addition to documenting their findings, the audit team should hold meetings to present and explain their findings to the development team.

8.4.5 Implementation of Audit Team Recommendations

The audit team should help the development organization implement its recommendations. This may include training, or bringing in new tools or technologies.

8.5 TESTING PROCESS

There are various definitions of software testing. The IEEE Standard Glossary of Software Engineering Terminology,[11] for example, defines testing as

> the process of exercising or evaluating a system or system component by manual or automated means to verify that it satisfies specified requirements or to identify differences between expected and actual results.

Hetzel[12] defines testing as

> any activity aimed at evaluating an attribute or capability of a program or system and determining that it meets its required results.
>
> Testing is the measurement of software quality.

Myers[8] defines testing as

> the process of executing a program with the intent of finding errors.

Each of these definitions provides valuable insights into the testing process. Specifically one sees the following:

- The essence of testing is verifying that life-cycle objects conform to specifications.
- Testing is not just for code; it should be done on all life-cycle products.
- The purpose of testing is to ensure software quality.
- Testing methods may be either manual or automated.
- The tester should believe that the software is incorrect, and that his or her job is to prove that software is incorrect by finding concrete examples of the incorrectness.

None of the preceding definitions describe testing as the process of showing that a software product is free of errors. There are several reasons for this. First, it is usually impossible to show that software is error free by testing it. Doing so would require one to test all possible inputs to the program, and verify that the program always behaved correctly. Almost always, the number of possible inputs is prohibitively large. For example, Shooman[13] has calculated the number of inputs required to test a program to find the roots of a quadratic equation exhaustively to be 64 trillion. He estimates that a reasonably fast computer might take 3 weeks to execute the tests, and that if a person was required to check the test results, he or she would need to look through 200 million pages of output! Testing cannot show that a program is correct; it can only increase our confidence that a program is correct.

When faced with the impossibility of showing program correctness by exhaustive testing, one response has been to urge that programs be proven correct using the axiomatic approach championed by Hoare, Djikstra, and Gries.[14] Unfortunately, this approach is currently no more practical than exhaustive testing, and there are convincing arguments that it will never be any more practical than it is today.[15]

Characterizing testing as an effort to show that software is error free also betrays a misunderstanding of the goals of the testing process, and promotes the wrong mind-set among testers. Because testing is expensive and difficult, and because software cannot be exhaustively tested, the best testing effort is the one that finds the most errors at the smallest cost. Thus test efforts ought to be oriented toward finding defects, not toward showing correct behavior. Furthermore, the best testers are motivated to turn up problems, and are not satisfied to execute test cases without finding any problems. Thus the mind-set of testers ought to be to find errors, not to show correctness.

8.6 WHO SHOULD TEST SOFTWARE

The last point about the testing mind-set has an important consequence for the formation of test teams. It is virtually certain that any piece of nontrivial software contains bugs when it is first produced. It is also virtually certain that even small software systems contain bugs even after extensive testing and debugging. Despite frequent exposure to these facts, however, programmers usually believe that their code has no bugs, and that every bug found is the last bug. This is true even of programmers who swear that they do not believe that their code is bug free—deep down, they do not really think that there are any more bugs. Recent experiments[16] support this view, and indicate that traditional testing methods encourage this type of thinking.

Of course, it is understandable that programmers deny the existence of errors in their software. Programmers do not believe there are errors because programmers do not want errors. If there are errors, in some sense it means that the programmer did not do the job right the first time (although it is unrealistic to expect anyone to write error-free code). Furthermore, errors mean more work for the programmer, sometimes much more work, because finding an error and fixing it can be an arduous task. Programmer optimism about errors can also be explained in the more sophisticated terms of cognitive dissonance theory.[17] Whatever the reason for this attitude, such a mind-set is debilitating for a tester; a tester who does not think there are errors, and does not really want to find errors, probably will not find many. Consequently, software engineers should not test their own software.

There are several other reasons why software engineers should not test their own software. If a developer misunderstands requirements and writes a program that correctly conforms to his or her misunderstanding, then the error will be propagated to the testing process and will not be detected. Because programmers typically attempt to anticipate and forestall all the problems they can think of during development, programmers are unlikely to think of test cases to stress their software in unanticipated ways during testing. Finally, programmers will tend to make the same sorts of assumptions about program behavior during testing that they made during development, and so will be unlikely to create test cases that violate their assumptions.

The consequence of all these considerations is the cardinal rule of program testing: *programmers should never test their own code.* Ideally, test teams should be formed from staff not associated with the development effort in any other way; such individuals have the least to lose from discovering problems and errors in the system. Also, because testers are supposed to break things rather than make them work, the best testers tend to be people with a knack for finding problems, or for doing things in a slightly offbeat way. Such individuals have a rare and usually unappreciated talent that should be used to maximize testing effectiveness.

8.7 TESTING RESOURCE ALLOCATION

We have seen that it is impossible to test a large system exhaustively. Because limited resources are available for testing, an important practical question is how to allocate testing resources optimally. One approach to this problem is to allocate most testing resources to those parts of the system considered most crucial—that is, those parts of the system whose failure would lead to the worst results. Unfortunately, this approach may offer insufficient guidance when large portions of the system turn out to be crucial, which often is the case.

Another approach is to allocate testing resources based on estimates of where the most errors are likely to be found. Because the complexity of software is assumed to correlate with fault density, testing resource allocation is sometimes guided by complexity metrics. Many complexity metrics have been proposed.[18] [19] [20] Perhaps the commonest and easiest to compute indicator of complexity is NCSL, which we have discussed before in explaining our example program **ccount**. It has been shown that NCSL is highly correlated with several complexity metrics.[21]

As an example of the use of such methods for test resource allocation, consider a large software system composed of five hundred C functions. If testing resources are not adequate to exercise more than a fraction of these functions, certain functions must be selected as good candidates for concentrated testing. A metrics tool is used to calculate a complexity measure for each function. Functions with high complexity values according to project standards, or relative to the mean complexity value of all functions, are selected. Under the assumption that functions with high complexity values are likely to contain the most faults, a larger proportion of testing resources are allocated to testing them.

Unfortunately, complexity metrics are far from being perfect predictors of where faults will occur. A function with a high complexity value may have no faults, and a function with low values may contain many faults. Nonetheless, experience shows that functions with high complexity values will, in general, have more faults than functions with low complexity values.

Another testing resource allocation problem is how to decide when to stop testing. No matter how much testing is done, faults always remain in any nontrivial program. Testing stops when few enough faults remain in the system. The difficulty is in determining how many faults are yet to be found. This is an important piece of information: If a product is released with too many faults, the cost to fix them will be enormous, and customer satisfaction and confidence may be severely damaged. If a product remains in test too long, then testing resources are not used effectively, and other problems, such as missed market opportunities, may arise. Unfortunately, estimating how many faults remain in a program is difficult.

One way of providing such an estimate is to use a model that predicts the number of faults remaining in a program based on data about the rate of discovery of faults during testing of the system. The data is plotted as cumulative counts of faults against time, and a curve is fit to the data to model it. Such models are called *cumulative fault models*. Figure 8.1 is an example of a model of this type.

This figure illustrates the typical S shape of cumulative fault curves. Cumulative fault curves have this shape because of the following:

- Early in the testing phase of the life cycle, fewer faults are found as personnel are hired and trained, test cases and test scripts are developed, test procedures are defined, and so on.

- In the middle of the testing phase, productive test activity is high, and there are many faults to be found. Consequently the cumulative fault curve climbs steeply during this stage of testing.

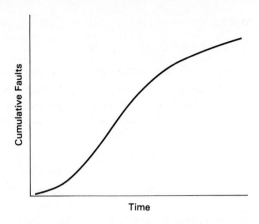

Figure 8.1   Example of Cumulative Fault Model.

- Toward the end of the test effort, most of the easily found faults have been discovered and corrected. The remaining faults are fewer and more obscure, and therefore take longer and longer to find. Because of this, the top of the curve flattens out as the rate of fault detection slows. The change in slope of the curve at this point must be considered in context. A change from 50 faults found per unit time to 10 found will produce a marked flattening in the curve. Ten faults per unit time may, however, not indicate that enough errors have been removed.

When the curve flattens out toward the end of the testing effort, it is assumed that few faults remain in the system, and it is safe to release it. It is clear, however, that in interpreting such a plot, one must rely heavily on background knowledge. Some of the things that one would need to know are the following:

- Have all subsystems been tested? To what degree have they been tested? Coverage metrics such as those supplied by test coverage tools like **nvcc** (discussed later) will be needed here.
- What testing methods were used? The various methods are complementary, so we need to know which have been used for the system.
- What other things might have caused the plot to tail off? Many factors other than having found most of the system faults might cause the top of the curve to flatten out. Some of these are the following:
  — The test machines were down.
  — The testers were on holiday, occupied with other duties, and so on.
  — The test cases were difficult to design for remaining faults. This often happens when trying to design test cases for unusual error conditions.
  — There has been a significant turnover in test personnel.
- Are the remaining faults critical? What other testing methods could be used to find them?

Without such background knowledge, it is impossible to interpret the cumulative fault curve correctly.

8.7.1 Stages in Testing Process

A software system is typically tested at several different levels.

- *Unit test.* A *unit* is a piece of software implemented by a single programmer. Units are typically single functions or small groups of functions that work together to accomplish some simple task. Programmers are usually responsible for testing units alone during their implementation before they are integrated with other parts of the system. This is called *unit testing*.
- *Integration test.* When several units are brought together to form a module, sub-system, or system, they are tested as a group. This is *integration testing*.
- *System test.* Once a system has been completely integrated, it must be tested as a whole, which is called *system testing*. System testing exercises a program with input generated from system requirements that may not reflect the use of the system by its intended users.
- *Acceptance test.* In acceptance testing, the whole system is exercised with data reflecting use of the system by its intended users. Often small groups of users participate in acceptance testing in an effort to provide a more realistic trial of the software.

We will now examine each of these phases in greater detail.

Unit Testing.   The purpose of unit testing is to show that a unit does not behave according to its specifications. Because units are (or ought to be) small, they present an opportunity for thorough, and sometimes even exhaustive, testing. It is important to take advantage of this opportunity, because it is always much easier and cheaper to correct errors at the unit test level than at higher test levels. Unfortunately, this opportunity is often missed, as witness the poor quality of unit testing in most development efforts.

The poor quality of unit testing was illustrated by a study we did on a large software project at AT&T. In this study, trouble reports of serious software faults found during system test were given to the programmers who wrote the code in which the errors were found and to the testers who found the faults. Both groups were asked to identify those faults that could have been detected during unit test. The programmers admitted that more than 40 percent of the faults could have been found at the unit test stage. The testers estimated that more than 60 percent of the errors could have been found at unit test. Clearly, many errors could have been detected and corrected at great savings during unit test.

In general, units cannot be tested in isolation from the rest of the system without supporting code and data. This supporting code and data is called a *test harness*. Test harnesses may require enormous development time and effort, sometimes amounting to as much as 50 percent of the size of the code for a finished system. If the function or functions making up a unit are functionally cohesive and loosely coupled with other units, however, and if the unit has a clean and well-defined interface, the effort required to develop a test harness is minimized. Thus good principles of program design and implementation pay off immediately during the development process.

Programmers often discard test harnesses once a unit has been tested. This is not a wise practice for several reasons. First, most units end up being changed at some point in the life cycle, either in the process of fixing bugs, or when making changes to the system during maintenance. Unit testing should be redone whenever a unit is altered (this is the principle of regression testing, discussed later), so it pays to save the test harness. Second, test harnesses can often be largely reused when testing other, similar units, saving some of the effort required to build a harness from scratch.

Unit testing is traditionally done by the programmer who wrote the unit. This may be a poor practice because, as we have noted, it is usually difficult for programmers to find errors in their own code. It may be better, even on small projects, for programmers to unit test each others' code.

Integration Testing.   In the integration test process, several units forming a module or subsystem are combined and tested together. For example, units that collectively scan and parse input might be tested together. The focus of integration testing is on finding errors in interfaces between program units.

Unit integration and test may be done in one of the three following ways:

- In *top-down integration and testing*, top-level routines are first combined, tested, and debugged. The top-level portion of the system then becomes the integration test harness for lower-level units, which are integrated and tested singly or in small groups. Top-down testing fits in with top-down development.

  As an example of top-down implementation and testing consider the task of implementing and testing an information retrieval (IR) system. We might begin by first implementing the main function, that is, the highest-level function, as follows:

```
#include "irsys.h"
void
main ()
   {
   while (TRUE) {
        /* Display menu and get desired operation */
      switch( irmenu(); ) {
         case ADD:    adddocs();
                      break;
         case DELETE: delete_docs();
                      break;
         case SEARCH: search_for_docs();
                      break;
         case EXIT:   exit( SUCCESS );
                      break;
         }
      }
```

To compile and test this function, one will also need to implement **irmenu**, **add_docs**, **delete_docs**, and **search_for_docs** as stubs. A *stub* is a function that performs only a subset of the tasks it will eventually perform. A possible implementation of these stub functions can be seen in the following example:

```
/* irmenu - print menu of choice and get response */
short irmenu()
    {
    short choice;    /* ordinal of choice selected by the user */

    printf( "What do you want to do?\n" );
    printf( "1) Add a document\n" );
    printf( "2) Detach a document\n" );
    printf( "3) Search for a document\n" );
    printf( "4) Exit the system\n" );
    printf( "Your choice:  " );
    scanf( "%d", choice );

    return(choice);
    }

    /* Stub for add function */
short adddoc()
    {
    printf( "In ADDDOC\n" );
    return(SUCCESS);
    }

    /* stub for delete function */
short deletedoc()
    {
    printf( "In deletedoc\n" );
    return(SUCCESS);
    }

    /* stub for search_for_docs function */
short search_for_docs()
    {
    printf( "In search_for_docs\n" );
    return(SUCCESS)
    }
```

The stubs implemented here print a message and return a **SUCCESS** flag. Having implemented the main function and stubs in this way, the main function can now be compiled and tested. Once the main function has been tested, the lower-level functions can be tested and implemented the same way.

Top-down integration and testing has several advantages and a few disadvantages. On the positive side, design errors tend to manifest themselves sooner when a system is integrated from the top down. When combined with a top-down implementation strategy, top-down integration and testing distributes integration and testing throughout the implementation phase of the life cycle, and tends to make debugging easier. A working version of the system is available at an early stage of implementation, which helps morale and can be valuable as a demonstration program. Top-down integration and testing also has the advantage of minimizing test harness creation effort, because the system itself serves as the integration test harness. Unfortunately this gain is largely offset by the effort required to create stubs that provide good simulations of unimplemented portions of the system; sometimes, this may not even be possible if a high level of functionality is required of the stubs. It may also be impractical to use an entire large system as a test harness for each unit as it is integrated. Thus a purely top-down strategy is usually not desirable.

- *Bottom-up integration and testing* proceeds by combining low-level units into modules and subsystems, testing them, and continuing to combine and test gradually larger pieces of the system until the entire program is constructed. This approach tends to work well early in the integration process, because it is possible to do thorough testing, and easy to find and fix bugs when small units and modules are combined and tested. Difficulties arise later in the process when several large, complex subsystems are combined, because it is then harder to test the code and often much harder to locate bugs. Design errors tend not to show up until late in the integration process, which is also undesirable. The bottom-up approach also requires much effort in the creation of test integration harnesses. Because of these difficulties, a pure bottom-up strategy is rarely practical.

- *Sandwich integration and testing* is mainly a top-down approach with bottom-up integration and testing applied to certain widely used components, such as libraries of utility routines or input-output and user interface routines. Sandwich integration and testing is a practical compromise between top-down and bottom-up integration and testing strategies that attempts to capture the advantages of both. Sandwich integration and testing seems to be the method used most often in real projects.

On large projects, integration testing will probably be done by a testing organization. On smaller projects, integration testing is usually done by the programmers who wrote the integrated units, although, as we have noted, this is not the ideal arrangement.

System and Acceptance Testing.   Once a system has been completely integrated, it must be tested as a whole. System test, sometimes called *alpha test*, exercises the completed system against its requirements, and to a lesser extent, consideration of the use of the system by its intended users. System testing may be done by the development team, but more often it is done by a testing organization. The documentation for the system, such as users' manuals, administrators' manuals, and particularly the requirements document, are used to design test cases for system test.

The acceptance test, also called *beta test*, exercises the system as a whole in a way that reflects the activities of its intended users. Often acceptance testing is done by selected groups of friendly users. This has the advantage of providing a realistic test of the system, because real users incorporate the software into their daily activities just as they would if the software were already a product. Serious problems and errors often come to light when the system is confronted with genuine data and knowledgeable users. Unfortunately, shortcomings of the system requirements often come to light in this phase of testing as well, which may lead to expensive last-minute changes.

Table 8.1: Phases of Testing Process

Test Phase	What is Tested	Goal
Unit	Individual units	Show that a unit fails
Integration	Module or subsystem	Show that a subsystem fails
System	Entire system	Show that system does not meet requirements
Acceptance	Entire system	Show that system fails for real users

8.7.2 Test Cases

A *test case* is a trial input used to exercise a system in an effort to make it fail. Test cases have the three following components:

- *Test case type*, which is the aspect of the system that the test case is designed to exercise.
- *Test conditions*, which are the input values and environmental state used in the test.
- *Expected behavior*, which is the correct response expected of the system under the test conditions.

Note that test conditions are not merely input values, because a system's configuration, the load on the computer, the state of peripheral devices, the speed of communications devices, and so forth may all influence system response. Likewise, the expected behavior is not merely output values, because proper behavior may include the correct control of peripheral devices, adequate response time, and so forth.

Test cases may be divided into two broad classes: black box and white box tests. *Black box tests*, also known as *data-driven tests* or *input-output tests*, exercise a system without regard to its internal structure, deriving test cases from requirements or other documentation. *White box tests*, also known as *glass box tests* or *structural tests*, exercise specific components of a system, and therefore are based on the internal structure of the system.

Black Box Test Cases.   Ideally, a system should be tested with all possible test cases, but in general, this is impossible. The goal of black box test generation, then, is to identify a set of test cases that will exercise the software as effectively as the entire range of possible test conditions.

One way of doing this is by *equivalence partitioning*, which groups test conditions into classes based on common attributes. A few members of the group can then represent the entire class during testing. For example, consider testing the part of a computer login procedure that accepts the user's name. Some examples of the equivalence classes one might select to test this software are the following:

- Valid user names typed with no line edits (backspaces, line erasures, and so on).
- Completely invalid user names typed with no line edits.
- Invalid user names with a valid user name prefix typed with no line edits.
- Valid user names typed with line edits.
- Invalid user names typed with line edits.
- Invalid user names with a valid user name prefix typed with line edits.

An assumption in using equivalence classes is that all classes taken together cover the entire range of possible execution conditions. If a class of conditions is not identified and represented, testing will be incomplete.

Once equivalence classes are defined, test cases to represent the classes are selected. Test cases are chosen so that those selected for a given class will identify or fail to identify the same faults as any other cases we might have chosen from that class. If poor class representatives are selected, testing may not be effective.

An effective method for choosing equivalence class representatives is *boundary value analysis*, the technique of choosing test cases that either themselves fall near the boundaries of test case equivalence classes, or produce system responses that are near the boundaries of system response equivalence classes. For instance, for the class of valid user names in the preceding example, selected test cases might include the following:

- Short (1-character) user names.
- Long (256-character) user names.
- Names containing white space at the beginning, in the middle, and at the end.
- Names with nonprintable characters.

Boundary checking is based on the observation that more errors tend to occur at the boundaries of classes than elsewhere. A common example of this occurrence is the "one off error" or "off by one error" in which a procedure works correctly, except for the first or last element processed.

Another difficult problem that often confronts testers during test-case generation is how to verify that a system response is correct. If a system makes complex mathematical calculations, it may not be possible to check the answers by hand, except in a few simple cases. For systems like this, another program is sometimes developed to compute the same answers in a different way, or to calculate an approximation of the correct solution. The answers obtained from the two systems are then compared. If they conflict, however, the tester is left with the problem of figuring out which of the conflicting answers is incorrect—perhaps they both are! Output verification is often an extremely difficult task.

White Box Test Cases.   Ideally, a structural test of a program would exercise every possible execution path through the program. This is impossible, so compromise is necessary. Such compromises usually involve selection of test cases that collectively cover some subset of all execution paths. Test cases that jointly execute every statement in the program at least once are an example. The following are common white box test generation criteria:

- *Statement coverage* is the percentage of program statements that have been executed at least once in executing some set of test cases.

- *Decision or branch coverage* is the percentage of branch directions that have been traversed at least once in executing some set of test cases. A *branch direction* is a logical path from a decision point such as an `if` condition.

- *Logical path coverage* is the percentage of all logical paths through the program traversed in executing some set of test cases. A *logical path* is defined in some way that accounts reasonably for loops without leading to infinitely many paths through programs with loops.

The goal in white box testing is to devise a set of test cases that will collectively obtain some high percentage of statement, branch, or logical path coverage. Although 100 percent coverage is ideal, it is often difficult to achieve in practice. Typically, it is difficult to provide test data that will trigger unusual error or processing conditions. Standards for acceptable coverage should be part of a project methodology.

Manual determination of test coverage metrics can be extremely difficult. Fortunately, tools exist to help with this task.

8.7.3 White Box Testing Tools

Several tools for white box testing are available in the UNIX/C environment. These tools fall into two categories: those that instrument the assembler code output by a compiler, and those that instrument the source code. Instrumentation is the insertion of extra code to generate measurement data. The assembler method offers the advantage of portability across languages on the same machine, because most compilers are capable of producing assembler. This would allow, for example, the same testing tool to be used for both C and Fortran on a given machine. The disadvantage is that a new testing tool has to be written for each machine with a different assembler.

The source method offers the advantage of portability across machines because the C code that it instruments is more portable than assembler. Because C and C++ are becoming more of a standard, and the number of machines that support them is proliferating, the trend is toward the use of source instrumentation tools.[22] The most widely used in our experience are the following:

- **lprof**, an assembler instrumentation tool that calculates how many times each line of code in a program has been executed, can be used to help measure statement coverage (**lprof** is discussed in Chapter 7).
- **tcov**, a tool similar to **lprof** that is available under 4.2BSD.
- **nvcc** (new verifier for C code) inserts instrumentation code into a C or C++ source file. The instrumentation code is used to generate coverage information. This is the tool we will use to illustrate white box testing with **ccount**. The **nvcc** suite consists of several programs.
  - — **nvcc** inserts instrumentation code into C or C++ language programs at program branch points. During execution, this code writes information to a file used by **nvcs** and **nvcp** to produce test coverage reports.
  - — **nvcp** prints source files highlighting (underlining on a printer, reverse video on a CRT) the parts of the program that have not been executed.
  - — **nvcs** reports the cumulative percentage of branch points executed for each compile module. As more test cases are executed against the instrumented program, the test coverage file is modified to reflect cumulative branch coverage.

Our testing examples appear subsequently.

8.8 REGRESSION TESTING

Whenever software is changed in an effort to fix a bug or enhance a program, one of the following four things may occur:

1. The bug fix or program enhancement is successful, and no further errors are introduced.
2. The bug fix is unsuccessful and the program error remains, or the enhancement does not work as planned.
3. The bug fix or program enhancement works as intended, but at least one new error is introduced by the change.
4. The bug fix or program enhancement does not work as intended, and, in addition, at least one new error is introduced by the change.

Only the first of these outcomes is desirable, but one of the other three occurs surprisingly often. Data from some projects shows that as many as 30 percent of software changes result in one of the three undesirable outcomes; on average, undesirable outcomes seem to occur about 10 percent of the time. If this figure is accurate, then for every ten errors corrected, on average one remains or one new error is introduced. Testing and debugging productivity and quality must be ensured by checking to see that program changes fix or change the software as intended without introducing new errors. There only seems to be one way to do this: run all test cases over again after changing the software. Such retesting of changed code is called *regression testing*.

Manual regression testing is time consuming and cumbersome. Fortunately, tools are available to automate the process, including the UNIX shell itself. The strategy is simple: Write a UNIX shell script to generate output files from test input files, then use the UNIX **diff** program to compare the test results with the expected output. For example, suppose that we wish to regression test a program called **addnums** that reads pairs of numbers from **stdin**, adds them, and writes the result to **stdout**. Regression test input is placed in the file **rtst1.input**, whose contents are the following:

```
1 3
2 7
3 5
4 8
```

Given this input, **addnums** should produce the regression test output in **rtst1.output** as follows:

```
4
9
8
12
```

A UNIX shell regression test script using these two files is the following:

```
# This shell script runs a regression test on the program addnums.

echo This script tests addnums using the input file rtst1.input and
echo comparing output to the expected result in rtst1.output.
echo ""

# Run addnums with the test input and capture stderr and stdout.

addnums < rtst1.input > temp.output 2>&1

# Test for differences in the output file and the correct answer file.

diff temp.output rtst1.output > test.diffs

# If a difference was found diff will exit with status 1
# this value will be in the shell variable "?"

if test "$?" = 1
then
    echo An error has been found in addnums.  Following are the
    echo differences between the observed and expected output.
    echo the difference are in the file temp.output.
    cat test.diffs
```

```
else
    echo No error found in addnums for this test.
    rm temp.output
fi
```

It is possible to regression test a program automatically with many test cases, with various input and output files, and even with user interactions, thanks to the power of the UNIX shell to redirect input and output to and from various sinks and sources.

Regression test systems that offer more capabilities than the UNIX shell have been developed. Totally Automated Regression Test System (TARTS)[23] is an example of such a system. TARTS consists of a test driver and smart comparison programs for both binary and ASCII files. The **diff** command will report *any* difference between numbers, whereas, for example, the TARTS **diff** program allows a tester to specify that only differences of a certain size are meaningful. TARTS can also do comparisons on nontextual output such as graphics or break sequences. TARTS consists of about seven thousand lines of shell and five hundred lines of C code.

Regression testing is an important technique for maintaining quality in the testing phase of the life cycle. Even when it must be done manually, it is worth the effort to incorporate it into the testing process. Given the ease with which it can be done using UNIX facilities, there is no excuse for not doing extensive regression testing in the UNIX/C environment.

8.9 DEBUGGING

Debugging is the process of finding the causes of faults in software and correcting them. Debugging is a difficult skill that makes severe demands on the programmer. Good debugging requires that the job be approached with the correct goals, expectations, and beliefs. Among these are the following:

- The goal of debugging must be the correction of a fault through understanding its *cause*, not correction of a fault by whatever change appears to work. Inevitably, bugs "fixed" without understanding their cause reappear later, or turn up as other bugs.

- Programmers should resist the temptation to blame, without proof, difficult bugs on some other parts of a system, such as the hardware, the operating system, the compiler, or someone else's code. It is most likely that an elusive bug is lurking in the code being exercised when failure occurs, no matter how difficult it is to find the bug.

- When debugging, programmers should never stop looking for faults in a code fragment after the first one is found. Finding one fault in a code fragment increases the probability that there are others. One reason for this is that failures are often caused by several faults, or several instances of the same error, and these will tend to cluster.

- Programmers should resist the urge to make quick fixes when debugging, because hasty changes usually either fail to correct the fault or lead to other faults. Care must always be taken to understand fully the consequences and side-effects of any changes to software during debugging.

Having established the appropriate mind-set, the debugging programmer then pursues a *debugging strategy*, or general approach to debugging, using various *debugging tactics*, or specific debugging techniques.

8.9.1 Debugging Strategy

The debugging process can be divided into the following four parts:

- *Stabilization* is the identification of test cases that reliably show the existence of the software fault. Finding and correcting a fault that shows up unpredictably is almost impossible. It is also helpful to identify a class of test cases that manifest the fault rather than a single test case, because this provides more information about the problem. For example, suppose during testing an incorrect output data item is identified. Suppose that this fault is stabilized by identifying a whole class of test inputs that lead to the same failure, namely those for which a certain summary statistic is requested and displayed. This not only provides a class of inputs for the debugging programmer to use in investigating the problem, but suggests that the request, computation, or display of the summary statistic may be the source of the failure.

- *Localization* is the process of isolating the problem to a small fragment, or several small fragments, of source code. Localization is usually the most difficult debugging task; once a bug has been isolated to a small code fragment, it is usually easy to spot. In general, the smaller the code fragment, the better, because localizing an error in a small code fragment makes the rest of the debugging task that much easier. Continuing our last example, suppose that the debugging programmer establishes that the output value is incorrect when the code gathering data to compute the summary statistic is executed, but not otherwise. This locates the problem in the code fragment where the data for the summary statistic is collected.

- *Comprehension* is the process of figuring out the cause of the failure by correlating incorrect program behavior with the algorithm described in the source code. In our example, corruption of the output data might be explained by an overwritten variable whose value is disturbed because an array index goes out of bounds. The faulty behavior of the array index is explained in turn by an incorrect test for loop termination during collection of data for computing the summary statistic. This completely explains the program's failure.

- *Correction* is the process of altering the program to remove the fault. Correction is often the easiest part of the debugging process, although it is also the most error prone because it is easy to introduce new bugs when changing unfamiliar code. In our example, the fault is corrected by changing the test for loop termination responsible for the problem.

Once a fault has been corrected, the correction must be verified, usually by regression testing, as discussed earlier.

8.9.2 Debugging Tactics

In carrying out debugging strategy, there are several common tactics that help achieve various goals including the following:

- *Execution tracing*. Monitoring the behavior of a function as it executes is often helpful for both localization and comprehension. There are several ways to do this. Programs can be executed by hand, but this is slow, error prone, and often will not catch bugs whose cause is that the computer is not doing what the programmer expects. Another way is to insert print statements at various places in the source program. During the isolation stage, this can help determine how far a program gets before it goes wrong; during the comprehension stage, printing the values of selected variables can make sure that they change as expected. The UNIX tool **ctrace** inserts print statements into programs automatically; unfortunately, the value of **ctrace** is limited because of the massive volumes of information that it tends to produce. Symbolic debuggers are perhaps the best mechanisms for tracing execution. Some debuggers, such as Sun's **dbxtool** have excellent facilities for single-stepping through programs and monitoring the values of variables during execution. A coverage trace, such as **nvcc** produces, can also help eliminate unexecuted code as a candidate for the location of the bug.

- *Interface checking*. A large percentage of software failures are caused by faulty interfaces. Simply checking an interface by making sure of agreement between number and types of function arguments, and the declarations and types of function return values, can turn up faults. Of course, this difficulty can be forestalled by proper use of C function declarations, particularly prototypes (when they are available) and the use of **lint**. Other interface problems go beyond syntactic difficulties to deeper semantic misunderstandings that require more detailed analysis. Often such problems can be found by checking the range or sanity of incoming values. This is a good defensive programming technique even when no errors are suspected, but it can be especially helpful when trying to isolate and understand a difficult bug.

- *Assertion-driven debugging*. Assertion-driven debugging is the tactic of inserting tests at crucial points in code and indicating test failures if they occur. This tactic is especially useful in localizing bugs. Assertions may be inserted using a debugger, or placed directly in the source code. Many versions of C, including the proposed ANSI standard, provide an **assert** macro that takes any scalar value as an argument and exits the program with a diagnostic error message if the assertion expression fails.

- *Skipping code.* When a certain code fragment is suspected of causing a bug, it is sometimes useful to test the software without executing the suspected fragment, to see whether the failure vanishes. This requires skipping code fragments. This can be done with the **goto**, or even better, by commenting out the suspected code fragment. The latter method may be preferable because it gives much finer control over the portions of code that are skipped.

8.10 TESTING OF CCOUNT

To illustrate many of the techniques discussed earlier, a regression test suite for **ccount** was developed using the following steps:

1. Develop test cases using both black and white box methods, the latter with the help of **nvcc**.
2. Execute the test cases using **ccount** and examine their outputs. If the output for a given test is acceptable, store the output in a regression test output file. If the output is incorrect, the software will need to be modified.
3. Write a regression test script for each acceptable test case.

ccount output is simple to check because CSL and NCSL can be counted by hand, and comment-to-code ratios computed by hand or with a calculator.

8.10.1 Equivalence Partition for ccount

In equivalence partitioning test cases for **ccount**, the highest-level partition chosen was between normal inputs and abnormal inputs. Abnormal inputs were further divided into cases in which no arguments are given to **ccount**, bad files are given, bad parameters are given, and so on. The complete partition can be seen in Table 8.2.

The focus of black box testing is to determine whether requirements have been met. A **ccount** requirement was that it produce a report of NCSL, CSL, and comment-to-code ratios for a syntactically correct C file. To test whether this requirement is fulfilled by the system, the following test case was used:

```
ccount hello.c > rtst14.output 2>&1
```

hello.c was determined to be syntactically correct by running it through **lint**. The output, both **stderr** and **stdout**, was stored in a file called **rtst14.output**. This output can be seen in the following display.

```
Output of regression test 14

hello.c        Sat Mar 25 16:30:11 1989

     Function        CSL   NCSL   CSL/NCSL
-------------------------------------------
       external        4     5      0.80
          total        4     5      0.80
```

Table 8.2: Equivalence Partition for ccount

			Test Case Number
Normal	No delimiter	Tab	13
		No tab	1
	Delimiter	Tab	9, 10, 11
		No tab	4, 12
Abnormal	Bad file(s)	Unreadable	5
		Object file	8
		Nonexistent file	7
		Executable file	19
	Bad argument(s)	File––file	2
		-vd	3
		-v	6
		Long delimiter	14
		-""	15
		""	16
		-?	17
		-d	18

To determine whether this output is correct, we must examine several issues. The first is whether **ccount** has produced accurate counts of CSL, NCSL, and the ratio of CSL to NCSL. To do this we must have an independent count of these values. One way to get these values would be to count them manually. Another would be to use one of the **ccount** prototypes discussed in Chapter 2. These prototypes, however, are not close enough to the final version of **ccount** to be used for this purpose. When we checked by hand, the values were correct.

Another thing that we needed to look at was whether the format of the output met requirements. This is a place where use of the JAD methodology (described in Chapter 2) would be extremely valuable, because it would provide testers with samples of user approved output. If, for example, users had agreed that the output of the **awk** prototype was acceptable, that output could be used to guide testing. Again, however, we did this step manually and determined that the output was acceptable. Having determined that the output was numerically correct and formatted correctly, we stored it as part of the regression test case.

In all, nineteen regression tests were developed for **ccount**. A test script and all test cases can be found in Appendix A. The first few regression tests were developed using black box methods. In addition to testing the requirements, however, we also wanted to be sure that a large percentage of the code had been exercised. Specifically, we set a target of 90 percent branch coverage. Ninety percent is a common goal in coverage analysis because higher figures usually require the testing of unusual error conditions, which can be extremely difficult. In **list.c** , for example, there are several tests of **malloc** failures such as the following:

```
/* Part 1:  Allocate the space for the new list node */

ptr = (count_list)malloc( sizeof(count_struct) );
if ( NULL == ptr ) Abort_Error( MALLOC_FAILURE );
```

Testing this code would require writing a dummy **malloc** procedure that returned **NULL** when called. Although this might be done for a critical application, we chose not to do it for **ccount** because a failure of **ccount** is unlikely to be critical.

To use **nvcc** on **ccount**, we first needed to change **ccount**'s makefile. Part of the **nvcc** suite is a tool called **vmake** that does this automatically. **vmake** is a **sed** script that transforms a standard makefile into the correct format and writes it to **stdout**. We captured the output as follows:

```
vmake Makefile > ccount.nvcc.mk
```

ccount.nvcc.mk is the makefile that will build the **nvcc** version of **ccount**.

The first step in our white box testing was to examine **nvcp** output for the first regression test. As can be seen in the following **nvcs** data, the first test case caused 68 percent of the total branch points in **ccount** to be exercised. Because this is below our target figure of 90 percent, we needed to find test cases that would increase this figure. **nvcs** output gave us the following information after the first test run:

```
nvcs: verif.out used
         Branch Point Analysis
     Executed    Possible   Percent Function or Filename
            3           3       100 ccount.c
           32          62        52 params.c
           12          16        75 counter.c
           64          71        90 classify.c
            9          15        60 report.c
           15          19        79 list.c
            0          13         0 error.c
          135         199        68 Total
```

We examined the code in **params.c** using **nvcp** and found that the following branch point had not been exercised. (This is shown by the underlining **nvcp** inserts for unexercised lines.)

```
/* process an option or list of options */
  for ( ch_ptr = (*argv)[arg_index]+1; *ch_ptr; ch_ptr++ )
  ------------------------------------------------
```

This indicates that code for processing options was not executed. If regression test 4 were run next, the following **nvcs** report would be generated:

```
nvcs: verif.out used
            Branch Point Analysis
   Executed    Possible   Percent Function or Filename
          3           3       100 ccount.c
         41          62        66 params.c
         15          16        94 counter.c
         67          71        94 classify.c
          9          15        60 report.c
         16          19        84 list.c
          0          13         0 error.c
        151         199        76 Total
```

As can be seen, the figure for module **params.c** has increased from 52 to 66 percent. Use of **nvcp** verified that the branch point had indeed been exercised by the new test case because **nvcp** now prints it without underlining as follows:

```
/* process an option or list of options */
for ( ch_ptr = (*argv)[arg_index]+1; *ch_ptr; ch_ptr++ )
```

We repeated this process, summarized in Figure 8.2, until 91 percent branch coverage was achieved.

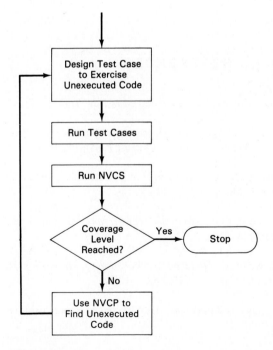

Figure 8.2   NVCC Testing Process.

The summary plot in Figure 8.3 shows the increase in total cumulative branch coverage as a function of test cases (in this case run in numeric order). The general form of this plot is typical: large increases as new test cases are added early, smaller increases as the target level is approached.

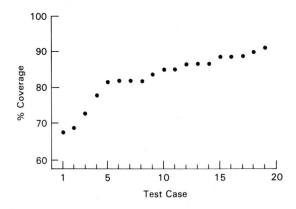

Figure 8.3 Total Cumulative Branch Coverage as Function of Test Cases.

nvcc is a valuable testing tool that can often improve the quality of testing. Unfortunately, it helps with only a limited part of the testing process. It can only show that C code has been exercised by a test case, *not* that code has been adequately tested. Adequate branch or line coverage is a necessary, but not a sufficient condition for good testing.

REFERENCES

1. Juran, J. M., *Juran's Quality Control Handbook* (4th ed.). New York: McGraw-Hill, 1988.

2. Parnas, D. L., and D. M. Weiss, "Active Design Reviews: Principles and Practices," *Eighth International Conference on Software Engineering* (August 1985), 132–136.

3. Fagan, M. E., "Design and Code Inspections to Reduce Errors in Program Development," *IBM Systems Journal*, 15, no. 3 (March 1976), 219–248.

4. Fagan, M. E., "Advances in Software Inspections," *IEEE Transactions on Software Engineering*, SE-12, no. 7 (July 1986), 744–751.

5. Freedman, D., and G. M. Weinberg, *Handbook of Walkthroughs, Inspections, and Technical Reviews* (3rd ed.). Boston: Little, Brown and Company, 1982.

6. Buck, F. O., *Indicators of Quality Inspections*. IBM Technical Report IBM TR21.802 (September 1981).

7. Bentley, J. L., *Writing Efficient Programs*. Englewood Cliffs, N.J.: Prentice Hall, 1982.

8. Myers, G. J., *The Art of Software Testing*. New York: Wiley, 1979.

9. Dunn, R., *Software Defect Removal*. New York: McGraw-Hill, 1984.

10. Crawford, S. G., and M. H. Fallah, "Software Development Process Audits—A General Procedure," *Eighth International Conference on Software Engineering* (August 1985), 137–141.

11. *An American National Standard IEEE Standard Glossary of Software Engineering Terminology*, ANSI/IEEE Standard 729, 1983.

12. Hetzel, W., *The Complete Guide to Software Testing*. Wellesley, Mass.: QED Information Sciences, 1984.

13. Shooman, M., *Software Engineering*. New York: McGraw-Hill, 1983.

14. Gries, D., *The Science of Programming*. New York: Springer-Verlag, 1982.

15. DeMillo, R., R. Lipton, A. Perlis, "Social Processes and Proofs of Theorems and Programs," *Communications of the ACM*, 22, no. 5 (May 1979), 271–280.

16. Selby, R. W., V. R. Basili, and F. T. Baker, "Cleanroom Software Development: An Empirical Evaluation," *IEEE Transactions on Software Engineering*, SE-13, no. 9 (September 1987), 1027–1037.

17. Weinberg, G., *The Psychology of Computer Programming*. New York: Van Nostrand Reinhold, 1971.

18. McCabe, T., "A Complexity Measure," *IEEE Transactions of Software Engineering*, SE-2, no. 4 (April 1976), 308–320.

19. Halstead, M., *Elements of Software Science*. New York: Elsevier North-Holland, 1977.

20. Nejmeh, B., "NPATH: A Measure of Execution Path Complexity and Its Applications," *Communications of the ACM*, 31, no. 2 (February 1988), 188–200.

21. Crawford, S., A. A. McIntosh, and D. Pregibon, "An Analysis of Static Metrics and Faults in C Software," *Journal of Systems and Software*, 5, no. 3 (March 1985), 37–48.

22. Neal, D., *NVCC Tutorial*. Department 45327 Technical Report, AT&T Bell Laboratories, August 1988.

23. Grinthal, E. T., "Software Quality Assurance and CAD User Interfaces," *IEEE Proceedings of the International Conference on Computer Design: VLSI in Computer* (1985), 95–98.

9

Software Maintenance
and Configuration
Management

The IEEE Standard Glossary of Software Engineering Terminology[1] defines *software maintenance* as "modification of a software product after delivery to correct faults, to improve performance or other attributes, or to adapt the product to a changed environment." *Maintainability* was defined in Chapter 1 as the ease with which a software system can be corrected, changed, or enhanced. Software maintenance, then, is about how to make and manage software changes.

The first section of this chapter discusses the software maintenance problem, maintenance costs and cost factors, some proposals that have been made for improving maintenance, and tool support for maintenance in the UNIX environment. The second section discusses a problem important throughout the life cycle, but especially critical during the maintenance phase. This problem of software configuration management can be posed as the question: *How can constant change to all software project work products be monitored, controlled, and coordinated to produce consistent sets of software work products and correct releases of customer deliverables?* Our discussion of configuration management emphasizes the use of UNIX tools that help solve this problem.

9.1 SOFTWARE MAINTENANCE

Lientz and Swanson[2] have identified three types of changes made to systems during maintenance, and have surveyed 487 business data processing centers about the amount of effort expended on each.

Perfective maintenance is the activity of adding functionality to a system, usually in response to requests from users or programmers. Lientz and Swanson[2] found that perfective maintenance accounted for 51.3 percent of total maintenance effort in their sample. *Adaptive maintenance* is the activity of altering a system because of changes in the system's operating environment. For example, moving a program from a computer running the UNIX operating system to a microcomputer running DOS is an example of adaptive maintenance. Lientz and Swanson[2] found that adaptive maintenance accounted for 23.6 percent of maintenance effort. *Corrective maintenance*, the activity of fixing system errors, accounted for 21.7 percent of maintenance effort. The last 3.4 percent of effort was spent on other activities.

Arnold and Parker,[3] however, have reported maintenance figures that are inconsistent with those of Lientz and Swanson.[2] Using more careful analysis techniques, they found that enhancements accounted for 38 percent of maintenance activity; error fixes, 36 percent; and other activities such as bad data and hardware problems, 26 percent. These figures are for eight year's worth of NASA maintenance data.

The findings of Lientz and Swanson[2] suggest that most maintenance activity is not fixing bugs, as many people believe, but adding functionality to programs. The Arnold and Parker[3] data also show significant maintenance activity expended on enhancements, though at a lower level. Changes of this sort can be far reaching, demanding modification of requirements, design, implementation, and user documentation, and requiring extensive retesting. Perfective maintenance requires a full life cycle of its own to accomplish such drastic change.

9.1.1 Maintenance Costs and Cost Factors

The maintenance phase of the life cycle is the most expensive for most projects, often accounting for 50 percent or more of total software development and maintenance costs.[2] Boehm[4] has reported maintenance to development cost ratios of up to 40 to 1. According to these figures a system that cost \$100,000 to develop might cost \$4,000,000 to maintain!

Many factors, both technical and nontechnical, affect system maintenance costs.[5] Some of these nontechnical factors include the following:

- *Novelty and complexity of the application being supported.* Projects with large research components, for example, are more likely to produce programs that need to be changed than projects using established technology.

- *Staff stability.* If the programmer who wrote the code maintains it, maintenance costs should be lower because the learning and understanding parts of maintenance are simplified.

- *Program lifetime.* The longer a system exists, the more changes will be made to it and to its operating environment. Besides the costs of perfective and adaptive maintenance, corrective costs are higher for older programs because they suffer from a form of deterioration. Old programs that have been patched and hacked for years eventually become so disorganized and incomprehensible that they are almost impossible to fix.

- *Dependence of the program on the external environment.* A tax program probably needs more change because of continual changes in tax laws than would a program to analyze production data, for example.

Some of the technical factors affecting maintenance costs include the following:

- *Module independence.* Systems are easier to maintain when one part can be changed without affecting other parts.
- *Programming language.* Programs written in a high-level language such as Pascal are normally easier to maintain than programs written in low-level languages such as assembler. C is intermediate between these two levels.
- *Programming style.* The programming standards, guidelines, and practices used in writing a program affect its readability and therefore directly affect maintenance costs.
- *Program validation and testing.* Appropriate use of validation and testing techniques like those discussed in the last chapter can increase quality and decrease corrective maintenance costs.
- *Documentation quality.* The correctness, completeness, and readability of both user and engineering documents can decrease maintenance costs.

Why does maintenance require such a large share of project resources? Several explanations are proposed in the literature.[6] One reason is that much software is poorly written. Many programs were written before the advent of effective design methods and structured programming. Some programs are poorly written because their builders were inadequately trained, or were not given adequate resources.

Another reason for high maintenance costs is that it is difficult to determine how a change to one part of a software system will affect other parts of the system. This can lead to unwise changes and unexpected problems. The use of modularity and good interface design are of paramount importance in overcoming this problem. Another source of high cost is that software is often not designed for maintenance. That is, maintenance is not considered throughout the life cycle but only late in the life cycle. When this happens, poor design choices are often made, systems are inadequately documented, there is too much reliance on a particular operating environment, and so forth.

An especially common reason (in our experience) for high maintenance costs is failure to make and document changes completely. Too often, a quick fix is made to code without parallel changes to comments, engineering documents like requirements and design documents, and user documents like reference manuals. Careless changes like this lead to increased costs in the next round of maintenance activity, when much effort is wasted figuring out and documenting how the program really works, before further changes make the problem even worse.

A final reason for high maintenance costs is that insufficient resources may be devoted to maintenance tasks. Maintenance is often assigned to junior programmers without the skill and experience to do it properly. Maintenance activities are often slighted in budgets and rushed in practice, resulting in the sort of careless changes mentioned earlier.

9.1.2 Lowering of Maintenance Costs

What then is needed to attack the maintenance problem? Some of the reasons for high maintenance costs, such as the difficulty of predicting the consequences of changes, are difficult problems that will likely remain. Many others, however, can be addressed. First, practices should be improved. Proven software engineering practices are not always used on software projects. Software engineers must learn more about the best available tools, techniques, and methods, and discipline themselves to use them. Many of the techniques we discussed in earlier chapters, such as modular design, good program readability, and the use of software inspections and regression test methods, can all improve system maintainability.

Second, management policies must be improved. Maintenance must be allocated adequate resources, and better personnel policies, such as rotating personnel between design, test, and maintenance, must be established. Maintenance activities must be monitored and measured.

Other improvements can come from continued research and development. Better design approaches, such as evaluating designs for complexity, could lead to better designs and more maintainable systems. Improved tools used to support maintenance activities could increase maintenance productivity.

9.1.3 UNIX Tools for Maintenance

Maintenance requires that a software engineer first understand how a system works. Understanding someone else's code is always difficult. Considering how poorly many systems are designed and coded, it can be nearly impossible. Fortunately, the UNIX environment provides tools to help with this difficult task. Once the system is understood, the software engineer must change it. The UNIX system has tools to help make wide-ranging program changes. Once the change has been made, someone needs to verify that the change has achieved its aim, and that errors have not been introduced as a result of the change. Regression testing (described in Chapter 8) is the technique of choice for this verification step. UNIX tools can help verify changes as well.

Following is a list of tool categories that have been proposed[7] [8] for helping maintenance programmers to understand software, change it, and verify that changes have been made properly. In each category we list the UNIX tools (if any) that fit the category.

- Tools that help maintenance personnel see structure in code when trying to understand it.
  - The highest-level structure of a C software system is at the compile module and header file level. C compile modules and header files are UNIX files containing C source code. The **make** utility is the primary means of specifying

system structure at this level. A system's **makefile** can tell a maintenance programmer both which source code files make up the system and how those files depend on each other.

— A lower level of structure is the hierarchy and calling sequence of C functions. The calling hierarchy of functions that tools like **cflow**, **cscope**, and **cia** report, for example, is an important piece of information about a system.

— Flow of control is another type of structure. It can be traced with the step functions in symbolic debuggers such as **sdb**, and **dbx**, and with tools like **ctrace**.

— Symbolic debuggers and **ctrace** can help determine how data is structured and how it changes during execution. **cflow** provides information about how data is passed between system modules and functions within the system.

- Tools that help programmers find common data referenced by different variable names. Extensive use of pointers in many C programs makes this task important and difficult. Unfortunately no UNIX/C tool for this task is generally available.

- Tools to restructure code. **cb** helps with restructuring source code for readability, but no tools that restructure program logic are generally available for C.

- Tools to store test cases and examine test output. The UNIX file system can be used to store test cases, and UNIX shell scripts can be written to automate the testing process. **diff** can be used to compare program output with expected output.

Although the UNIX system offers many tools to help the C maintenance programmer, there are a few categories in this list where it is deficient, and several where better tools would be useful.

9.2 SOFTWARE CONFIGURATION MANAGEMENT

Software development projects produce development documents, code, test cases, user documents, and so forth. This material changes throughout the life cycle. Work products have successive versions, with versions of one item matching various versions of the others. For example, a major enhancement during the maintenance phase may require new requirements documents, leading in turn to new designs, changed code, new or revised test cases, and so forth. Eventually a new release of the software product results. The new versions of the documents—code, test cases, and so on—usually do not match the old versions. The old versions must be recoverable so they can be used to fix mistakes, answer questions about, or make corrections to previous releases, and so forth. In even a medium-sized project with several people changing the work products, chaos can quickly result.

In *software configuration management* one monitors and controls changes to software work products. One also coordinates work products to produce correct and consistent product releases.[9] Even though we discuss this topic with the maintenance phase, software configuration management is an important activity throughout the life cycle.

We divide configuration management into the following three activities:

- *Version control.* As software work products change, they form successive versions. Version control is the activity of keeping track of these versions.
- *Change control.* Change control is the procedure for requesting changes, deciding what changes to make, making changes, and recording and verifying changes.
- *Build control.* Keeping track of which versions of work products go together to form a release, and generating derived work products correctly, is called build control.

We discuss each of these component activities in turn.

9.2.1 Version Control

A *software configuration item*, or *item* for short, is any software project work product treated as a unit for version control. Examples of items include requirements and design documents, sets of test cases, header files, and user documents. Items are often changed producing variants. Variants are sometimes distinguished as *versions* to be kept track of in the version control system. The first version of an item is called a *baseline*. For example, a design document may have a baseline at the end of the design phase. A second version might be generated during the coding phase, a third version created for the second release of the product, and so on.

Except for baselines, versions are always created by changing previous versions, called *predecessors*. Naturally, a version is called a *successor* of its predecessor. We can distinguish two kinds of versions: A version is a *revision* if it is a replacement for another version. A version is a *variation*, or *branch*, if it is one of several alternative versions. Variations may be created from other versions, or may be a baseline. Revisions are produced because it is constantly necessary to correct errors, remove or add information, and so forth. Variations are generated because of the need to tailor systems to different environments and users.

To illustrate, suppose that a baseline requirements document is changed to correct several mistakes. The new version is a revision of the baseline because it is meant to replace it. Now suppose that two additional requirements documents are generated from the corrected version describing two slightly different products for two new markets. Because these three requirements documents are alternatives, with none meant to replace the others, they are variations, not revisions. In large projects generating multiple releases or multiple variations of releases for different operating environments or markets, there may be many variations and revisions of all items. Version control systems must keep track of all versions of items including successor and predecessor information.

Version control is primarily a database system function, or a record keeping function. On small projects with few developers, an informal paper system may suffice; usually, however, the task is large and complex enough that mechanized tools like the Source Code Control System (**SCCS**)[10] or Revision Control System (**RCS**)[11] must be employed. These tools have similar functionality. We discuss **SCCS** for purposes of illustration.

SCCS is a popular version control tool for items stored as UNIX files. **SCCS** also provides several change and build control features. **SCCS** services include the following:

- *Version storage.* **SCCS** records changes to files and forms new versions. Version dates and comments about the version are recorded. **SCCS** stores only changes to files rather than a complete file for each version. This economizes on storage and allows **SCCS** to keep many versions in only a little more space than would be needed for one version. These changes are known as *deltas*.
- *Version retrieval.* **SCCS** allows retrieval of any version of any file.
- *Version deletion and combination.* **SCCS** allows versions to be deleted and combined to simplify the version tree.
- *Support for revisions and variations.* **SCCS** supports the creation of variations under the name of *branch deltas*. Variations are created automatically when a version that already has a successor is checked out for editing.
- *Administration features.* **SCCS** provides facilities for maintaining comments about versions, printing version histories of items, comparing versions, inserting version information into files automatically, and so forth.
- *Change control features.* All official changes to files must be made by checking out the affected file for editing, and then submitting the changed file to **SCCS** as a new version. When a file is checked out for change, no one else may check out the file, precluding the possibility of inconsistent revisions. **SCCS** keeps a list of users allowed to change files and only allows registered users to check out files for editing. **SCCS** also provides a special field for modification request (MR) numbers (we discuss MRs later).
- *Build control features.* **make** is able to interrogate **SCCS** about file creation times in computing file dependencies. Makefiles can contain **SCCS** commands to retrieve versions for compilation.

The **SCCS** system is composed of three principle commands and several subsidiary commands (that we do not discuss). The principle commands are as follows:

- **admin** is used to place a file under **SCCS** administration (that is, register a baseline), and control its use.
- **get** is used to check out versions of files for reading or editing.
- **delta** is used to check in a new version of a file.

A diagram of the basic **SCCS** activities is presented in Figure 9.1.

Every **SCCS** version has a version number called a *SID* of the following form:

```
release.level.branch.sequence
```

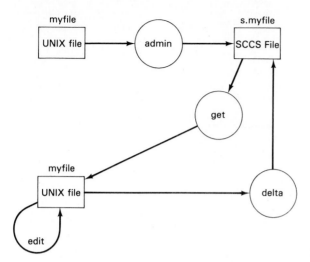

Figure 9.1   SCCS Activities Diagram.

Every version has a release and level; the release number is used to distinguish major revisions, and the level number is used to distinguish minor revisions. The branch and sequence numbers are added to variations, the branch number distinguishing the variation, and the sequence number distinguishing revisions of the variation.

To illustrate, suppose we wish to place the file **myfile.c** under **SCCS**. The command **admin −imyfile.c s.myfile.c** causes **SCCS** to produce a baseline file called **s.myfile.c** containing **SCCS** administration information and the original contents of **myfile.c**. (The prefix "s." is a required **SCCS** convention.) The baseline version of **myfile.c** has SID 1.1. The **get** command can be used to access **myfile.c** for editing by typing **get −e s.myfile.c**. Once **myfile** has been changed, it is checked back in with the command **delta s.myfile.c**. The SID for the new version of **myfile.c** is 1.2.

Suppose that **myfile.c** has been checked out, changed, and checked back in several times, producing the string of revisions with SID's 1.1, 1.2, 1.3, and 1.4. Suppose we want to create a variation of version 1.3. The command **get −e −r1.3 s.myfile.c** will retrieve version 1.3 for editing. **SCCS** recognizes that the new version is a variation of 1.3 (because it has a successor, version 1.4), and assigns it the SID 1.3.1.1 when the **delta** command is used to check in the variation. This number shows that the new version is a variation of version 1.3. Revisions of version 1.3.1.1 will be numbered 1.3.1.2, 1.3.1.3, and so on, whereas new variations of version 1.3 will be numbered 1.3.2.1, 1.3.3.1, and so on. A summary of this numbering scheme can be seen in Figure 9.2.

9.2.2 Change Control

Change control is the activity of considering, deciding on, delegating responsibility for, and monitoring changes to items. Change control is instituted as a collection of procedures, usually focused on a database system for documenting and tracking changes.

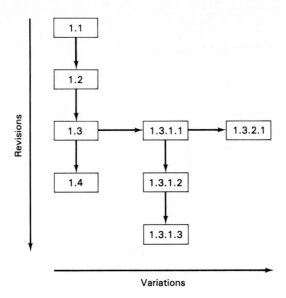

Figure 9.2 SCCS Number Generation.

Such a change documenting and tracking database system is called a *change control system*. Change control may be informal on small projects, perhaps using a logbook to document and track changes. On larger projects, strict change control procedures must be instituted along with a mechanized system for documenting and tracking changes.

The basic activities and processes of change control are the following:

1. Someone submits a request for a change. Such requests are called MRs, and submitting a request is called *opening* an MR. Usually a form, either paper or electronic, called a *modification request form* (MRF) is used to open an MR. An example of an MRF follows:

```
Modification Request #0001              Date of MR: 8/10/88

APPLICATION:  ccount       TYPE:     SW     RELEASE OCC:   1.0

ORIG. NAME:   Bill Frakes  PHONE:    7186   DEPT:          45327
ROOM:         2J-502       MACHINE:  SUN 3/50  DATE OCCURRED: 8/2/88

ATTACHMENTS:  None.

ABSTRACT:     Incorrect CSL output.

DESCRIPTION:  The CSL count produced by ccount on correct C files
              is one too small.  The problem occurs for all
              per-function counts; try list.c for an example and
              check the output by hand.

RELATED MRs:  None.
```

```
EXPLANATION:    Per-function CSL counting was turned off at the sight
                of a left curly bracket closing a function definition,
                not at end of the line with the closing curly bracket
                on it, thus failing to count comments on the last line
                of the function definition.

STATUS:         Closed       PRIOR STATUS: Open     DUE DATE: 08/08/88

TESTER:         Bill Frakes

CATGORY CHNG:   Bug fix.

RES. SUMMARY:   Bug was fixed by programmer C. Fox.

RESOLUTION:     Changed where end-of-function flag was set in
                counting routine.

IMPACT:         Local change to counter.c module.

CHILDREN:       None
```

MRs may be opened by customers, developers, managers, testers, documenters, or some selected subset of these groups. MRs may mention faults, errors, enhancements, typos, and so forth.

One notable concept is the child MR, best illustrated by example. If an MR is written against a requirement during the latter part of the life cycle, it is likely that the change will also require changes in the design, code, test plans, and other later life-cycle products. The MRs written to change these later life-cycle products are said to be *child MRs* of the original MR. Another example of child MRs are changes in individual compile modules dictated by a change in a common header file. Here, MRs to change the compile module are child MRs of the MR for the header.

2. MRs are reviewed by a *change control authority* or an *MR review board* that examines each MR and decides on an appropriate action. The MR review board is composed of developers, managers, testers, and so forth. Often the decision involves classifying the MRs according to their severity. A classification system like the following is sometimes used:

- *Severity level 1*. The item is unusable, incomprehensible, or unmanufacturable because of a problem reported by the MR. For example, an MR reporting a software fault causing the system to crash during typical use would rate a severity rank of 1.
- *Severity level 2*. The item is usable but unacceptable because of the problem reported in the MR. For example, a test case with partially incorrect input conditions might be given this severity classification.
- *Severity level 3*. The item is usable, but the MR reports a failure to conform to standards, guidelines, or practices. For example, an MR reporting improperly

formatted section headings in a user document would receive a Level 3 severity ranking.

- *Severity level 4*. The MR requests an enhancement or adaptation. For example, a request for a port to a personal computer would rank as a severity Level 4 MR.

Once MRs are classified, the MR review board decides how to dispose of each MR. Among the possibilities are the following:

- Investigate the MR and make the change immediately.
- Schedule investigation and change when resources become available.
- Defer a decision about the disposition of the MR until later.
- Deny the request made in the MR.

3. Once a change is approved, a *change tracking authority* is notified and proceeds to track the progress of the change. The change tracking authority might be a project manager, a staff member responsible for change tracking, or the MR review board.

4. The change must be planned, scheduled, assigned to a developer, implemented, reviewed, and verified. Once this is done, the change control authority is notified that the change is completed. The MR is *closed*, and the change becomes part of the next version of the software configuration item.

Change control systems can usually report the status of MRs, generate statistics and reports summarizing the change activity of a project, and direct notifications and information about changes to people. Figure 9.3 illustrates the change control process.

Formal change control systems introduce significant management overhead in development and maintenance. Consequently software configuration items are usually placed under change control at the same time they are placed under version control, usually as late in the life cycle as possible.

9.2.3 Build Control

A *software configuration* is a collection of versions of items. An initial configuration might consist of initial versions of requirements and design documents, and an implementation plan. A second configuration might consist of the initial requirements document and implementation plan, a revised design document, and several software modules and unit test cases. Later configurations would likewise consist of certain versions of items. An important group of items that are part of software configurations are *derived items*, items generated from other items, usually by the computer. Examples of derived items include object modules, executable files, test data, and so forth. Other items are called *nonderived items*.

Build control is the activity of specifying, tracking, and forming software configurations. Build control centers around the database activity of maintaining complete specifications of software configurations as items change through the life cycle. Nonderived item build control is not difficult until there is more than one release of a

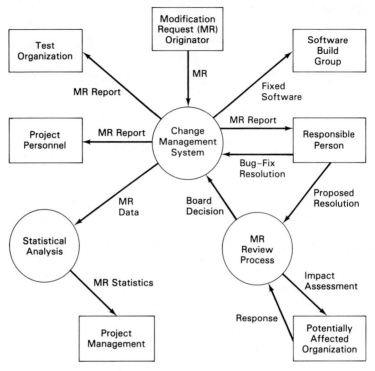

Figure 9.3   Change Process Diagram.

system; then it can become a difficult problem. Nonderived item build control is usually done by hand. Efficient derived item build control is a difficult problem, but it yields to mechanization; many tools for derived item build control exist.[12]

The primary build control tool in the UNIX environment is **make**, which automates the generation of derived items. **make** is discussed in Chapter 7. **SCCS** provides crude support for build control of nonderived items in its version numbering system.

9.2.4 Project Monitoring and Configuration Management

Besides the primary activities of configuration management, configuration management tools can produce data to help with project tracking. For instance, **SCCS** can report how many lines have changed in project files. These changes, or deltas, are often equated with corrected errors and are used in metrics to estimate fault density. Automated change management tracking systems can generate more detailed project data, such as the number of MRs subdivided by severity category. They can also report the length of time taken to close MRs. Both the number of MRs and the time taken to close them figure largely in project reports used by project management for decision making. **make** can be used to invoke programs to record the number of times an item has been compiled. This data can be useful in estimating the fault proneness of source modules, and the efficiency of bug-fixing or program-enhancement efforts.

9.2.5 Summary

Configuration management includes three inter-related activities: version control, change control, and build control. The UNIX system offers tools to support these activities separately, with some features to integrate their use. This is one area where more sophisticated tool support would be welcome, however.

REFERENCES

1. *An American National Standard IEEE Standard Glossary of Software Engineering Terminology*, ANSI/IEEE Standard 729, 1983.

2. Lientz, B., and E. Swanson, *Software Maintenance Management*. Reading, Mass.: Addison-Wesley, 1980.

3. Arnold, R., D. Parker, "Using Post Facto Validation for Gathering Empirical Data on Software Maintenance," *Proceedings of the Eighteenth Annual Hawaii International Conference on System Science* (January 1985), 435–446.

4. Boehm, B., "Software Engineering—R&D Trends and Defense Needs," in *Research Directions in Software Technology*, pp. 44–86, ed. P. Wegner. Cambridge, Mass.: M.I.T. Press, 1979.

5. Sommerville, I., *Software Engineering* (2nd ed.). Reading, Mass.: Addison-Wesley, 1985.

6. Schneidewind, N. F., "The State of Software Maintenance," *IEEE Transactions on Software Engineering*, SE-13, no. 3 (March 1987), 303–310.

7. Martin, J., and C. McClure, *Software Maintenance: The Problem and Its Solutions*. Englewood Cliffs, N.J.: Prentice Hall, 1983.

8. Kishimoto, Z., "Testing in Software Maintenance and Software Maintenance from the Testing Perspective," *Proceedings of the Software Maintenance Workshop* (1983), 166–177.

9. Babich, W. A., *Software Configuration Management*. Reading, Mass.: Addison-Wesley, 1986.

10. Rochkind, M. J., "The Source Code Control System," *IEEE Transactions on Software Engineering*, SE-1, no. 4 (April 1975), 255–265.

11. Tichy, W., "RCS—A System for Version Control," *Software Practice and Experience*, 15, no. 7 (July 1985), 637–654.

12. LeBlang, D. B., and R. P. Chase, "Parallel Software Configuration Management in a Network Environment," *IEEE Software*, 4, no. 6 (November 1987), 28–35.

10

Future Trends

Software engineering has progressed, but many problems remain. In this chapter, we consider trends in software engineering that may improve software engineering practice, including the evolution of the UNIX system as a CASE environment, data repositories, front-end support tools, project management support, and document management support.

10.1 EVOLUTION OF UNIX PROGRAMMING ENVIRONMENT

Despite its popularity, the UNIX system does not provide an ideal environment for software engineering. A comprehensive software development environment provides support for creating, storing, controlling, retrieving, and transforming software project information from development and planning documents, through program code and data, to support programs and test cases. Criticisms of the UNIX system as a software development environment include the following:[1]

- UNIX software development environments (SDEs) are almost exclusively for programmers and focus almost exclusively on the implementation and testing portions of the software life cycle. For example, most UNIX SDEs lack tools for managers (like project planning and tracking tools) and testers (like code coverage analyzers). UNIX SDEs also often lack "what you see is what you get" (WYSIWYG) document production facilities, and strong front-end CASE tools with code generation capabilities.
- Most UNIX shells have a terse and difficult command language, and UNIX tools do not provide helpful error and warning messages, making the system difficult

for all but experts to use effectively. For example, a cardinal rule of user interface design[2] is to avoid giving punctuation symbols important meaning because punctuation is not very important in English, and punctuation symbols are easy to misread or overlook. UNIX shells violate this rule by giving punctuation symbols important and subtle functions. For example, UNIX shells have three kinds of quotation marks that mean different things. This makes the UNIX system difficult to learn, remember, and use.

- The UNIX system does not provide an integrated user interface in part because it has weak user interface standards. For example, some commands with option arguments insist that white space appear between the option and its argument; others insist that none appear; and others will work either way. Some UNIX tools expect input on **stdin**; some will accept a list of files as input; and others will work either way. Taken together, these and other user interface inconsistencies make it difficult to work with the UNIX system.

- UNIX shells and tools implicitly assume a command line user interface model. Although such interfaces offer some advantages for expert users, they are difficult for novices. They also severely constrain interaction mechanisms. For example, many interactive tools benefit from user interfaces designed to update display fields, graphics, gauges, sliders, and so forth, continuously, monitoring the progress of computation. This is difficult with a command line interface.

- UNIX tools are not strongly integrated because the data interface is based on files and byte streams. For example, **make** works at the compile module level by checking file date stamps. If a file is changed, then all less recently compiled dependent files must be recompiled, even if the change does not require it. If a finer-grained data interface were available, **make** could restrict recompilation to only those dependent files that needed to be recompiled.

Recent software engineering research has pointed out ways to overcome some shortcomings of the UNIX system as a CASE environment. If the UNIX system is to maintain its popularity and continue to be a first-rate software development environment, it must evolve in response to its critics and to advances in CASE technology. Fortunately, the path for UNIX system evolution is smoothed because the UNIX system is a popular environment for many emerging CASE technologies. Thus we may expect to see improvements in UNIX software engineering support as the UNIX system evolves to keep pace with progress in CASE technologies.

     In this section we consider some likely directions for UNIX system evolution based on recent CASE environment research and product introductions.

10.2 USER INTERFACES

Character-based terminals lacking high-resolution graphics have been the standard for the UNIX system since its inception. This restriction has impeded efforts to build better user interfaces despite development of sophisticated character based screen handling packages like **curses**.[3] Lack of high-resolution graphics has also made it difficult to provide automated tool support for the early phases of the life cycle, where graphical tools and techniques like dataflow diagrams, hierarchy charts, and Pert charts, predominate. The emergence and spread of high-resolution, high-speed graphics workstations, coupled with standard windowing systems, like the X Window System from the Massachusetts Institute of Technology[4] provide the necessary technology for improvement.

The final step to a firm foundation for an improved UNIX system user interface is a standard for user interface look and feel. Several such standards, like the *OPEN LOOK*[5] and *Motif*[6] graphical user interface standards, have been proposed. These standards specify visual aspects and principles of operation of conforming applications including features such as the following:

- Types, properties, and look of windows, menus, buttons, scroll bars, and so on.
- Operations and mechanisms for manipulating graphical objects.
- Mouse and keyboard functions.
- Visual cues and feedback, such as use of color, shading, and highlighting.

These standards support many hardware environments (different size and resolution screens, different input devices), handle existing user interfaces, and have open architectures.

As these standards become more widely used, interfaces will improve considerably in several ways. Throwing out the assumption of a character-based terminal allows shells and tools to take advantage of an interface with separate windows, full-screen display capabilities, graphics, and pointing device input. An example is **dbxtool** (see Chapter 8), a rewrite of the UNIX debugging tool **dbx**. **dbxtool** uses multiple windows to display program execution, list the program, display values of variables, and so forth. **dbxtool** is much easier and faster to use than **dbx**. The improvement is so dramatic that **dbxtool** almost seems like another (better) debugger, although its functionality is almost identical to **dbx**.

Difficulties with UNIX shell command languages are alleviated by menus, icons, and an extensive help system. Menus are good reminders and good grouping mechanisms. Commands chosen from menus also prompt for the input they need. A help system integrated with a menu system can provide reminders and supplementary information about commands, options, and arguments.

Powerful workstations and user interface standards address some of the most serious criticisms of the UNIX system as a CASE environment, and should help maintain UNIX as a leading software development environment.

10.3 DATA REPOSITORIES

Software engineering activities produce huge volumes of data including requirements documents, design documents, architectural diagrams, dataflow diagrams, structure charts, hierarchy charts, source code, test scripts, quality assurance reports, project plans, user documentation, and so forth. Versions of all work products must be controlled, and relationships between work products must be maintained for configuration management and requirements traceability. The tasks of creating, storing, retrieving, controlling, and manipulating software project data are attractive candidates for automation. The diversity of the data, its volume, the size and frequency of database transactions, the number and complexity of relationships between objects, and storage of project data in many locations in a system of networked computers create difficult problems, however. Traditional database systems and simple file systems like the UNIX file system do not provide adequate solutions to these problems.[7] Hence data management is an important and difficult issue for CASE environments. In particular, the file system mechanisms of the UNIX system are not adequate to the demands of advanced CASE environments.

Several strategies for solving the CASE data repository problem have been investigated by researchers and in commercial products. A simple approach is to enhance the file system to do version and configuration control, and to maintain type information about files. One example of this approach is the Domain Software Engineering Environment (DSEE).[8] The DSEE runs on Apollo workstations under a version of the UNIX system that supports typed files. The DSEE uses a description of system components, a specification of a software configuration, and a derived object pool to build all or parts of a system.

A second approach is based on object-oriented database technology.[9] Object-oriented databases store complex, highly inter-related objects rather than structured data in simple relations. Objects have attributes that may be inherited from other objects, and they may contain methods that define or constrain database transactions. The object management system is responsible for version and configuration control, and for propagating changes triggered by transactions. For example, an object-oriented database system might provide objects like bug reports. A bug report might have attributes like the reporter's name, the bug's severity, whether the bug was fixed, and conjectures about the cause of the bug. Furthermore it would have relations to other objects. For example, it might have the *shown-by* relation to a set of test cases that illustrate the bug, the *in-module* relation to the module where the bug resides, the *fix-described-by* relation to a bug-fix report, and so on. Among the methods that might be supported by this object is a method for setting the *is-fixed* attribute. Such a method might set the *is-fixed* attribute by checking whether there was a bug-fix report related to the bug report by the *fix-described-by* relation. The object-oriented database approach seems the most promising for solving the CASE data repository problem, but it is still under research.

Another approach to the CASE data repository problem is using a hypertext system to maintain software project work products.[10] [11] Hypertext systems store information in chunks regarded as nodes of a graph connected by arcs representing relationships between nodes. The nodes can be textual, graphical, video, sound, or raw data. Hypertext systems offer promise in CASE environments because they can handle information at any level of granularity, and because they provide mechanisms for constructing arbitrary links between chunks of information. Thus, for example, individual requirements could be stored in separate nodes, and linked to corresponding design elements. These nodes could in turn be linked to segments of source code that implement the design elements. Source code segments could be linked to test cases that verify whether the system satisfies the requirements at the start of the chain. Automatic checks could be run on the system to verify that all requirements are linked to design elements, all design elements are implemented in code, all code is linked to test cases, and so on. Thus hypertext systems could provide an adequate data repository for CASE environments.

There are at least two important problems that must be overcome before hypertext can be used in CASE environments. First, there is a lack of support for version and configuration control in most hypertext systems. Version and configuration control are essential features of a CASE data repository. Second, most hypertext systems do not provide a rich enough variety of links to handle the interconnections between objects that must be maintained in CASE data repositories. At least one research project is addressing these problems.[12]

The European Community has been working on the CASE environment repository problem for some time and has proposed the *Portable Common Tool Environment* (PCTE) as a standard.[13] PCTE is based on a modified binary entity-relationship model in which all objects are typed and form a type hierarchy. Relationships between objects can be established. The standard also covers access control, configuration management, and transaction management. There is already a UNIX implementation of the PCTE standard. Standards have also been proposed for data exchange between CASE tools.[14]

One difficulty common to all approaches to the data repository problem is collecting and organizing data without overburdening the software engineer. The overhead of data collection and organization in many software projects is already a huge burden. The additional effort of providing information for a sophisticated CASE environment data repository may be overwhelming. If too much is demanded of software engineers, they may simply refuse to cooperate—examples of this kind of failure have already occurred. In the long run, the most difficult aspect of the CASE environment data repository problem may be finding a good way to collect the data.

10.4 PROJECT MANAGEMENT SUPPORT

A shortcoming of UNIX-based software development environments is their lack of support for software project management activities such as project costing, scheduling, and resource allocation. There are several project management support tools that run under UNIX. For example, ISTAR[15] is an integrated project support environment that includes the following tools:

- A resource definition tool for defining and changing resource descriptions.
- A scheduling tool computes a critical path schedule for a project based on task descriptions and resource descriptions.
- A resource allocation tool tracks resource allocations.
- A resource usage-reporting tool records time spent on tasks.
- A monitoring tool reports on status and resource usage data and compares it with planned progress and resource consumption.

10.5 DOCUMENT PRODUCTION SUPPORT

UNIX batch-oriented word processing tools (e.g., `troff, pic, eqn`) do not fill all software engineering document production needs. Several WYSIWYG editors are now available for UNIX and are a valuable supplement to the older document preparation tools. The Technical Publishing Software system from Interleaf[16] and FrameMaker from Frame Technology Corporation[17] are popular WYSIWYG editors in UNIX environments. In addition to traditional document preparation facilities, these systems provide facilities supporting traceability, group review, and change coordination on documents.

10.6 FRONT-END SUPPORT

One concern about front-end requirements and design tools is their lack of code generation capability. We are beginning to see the introduction of new methods for generating code from system descriptions.

Statemate from I-Logix, Inc.,[18] is an example of a tool providing strong code generation support based on the underlying formalism of *statecharts*, an extension of standard state diagrams. Statemate accepts graphical and textual specification and analysis of three views of a system: behavioral, functional, and structural. The statechart extensions include the ability to specify behavior hierarchically, to deal with concurrency (both synchronous and asynchronous), and the ability to base current system behavior on past behavior. The statechart language defines the behavioral view of the system by allowing the user to specify the states of the system and the conditions, events, and actions that cause transition between them. The activity-chart language defines the functional view of the system including the system's functions and activities, and the signals and the flow of data items between the system's components. The module-chart language defines the structural view of the system including the actual modules, components, and subsystems and their interconnections via channels and lines. Statemate provides simulation tools that confirm the accuracy of the system specification by simulating the system's behavior.

10.7 SUMMARY

UNIX began as an operating system, and developed into a programming environment as individuals wrote or improved tools and made them available to others. The best tools were widely distributed, gradually recognized as important, and eventually became part of the standard toolset. This process continues, with areas of great promise in user interface tools, the early phases of the life cycle, and tasks other than programming and testing. Such efforts cannot move forward, however, without environments to support graphical interfaces and agreement on standards. As these prerequisites are satisfied, the UNIX programming environment continues to evolve at the forefront of CASE environments.

REFERENCES

1. Penedo, M. H., and W. E. Riddle, "Guest Editors' Introduction: Software Engineering Environment Architectures," *IEEE Transactions on Software Engineering*, SE-14, no. 6 (June 1988), 689–696.

2. Rubinstein, R., and H. Hersh, *The Human Factor*. Bedford, Mass.: Digital Press, 1984.

3. Strang, J., *Programming with Curses*. Newton, Mass.: O'Reilly & Associates, 1986.

4. Scheifler, R. W., J. Gettys, and R. Newman, *The X Window System C Library and Protocol Reference*. Bedford, Mass.: Digital Press, 1988.

5. AT&T, *OPEN LOOK Graphical User Interface Style Guide*. New York: AT&T, 1989.

6. Open Software Foundation, *OSF/Motif Style Guide*. Englewood Cliffs, N.J.: Prentice Hall, 1990.

7. Bernstein, P. A., "Database System Support for Software Engineering," *Proceedings of the Ninth International Conference on Software Engineering* (March 1987), 166–178.

8. Leblang, D. B., and R. P. Chase, "Parallel Software Configuration Management in a Network Environment," *IEEE Software*, 4, no. 6 (November 1987), 28–35.

9. Hudson, S. E., and R. King, "The Cactis Project: Database Support for Software Environments," *IEEE Transactions on Software Engineering*, SE-14, no. 6 (June 1988), 709–719.

10. Conklin, E. J., "Hypertext: An Introduction and Survey," *IEEE Computer*, 2, no. 9 (September 1987), 17–41.

11. Smith, J., and S. Weiss, "Hypertext," *Communications of the ACM*, 31, no. 7 (July 1988), 816–819.

12. Garg, P., and W. Scacchi, "A Hypertext System to Manage Software Life Cycle Documents," *Proceedings of the Twenty-First Annual Hawaii International Conference on System Sciences* (January 1988), 337–346.

13. Gallo, F., R. Minot, and I. Thomas, "The Object Management System of PCTE as a Software Engineering Database Management System," *Proceedings of ACM SIGSoft/SIGPlan Software Engineering Symposium on Practical Software Development Environments* (December 1986), 12–15.

14. Hecht, A., and M. Harris, "A CASE Standard Interchange Format: Proposed Extension of EDIF 2.0.0," *Proceedings of Twelfth Structured Methods Conference* (August 1987), 112–123.

15. Dowson, M., "Integrated Project Support with ISTAR," *IEEE Computer*, 4, no. 6 (June 1987), 6–15.

16. Interleaf, Inc., *Interleaf Sun Reference Manual, TPS 4.0.* Cambridge, Mass: Interleaf, 1989.

17. Frame Technology Corp., *FrameMaker Reference Manual.* San Jose, Cal.: Frame Technology, 1989.

18. Harel, D., "STATEMATE: A Working Environment for the Development of Complex Systems," *Proceedings of the Tenth International Conference on Software Engineering* (April 1988), 396–406.

A

ccount **Project Documents**

This appendix contains software engineering project documents for our example software metrics program **ccount** including the following:

- **ccount** C Metrics Tool Concept Exploration.
- **ccount** C Metrics Tool Requirements.
- **ccount** C Metrics Tools Design.
- **ccount** Project Coding Standards.
- **ccount** Regression Test Script and Test Cases.

Also included is the **ccount** user documentation, a manual page.

A.1 CCOUNT C METRICS TOOL CONCEPT EXPLORATION

A.1.1 Problem Definition

A primary purpose of software engineering is to manage the complexity of software. Tools are needed to measure the complexity of parts of a software system so that the parts can be changed to make them less complex, or so that they can be given special attention, such as extra testing.

In general, as the size of code increases so does its complexity. Thus, one type of measurement that reflects complexity is the count of noncommentary source lines (NCSL) in a piece of software. The tool proposed, **ccount**, will provide NCSL counts for C source code files. Specifically, **ccount** will report NCSL for the file as a whole, for each C function definition in the file, and for code, such as macro definitions and variable declarations, outside any function definition in the file.

Counts of the commentary source lines (CSL), and comment-to-code ratios (CSL/NCSL), can be useful as rough estimates of the adequacy of program documentation. **ccount** will also count the CSL and compute comment-to-code ratios for the whole file, for each function definition, and for code external to function definitions in the file.

A.1.2 System Justification

There are about twenty C programmers in our shop and hundreds in the company. All could benefit from a simple metrics tool like the one proposed. Although other metrics tools exist, none provide the simple metrics we describe in a small, efficient, and portable tool.

A.1.3 User Characteristics

The proposed tool would be used by C programmers and testers during the coding and testing phases of the life cycle. Users can be assumed to have a good knowledge of the C programming language and the UNIX operating system, and to be familiar with a wide range of UNIX/C programming tools.

A.1.4 Goals for System and Project

ccount should be simple to learn and use, and the metrics it reports should be easy to interpret. Response time should be short to encourage programmers to use the tool often. Project management and program maintenance should be minimal.

A.1.5 Constraints on System and Project

Development of this system must not require the purchase of new hardware or software. Development cannot require more than two person months of effort. Because programmers in our shop and in the company work in a variety of environments, the program should be easy to port to environments with a C compiler.

A.1.6 Solution Strategy

To save time and to check requirements, **ccount** will first be implemented as a prototype with the major features of the target system. The prototype will be written using the UNIX shell and UNIX tools. If the prototype is fast enough, it will be enhanced to attain full functionality, and revised for robustness, reliability, and maintainability. If the prototype is too slow, the final program will be written in C.

A.1.7 Development, Operation, and Maintenance Environments

ccount will be developed on a Sun 3/50 workstation under Sun OS,®* a version of the UNIX operating system. The prototype will be written in the UNIX shell language, with major portions written in the **awk** programming language. If the prototype is inadequate, the final program will be written in C. **ccount** will be maintained for UNIX systems and perhaps for DOS as well.

A.1.8 Feasibility Analysis

Technical Feasibility.   Preliminary study shows that this tool is technically feasible because simple source code metrics can be generated by parsing source code using well-known techniques.

Political Feasibility.   The two following questions must be addressed in determining political feasibility:

1. *Will the tool meet the needs of, and can it be made available to, a large enough population of users to justify its creation?* This tool is almost certain to be successful because enough programmers will use it our development shop to justify the small cost of its creation. Wider distribution in the company can be done by publishing a technical memorandum describing the tool. All employees have access to these memoranda, so information about **ccount** will be widely dispersed. We will give a copy of the tool to any employee who asks for it.
2. *Are resources to build the project available?* Many tools of this size and complexity have been built before in this environment. The software engineer responsible has two months for the task, which is adequate.

In summary, **ccount** is both technically and politically feasible.

A.2 CCOUNT C METRICS TOOL REQUIREMENTS

A.2.1 Product Overview

A primary purpose of software engineering is to manage the complexity of software. Tools are needed to measure the complexity of parts of a software system so that the parts can be changed to make them less complex, or so that they can be given special attention, such as extra testing.

In general, as the size of code increases so does its complexity. Thus, one type of measurement that reflects complexity is the count of noncommentary source lines (NCSL) in a piece of software. The tool described in this requirements document,

---

*Sun OS is a registered trademark of Sun Microsystems Inc.

ccount, will provide NCSL counts for C source code files. Specifically, ccount will report NCSL counts for the file as a whole, for each C function defined in the file, and for code outside any function definition in the file (such as macro definitions and variable declarations).

Counts of the commentary source lines (CSL), and comment-to-code ratios (CSL/NCSL), can be useful as rough estimates of the adequacy of program documentation. ccount will also report CSL counts and compute comment-to-code ratios for the whole file, for each function definition, and for code outside function definitions.

A.2.2 Development, Operation, and Maintenance Environments

Development Environment.   ccount will be developed on a Sun 3/50 workstation under Sun OS,®* a version of the UNIX operating system. It will be written in the C programming language.

Operating Environment.   ccount should be portable (with minor changes) to other environments with a C compiler. This requirement will be tested by porting ccount to two other environments: a Vax running UNIX System V, and a PC running DOS.

Maintenance Environment.   ccount will be maintained in its development environment.

A.2.3 Conceptual Model

ccount is built on the model of a standard UNIX filter.

Options and Input.   Options and input files are specified on the command line, however the default function delimiter (see later) can be stored in an operating system environment variable, and input can also be supplied on **stdin**.

Data Output.   Data output is directed to **stdout**.

Error Output.   Error output is directed to **stderr**.

Conceptual Model.   Figure A.1 is the conceptual model for ccount.

A.2.4 User Interface Specifications

This section specifies the input user interface. The output formats are specified in the next section.

---

*Sun OS is a registered trade mark of Sun Microsystems, Inc.

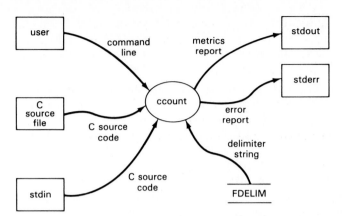

Figure A.1   Conceptual Model for **ccount**.

Command Line Format.   **ccount** is invoked by the command "**ccount**," possibly followed by options, possibly followed by a list of input source code file names. The allowed options are **t** and **d**. Schematically, the **ccount** command line looks as follows:

ccount [-t] [-d *function_delimiter*] [*file_name* ...]

Option Format.   As with other UNIX tools, the options may be listed separately as shown, or they may be put together (i.e., as **-td**). The white space separating the **-d** option from its argument is optional. Repeated options are allowed; the argument for the last **-d** option is used as the *function_delimiter*. Options and file names may be interspersed. A double dash can be used to mark the end of the options list and the start of the filenames.

Option Actions.   The **-t** (for "tabbed" option specifies that each field in the output should be separated by a single tab. The **-d** (for "delimiter") option specifies a function start delimiter string. This string must either not contain white space or characters significant to the UNIX shell, or it must be quoted. Details about the functions of these options are provided in the next section.

Input File Specification.   A *file_name* is a path to a C source file. When files are named on the command line, **ccount** uses the named files for input; if no file is named on the command line, **ccount** reads **stdin**.

A.2.5 Functional Requirements

Incorrect Input.   **ccount** assumes that its input is syntactically correct. There is no need for **ccount** to make estimates of CSL and NCSL for incorrect programs; consequently **ccount** is required to work properly only on syntactically correct programs. **ccount** should not core dump on incorrect input, but otherwise its behavior is undefined.

Definitions of NCSL and CSL.   These definitions are as follows:

- NCSL—a line of a (syntactically correct) source file is a NCSL if it contains at least one token of the language that is not part of a comment.
- CSL—a line of a (syntactically correct) source file is a CSL if it contains at least one nonwhite space character that is part of a comment.

Note that a blank line is considered neither a CSL nor a NCSL, and that a line containing both code and comments is both a CSL and a NCSL.

Definition of Function Delimiter String.   It is possible to tell by parsing a source code file where a function definition's *code* begins, but it is not possible to tell where the *comments* that go with a function definition begin. Therefore, if **ccount** is to report accurate counts of CSL by function definition, a special character string marking the beginning of the comments for each function definition must be placed in the source file, and provided to **ccount**. Such a string is called a *function delimiter string*, and it marks the line at which counting for a function definition begins. Once counting for a function definition begins, all lines up to and including the line containing the brace (**}**) ending the definition are included in the counts for the function. The line containing the function delimiter string itself counts as a CSL or NCSL for the function, as appropriate.

Missing Function Delimiter.   If no function delimiter string is specified, then all lines are regarded as external to any function definition, and no per-function counts are reported.

Function Header Recognition.   A quick look at the grammar for the C programming language suggests that recognizing function definition headers, necessary for finding function names, will be difficult. The problem arises for two reasons: C declarators can be complex, and identifiers can name types using the **typedef** facility. Handling arbitrary function definitions would probably require sophisticated parsing algorithms, a symbol table to track type definitions, and header file processing. Because limited development resources are available for this project, the final program is only required to recognize simple function definition headers. Specifically, the program need only recognize function definition headers in which the function name is not contained in a parenthesized declarator. This restriction simplifies parsing without unduly damaging **ccount**'s usefulness.

Output Report Contents.   For each C source file, **ccount** will report the following:

- NCSL, CSL, and the ratio of CSL to NCSL for each function definition whose start is marked by the function delimiter string.
- NCSL, CSL, and the ratio of CSL to NCSL for lines external to any function definition.

- NCSL, CSL, and the ratio of CSL to NCSL for all lines in the file.

Output Report Formats.   The output report will contain a section for each file provided as input. The report is produced in either of two formats: tabbed format (specified by the **-t** option on the command line), and nontabbed format (the default). Report sections consist of a *header* and a *body*.

Report Section Header Contents.   Report section headers contain file names and dates, though their exact contents depends on the output format, as specified subsequently.

Report Section Body Contents.   Report section bodies start with lines reporting counts for each function defined in the file, followed by a line reporting counts of source file lines external to any function definition, followed by a line reporting file totals. As noted earlier, when no function delimiter string is specified, all lines are regarded as external to any function definition, and only the external and total lines appear in the report section body.

Report Section Body Fields.   Each line in a report section body contains four fields: the first field is a function name, or "external," or "total," for data lines reporting counts for a function definition, for code external to any function definition, or for all code in the file, respectively. The second field is a CSL count, the third field is a NCSL count, and the fourth field is the ratio of CSL to NCSL expressed as a decimal number rounded to two decimal places, with a leading whole number digit or digits. When the NCSL count is 0, this ratio is undefined, so the report shows a dash (-) in place of the decimal number.

Tabbed Format Header Layout.   In tabbed format, if the program is reading its input from **stdin**, the header is empty; otherwise it contains the name of the current file.

Tabbed Format Body Layout.   Each field on a line in the body of the report section is left justified and separated from its predecessor by a single tab.

Tabbed Format Output Example and Discussion.   An example of a tabbed format output report section is the following:

```
main.c
function1    23    29    0.79
function2    69    172   0.40
function3    30    111   0.27
function4    46    60    0.77
external     143   212   0.67
total        313   584   0.54
```

Tabbed format is intended to make it easy to use **ccount** in pipelines with other UNIX filters. For example, the filter **cut** can be used to select fields from a data stream when these fields are separated by tabs. So if portions of **ccount**'s output are to be directed to other filters, **cut** can be used to select data from **ccount** output delivered in tabbed format. Similarly, if the header line in **ccount** output is not desired, then files can be piped to **ccount** through **stdin** and the header line will not appear in tabbed format output.

Nontabbed Format Header Layout.   In nontabbed format, report section headers are five lines long. The first and third lines are blank. The second line contains the current file name, or "stdin" if the program is reading from **stdin**, followed by a tab, followed by the date and time in the format shown below in the example. The fourth line contains column labels identifying the output fields, and the fifth is a line of 45 dashes separating the header from the body of the report section.

Nontabbed Format Body Layout.   Each field in each line in the body of the report section provides four fields of right justified output. The first field occupies 20 character positions. Function names too long to fit in this space are truncated to 20 characters. The CSL and NCSL fields are 6 characters wide; the CSL-NCSL ratio field is 8 characters wide. Fields are separated from one another by a single blank.

Nontabbed Format Output Example and Discussion.   An example of a nontabbed format output report section is the following:

```
main.c    Thu Mar 3 16:39:21 1988

          Function        CSL    NCSL   CSL/NCSL
---------------------------------------------
          function1        23      29     0.79
          function2        69     172     0.40
          function3        30     111     0.27
          function4        46      60     0.77
           external       143     212     0.67
              total       313     584     0.54
```

Nontabbed format is intended for use by software engineers working at their terminals. Consequently this output format is spaced to ease reading and avoid confusion.

Function Delimiter String Restrictions.   The **ccount** function delimiter string can be any string of printable ASCII characters, up to 63 characters in length, that contains at least one nonwhite space character.

Function Delimiter String Determination.   The function delimiter string is determined as follows:

- **ccount** uses the last string specified by the **-d** option on the command line used to invoke **ccount**. For example the command line:

```
ccount -d "/* FN */" prog.c
```

  tells **ccount** to use the comment "**/* FN */**" as a function delimiter string. Note that the function delimiter string, as in this example, may have to be enclosed in quotes if it contains several words, or characters (like the asterisk) with special meaning to the UNIX shell.
- If no function delimiter string is specified on the command line, **ccount** uses the string specified in an operating system environment (shell) variable named **FDELIM**.
- If no function delimiter string is specified in the command line or in an environment variable, **ccount** will not use a function delimiter string and will not report per-function metrics.

Function Delimiter String Recognition.   **ccount** will recognize a function delimiter string only if it appears at the beginning of a line. This provision is made so that the function delimiter string can be mentioned in a file without upsetting the counting mechanism.

A.2.6 Nonfunctional Requirements

Performance.   On an unloaded Sun 3/50 workstation, **ccount** must be able to process a source file of forty thousand bytes in 2 seconds or less of CPU time as measured by the UNIX **time** command.

Input File Size.   **ccount** must be able to process a source file at least one Mbyte long.

A.2.7 Error Handling

Error Actions.   Errors will be handled in the following way:

Table A.1:   Handling of Errors

Error	Messages	Action
Bad option	Usage message	Issue message and halt
No string after –d	Usage message	Issue message and halt
Bad delimiter string	None	Process file without delimiter
Nonexistent file	No such file *filename*	Issue message, process next file
Unreadable file	Cannot read file *filename*	Issue message, process next file
Out of memory	Memory allocation failure	Issue message and halt
Internal error	Internal error	Issue message and halt

Usage Message Format.   The **ccount** usage message is the following:

```
Usage: ccount [-t] [-d <string>] [<file> ...]
```

The usage message should start on a new line and end with a new line character.

Error Message Format.   All **ccount** error messages have the format:

```
ccount: <message body>
```

Error messages should start on a new line and end with a new line character.

A.2.8 User Documentation

Because **ccount** is a simple UNIX filter, it need only be documented for the user with a manual page.

A.2.9 Foreseeable Changes and Enhancements

The most likely enhancement to **ccount** is improvement of the parsing mechanism to recognize function definition headers, and hence function names, no matter how complex the function declarator. Another desirable enhancement is the provision of regular expression patterns as function delimiters rather than fixed strings. This enhancement would allow more flexible function delimiter specifications. Another likely enhancement to **ccount** is to have it check a project specification file and report any files or functions out of specified bounds. For example, a project specification file might state minimum, maximum, and target values for **ccount** metrics. Functions or source files with values outside the extrema might be logged in a separate file.

A.3 CCOUNT C METRICS TOOL DESIGN

A.3.1 Overview

Structured design is the design method used for **ccount**. The dataflow diagram presented as the **ccount** conceptual model in the requirements document is elaborated into a detailed dataflow diagram. This dataflow diagram is converted into a structure chart. A data dictionary and mini-specs to go along with the dataflow diagram and the structure chart are presented. These products constitute the architecture of **ccount**.

Because **ccount** is so small and simple, several units identified in the structure chart for logical reasons are too small to be compile modules. In the detailed design, units are chosen from the structure chart to be compile modules. All module interfaces, error handling, internal structure, and so on are presented as the detailed design.

A.3.2 Architectural Design

The **ccount** conceptual model is a dataflow as shown in Figure A.2. The detailed elaboration of this diagram is shown in Figure A.3.

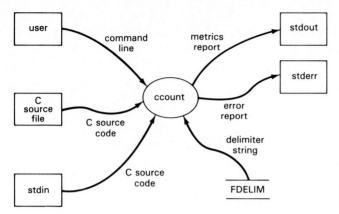

Figure A.2   Top-Level **ccount** Dataflow Diagram.

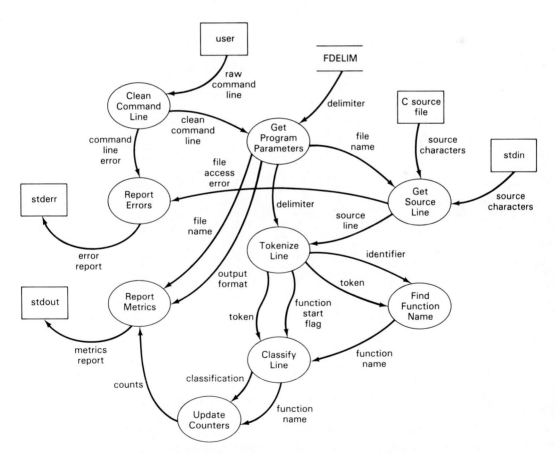

Figure A.3   Second-Level **ccount** Dataflow Diagram.

This dataflow diagram has a transform flow—that is, it has the overall form of a filter, with an input portion, a process portion, and an output portion. This form serves as the starting place for transforming the dataflow diagram into a structure chart, as shown in Figure A.4.

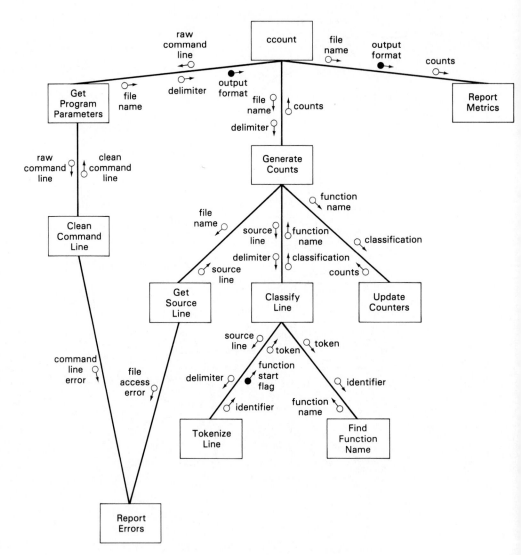

Figure A.4   Structure Chart of ccount.

Note that every dataflow from the dataflow diagram is captured in a data couple in the structure chart, and every transform bubble in the dataflow diagram is captured in a rectangle in the structure chart. Next we present a data dictionary describing each dataflow–data couple.

Table A.2: Data Dictionary

Data Item	Description
classification	Set of boolean values marking lines as CSL, NCSL, external, function ending
clean-command-line	Command line arguments array checked and rearranged
command-line-error	Error code indicating a command line error
counts	A list of triples of function names and counts of CSL and NCSL
delimiter	String with the text of the function delimiter string
error-report	Error and usage messages as specified in the requirements
file-name	String with the text of a C source code input file name
file-names	Array of strings with C source code input file names
file-access-error	Error code indicating a file access error
function-name	String with the text of a C function name
function-start-flag	Boolean value true when a line is a function start, false otherwise
identifier	String with the text of a C program name or a key word
metrics-report	Output reports as specified in the requirements
output-format	Boolean value indicating whether output is in tabbed format
raw-command-line	Original command line arguments in an array of strings
source-characters	Characters from a C source code input file
source-line	String with the text of a line from a C source code input file
token	Name of a C program lexical object

The final element of our architectural design is a mini-spec for each rectangle in the structure chart (corresponding to the transforms in the dataflow diagram).

- **ccount** is the root module coordinating the activities of other modules. It loops on **file-names** to generate and report metrics for each input file.
- **Get-Program-Parameters** obtains program parameters from the command line and the environment. It uses **Clean-Command-Line** to check **raw-command-line** arguments and put the command line in canonical form in **clean-command-line**. Then it extracts the **file-names** from **clean-command-line**, gets the **delimiter** from **clean-command-line** or the environment, and gets the **output-format** from **clean-command-line**.
- **Clean-Command-Line** checks options to make sure they are valid and that options with arguments have arguments. It rearranges the **raw-command-line** array so it contains all options and option arguments first, followed by a double dash, followed by **file-names**. Options are separated, and the last element of **clean-command-line** is **NULL**.
- **Report-Errors** receives **error-indications** and translates them into **error-reports**, sends the reports to **stderr**, and aborts the program if necessary.
- **Report-Metrics** writes **metrics-reports** to **stdout** according to the **output-format**. Headers are generated from the **file-name** and the current date and time, and bodies are generated from the data in the **counts** data structure.

- **Generate-Counts** processes each source file, returning its results in **counts**. Each file is opened and read a line at a time. Lines are classified by **Classify-Line**, and the **classifications** and function names are used by **Update-Counters**, which puts **function-names** and counts of CSL and NCSL in **counts**. Files are closed once processed.

- **Get-Source-Line** reads a **source-line** from a file.

- **Classify-Line** sends a line to the tokenizer and then asks for the line back a token at a time. The tokenizer also says whether the line starts a function. As tokens come in, **Classify-Line** figures out whether the line is a CSL, NCSL, or both, and whether it is external to a function or not. It records all this in a **classification**. When processing a function, **Classify-Line** asks **Find-Function-Name** to process the token stream to get the **function-name**.

- **Tokenize-Line** takes a line and returns a stream of C tokens. It also indicates whether the line is a function start line according to the function start delimiter string, and it provides the text of identifiers when asked.

- **Find-Function-Name** processes a token stream attempting to find function definition headers and then extract function names from them.

- **Update-Counters** takes a line classification and updates counters for per-function CSL and NCSL, external CSL and NCSL, and total CSL and NCSL. It also keeps track of function names, and places all this information in **counts**.

A.3.3 Module Overview

As discussed earlier, many of the modules in the structure chart are too simple to be compile modules. In choosing units to be compile modules, we have taken the internal nodes of the structure chart, and two leaf nodes that have logically distinct functions. This gives six modules. In addition, we formed another compile module to implement the only complex data type in the program, the count list used to accumulate data and send it from the counting module where it is collected to the reporting module that uses it to generate output. These modules are summarized in Table A.3.

Table A.3: Module Overview

Module	Description
ccount	Root module overseeing data and control flow
params	Checks command line and fetches program parameters
counter	Processes a file to generate line counts
classify	Parses lines and classifies them
report	Generates metric output reports
error	Generates error messages from error indications
list	Implements an abstract data type for lists of line counts

A.3.4 Module Descriptions

ccount.   This module contains the program's **main** function. Its job is to pipe data between the other modules.

- *Assumptions*. None.
- *Secrets*. None.
- *Constraints and limitations*. None.
- *Related requirements*. 4.4 Input File Specification.
- *Module packaging*. Main program.
- *Error handling*. None.
- *Internal structure*. This module contains four important data objects: the command line, the output format specifier, the delimiter string, and the array of C source files to be processed. The following processing is carried out by this module:

```
Get_Parameters(in: cmd_line, out: is_tabbed, delimiter, files);
do
   {
   Count_Lines(in: delimiter, file, out: count_list);
   Report_Metrics(in: is_tabbed, count_list, file);
   next file;
   }
while more files;
```

params.   This module accepts the raw command line as input, and returns a list of C source files to be processed, the delimiter string, and the output format.

- *Assumptions*. This module assumes that the command line description sent to it (**argc** and **argv**) is correct.
- *Secrets*. This module hides the name of the environment variable containing the delimiter string.
- *Constraints and limitations*. None.
- *Related requirements*. 4. User Interface Specifications, 5.17 Function Delimiter String Restrictions, 5.18 Function Delimiter String Determination, 7.1 Error Actions.
- *Module packaging*. This module exports no data types or objects, and only the following function:

```
int Get_Parameters(
      int argc,           /* in: argc from main */
      char *argv[],       /* in: argv from main */
      int *is_tabbed,     /* out: output format */
```

```
char **delimiter,   /* out: delimiter string */
char ***files       /* out: array of source files */
)
```

The **argc** and **argv** parameters are straight from the main function's parameter list. The output format parameter is **TRUE** if the output is supposed to be in tabbed format, and **FALSE** otherwise. The delimiter string is set according to the command line or the environment variable **FDELIM**. If the string has length 0 or does not exist, then **delim** is **NULL**, meaning that there is no delimiter string. Any string on the command line that is not an option and not a delimiter string is considered a file name. No further checking of file names is done. The parameter **files** is a pointer to an array of strings, so it is a pointer to an array of pointer to characters. The end of this array is indicated by a **NULL** pointer as the last element. Hence if no files are specified, the only element of the array is the **NULL** pointer. The return value is **SUCCEED** (0) on success and **FAIL** (1) on failure; however, all errors encountered by this module should cause a program abort.

- *Error handling*. This module detects and handles the following errors:
  — Bad option: Call the error routine and return **FAIL**.
  — Unrecognized option: Call the error routine and return **FAIL**.
  — Missing delimiter string: Call the error routine and return **FAIL**.
  — Memory allocation failure: Call the error routine and return **FAIL**.

- *Internal structure*. This module really has two major jobs: check the command line for errors, and then process the command line (and perhaps check the environment) to generate the necessary program parameters. The first job has been done before; we should take advantage of this work. Consequently we will reuse code from Thomas, Rogers, and Yates.[1] The rest of the processing is as follows:

```
Clean_Command_Line(in/out: argc, argv);
if ( error ) return( FAIL );

if ( -t on command_line )
   is_tabbed = TRUE;
else
   is_tabbed = FALSE;
if ( -d on command_line )
   set delimiter;
for all other strings on command_line
   add to list of files;

if ( !delimiter_set )
   set delimiter from environment;
if ( !delimiter_ok )
   delimiter = NULL;

return( SUCCEED );
```

counter.   The counter module accepts a C source file name and a delimiter string as input, and produces a list of counts for that source file as output.

- *Assumptions*. This module assumes that the contents of the files passed to it are syntactically correct C code.
- *Secrets*. This module hides all details of source file line counting.
- *Constraints and limitations*. None.
- *Related requirements*. 4.4 Input File Specification, 5.6 Output Report Contents, 7.1 Error Actions.
- *Module packaging*. This module exports no data types or objects and has only the following public function.

```
void Count_Lines(
         char *file,           /* in: C source file */
         char *delimiter,      /* in: delimiter string */
         count_list *counts    /* out: the count list */
         )
```

When **file** is the **NULL** pointer, data should be read from **stdin** rather than from a file. When the **delimiter** is **NULL**, no per-function counts are made. When the count list is empty, no data was generated.

- *Error handling*. This module detects file problems when it tries to access files. In particular, this module handles the following errors:
  — Nonexisting file: Call the error routine.
  — Unreadable file: Call the error routine.
  If a file access operation fails then an empty count list is returned. Hence the **report** module should not print anything when supplied with an empty count list.
- *Internal structure*. This module has only the one function; it maintains counters for the current function's CSL and NCSL, total CSL and NCSL, and external CSL and NCSL. Each line is sent to the **classify** module to be classified, and the counters are updated accordingly. When the end of a function is detected, its data is recorded and the function counters reset. At the end, the external and total data is recorded. The following shows this processing:

```
initialize counters;

Create_List(out: counts);

open( file );
if ( error )
   {
   Error( ACCESS_ERROR );
   return;
   }
```

```
        for each line in file
          {
          Classify_Line(in: line, delimiter,
                        out: classification);
          update counters based on classification;
          if ( end_of_function )
            {
            Append_Element(in: func_counters,
                           in/out: counts);
            reset function_counters;
            }
          }

      Append_Element(in: extern_counters,
                     in/out: counts);
      Append_Element(in: total_counters,
                     in/out: counts);

      close( file );
```

report. The report module accepts a file name, an output format indicator, and a count list for a file, and generates a formatted report on **stdout**. As a side-effect it also consumes the count list so that it is empty when it is finished.

- *Assumptions*. None.
- *Secrets*. The report module encapsulates all details about output formats.
- *Constraints and limitations*. None.
- *Related requirements*. 3.2 Data Output, 5.7 through 5.16 describing all output formats.
- *Module packaging*. This module exports no data types or objects and has only the following exported function:

```
      void Print_Metrics(
              char *file_name,     /* in: of C source file */
              int is_tabbed,       /* in: output format */
              count_list *counts   /* in/out: count list */
              )
```

The **file_name** parameter is needed because the file name appears in output reports. If the output format indicator **is_tabbed** is **TRUE** then a tabbed format output report is generated; otherwise a nontabbed format report is generated. The count list contains the data; if the list is empty then no report at all should be generated.

- *Error handling*. None.
- *Internal structure*. This module performs a simple task; the main algorithm is the following:

```
        if ( Is_Empty_List(in: cnts) ) return;

        if ( is_tabbed )
          print tabbed header;
        else
          print nontabbed header;

        for every element in counts
          {
          Delete_Element(in/out: cnts,
                         out: cnt_data);
          if ( is_tabbed )
            print tabbed cnt_data
          else
            print nontabbed cnt_data
          }
```

The only point of note here is that if **file_name** is **NULL** then in tabbed format the header is empty, and in nontabbed format the file name is "stdin."

classify.   This module parses C source lines and classifies them as CSL or NCSL, as external to any function or internal to a particular function, and as function ending or not. It also finds function names and returns these for use in the output report.

- *Assumptions*. This module assumes that the input is a syntactically correct C program. It also assumes that the preprocessor has not been used to make even syntactically correct programs unrecognizable by hiding braces and disguising C in other nefarious ways.
- *Secrets*. This module hides details about the way parsing is done.
- *Constraints and limitations*. The parser has several limitations. First, it cannot recognize parenthesized function names in function definition declarators. Second, it will confuse function delimiter strings beginning with a pound sign (#) with preprocessor directives.
- *Related requirements*. 5.1 Incorrect Input, 5.2 Definitions of NCSL and CSL, 5.3 Definition of Function Delimiter String, 5.4 Missing Function Delimiter, 5.5 Function Header Recognition, 5.6 Output Report Contents, 5.19 Function Delimiter String Recognition, 7.1 Error Actions.
- *Module packaging*. This module exports no data types or structures and has only the following public function:

```
    void Classify_Line(
           char *line,           /* in: source file line */
           char *delimiter,      /* in: delimiter string */
           int *is_CSL,          /* out: TRUE iff a CSL */
           int *is_NCSL,         /* out: TRUE iff an NCSL */
           int *is_extern,       /* out: TRUE iff external */
```

```
        int *is_func_end,    /* out: TRUE iff end of func */
        char **func_name     /* out: function name */
        )
```

The delimiter string is needed to watch for the start of a function. The four boolean variables suffice to completely classify the input line. The **func_name** parameter is set to point to a buffer with the function's name in it when the current line is the last line of a function (that is, when **is_func_end** is **TRUE**).

- *Error handling.* The only errors that this module watches for are errors in its own internal processing—sanity checks. Failed sanity checks cause the error routine to be called to report an internal error and abort the program.

- *Internal structure.* The **classify** module must do three complex tasks: scan the input line to tokenize it; parse the tokens well enough to classify lines; parse the tokens well enough to recognize function names. We design these in turn.

  — Tokenizing: Tokenizing depends on what tokens are recognized. For the task at hand, the following tokens must be recognized: identifiers (for function names), comment delimiters (for distinguishing CSL and NCSL), left and right parentheses (for recognizing function headers), left and right braces (for finding the ends of function definitions), line ends (to signal the end of processing), and all others. A private enumeration type for these tokens called **token_type** is defined as in Table A.4.

Table A.4: Recognized Tokens

Name	Token
ID_TKN	Identifiers and keywords
BEG_CMNT_TKN	Comment start delimiter
END_CMNT_TKN	Comment end delimiter
LPAREN_TKN	Left parenthesis
RPAREN_TKN	Right parenthesis
LBRACE_TKN	Left curly bracket
RBRACE_TKN	Right curly bracket
EOL_TKN	End of line
OTHER_TKN	Anything else

Recognizing these tokens requires character classification. The following character classes must be distinguished: letter, digit, slash, star, left parenthesis, right parenthesis, left brace, right brace, end of line, white space, and all others. A private enumeration type for these character classes called **char_class** is defined in Table A.5.

Input characters must be mapped to character classes. The standard way to accomplish this is with an array. A preloaded private ASCII array mapping characters to character classes must be defined.

Table A.5: Character Classes

Name	Description
WHITE_CH	White space characters
EOL_CH	The newline character
LETTER_CH	The uppercase and lowercase characters
DIGIT_CH	The digits
STAR_CH	The asterisk
SLASH_CH	The slash
L_PAREN_CH	The left parenthesis
R_PAREN_CH	The right parenthesis
L_BRACE_CH	The left curly brace
R_BRACE_CH	The right curly brace
OTHER_CH	Anything else

A private buffer for accumulating the text of identifiers must be defined.

Once all this machinery is in place, a scanner can be built as a simple finite state machine that takes the (remaining) input line and consumes it character by character until it recognizes a token. The token is returned along with the unconsumed portion of the input line. The scanner also accumulates the text of identifiers.

— Recognizing function names: The function name recognition problem is simplified if we assume that we only need to process tokens outside the braces delimiting a function definition (that is, tokens at nesting level 0), and outside macro definitions. We make these assumptions. Then we can recognize a function name by watching for an identifier immediately followed by a parenthesized expression, in turn immediately followed by either an identifier (a type specifier) or a left brace.

This job can be done with a souped-up finite state machine that works as follows: Watch for identifiers, and save them as candidate function names. Once an identifier is encountered, look for an argument list followed by an identifier or a left brace. If such a string is recognized, save the identifier as a function name. The machine is represented in Table A.6.

The A means "accept" and the D "do not accept." The algorithm must count unmatched left parentheses, and allow the transition from State 2 to State 3 only if this count is 0. Finally, whenever a transition is made to State 1

Table A.6: Transition Diagram

State	Identifier	(	)	{	Other
0	1	0	0	0	0
1	1	2	0	0	0
2	2	2	3	2	2
3	1(A)	0(D)	0(D)	0(A)	0(D)

on an identifier, the text of the identifier is saved. The saved text is returned when an accepting state is reached.

— Line classifying: The line classifier must watch every line for a function delimiter marking the start of function counting. It must keep track of comment delimiters and ignore everything but the end of a line when it is inside a comment. Outside a comment, it must count braces to find the ends of functions, to know when code is outside a function, and to know when to feed tokens to the function name finder. It must also keep track of whether a line is a preprocessor line, so as not to feed macro definition tokens to the function finder. This is not hard, but it is tricky. The following describes the algorithm used for this task:

```
if ( line starts with delimiter )
   in_function = TRUE;

while ( token != end_of_line )
   {
   if ( in_comment )
      {
      is_CSL = TRUE;
      if ( token == end_of_comment )
         in_comment = FALSE;
      }
   else if ( token == start_of_comment )
      is_CSL = in_comment = TRUE;
   else
      {
      is_NCSL = TRUE;
      if ( 0 == num_braces && !cpp_line )
         Find_Function_Name(in: token);
      if ( token == left_brace )
         num_braces++;
      else if ( token == right_brace )
         {
         num_braces--;
         if ( 0 == num_braces )
            {
            if ( in_function )
               {
               is_func_end = TRUE;
               Get_Function_Name(out: name);
               }
            in_function = FALSE;
            }
         }
      }
   }
```

error.   This module contains the error function.

- *Assumptions.* None.
- *Secrets.* This module hides the secret of where error messages are written, namely to **stderr**, and which errors cause program aborts. It also hides implementation dependent information about the global variable **errno** that is set to an error value when an error occurs. These error values differ in different environments (this was discovered during porting).
- *Constraints and limitations.* None.
- *Module packaging.* This module exports an **error_type** with the allowable error indications shown in Table A.7.

Table A.7:   Error Type

Error Indication	Description
BAD_OPTION	Option is not a character
MISSING_DELIMITER	Missing delimiter string
ACCESS_ERROR	Cannot access file
MALLOC_FAILURE	Memory allocation failure
INTERNAL_ERROR	Input scanner failure

The **error** module also exports the following function:

```
int Error(
        error_type indication,  /* in: what error */
        char *file_name         /* in: file name */
        )
```

This first issues error messages, aborts the program if appropriate, and returns **FAIL** (1) for error propagation.

- *Error handling.* None.
- *Internal structure.* The error function is a switch on error indications.

list.   This module implements the abstract data type of count lists. A count list is a list of elements consisting of a string and two long values. In this program, the string is used for the function name, and the long values are used for the CSL and NCSL counts for the function. The count list data type has four operations: a list creation operation, an empty list predicate operation, an append list element operation, and a delete list element operation.

- *Assumptions*. None.
- *Secrets*. This module hides the secret of how count lists are implemented. This implementation uses singly linked lists in a standard way.
- *Constraints and limitations*. Counts can only go as high as a **long** value will allow.
- *Related requirements*. None.
- *Module packaging*. The module exports a **count_list** data type and the following functions:

```
int Is_Empty_List(
        count_list list    /* in: list checked */
        )
void Create_List(
        count_list *list   /* out: list created */
        )
void Append_Element(
        count_list *list,  /* in/out: list changed */
        char *name,        /* in: name field */
        long CSL,          /* in: first count */
        long NCSL          /* in: second count */
        )
void Delete_Element(
        count_list *list,  /* in/out: list changed */
        char *name,        /* out: name field */
        long *CSL,         /* out: first count */
        long *NCSL         /* out: second count */
        )
```

  The function **Is_Empty_List** returns **TRUE** if its argument is the empty count list, **FALSE** otherwise. **Create_List** makes a new list. **Append_Element** adds a list element with the indicated values in its fields to the tail of the list, and **Delete_Element** removes an element from the head of the list, placing the values of its fields in the other parameters. These operations impose a queue discipline on count lists.

- *Error handling*. Memory allocation failures are detected and handled by calling the error routine.
- *Internal structure*. The count list data type is simple; a linked list implementation of the data type does not need elaboration.

A.3.5 Uses Relationships

Table A.8 indicates the uses relationships among **ccount** modules:

Table A.8: Uses Relationships among ccount Modules

Module	Uses
ccount	classify, counter, error, list, params, report
params	error
counter	classify, list
report	list, error
classify	error
list	error
error	

A.3.6 Rationale

The **ccount** problem is simple enough that there are few decisions to be made in the implementation, and certainly no difficult decisions. The decisions that were made are summarized subsequently.

- The tokenizer in the **classify** module was hand written rather than using **lex**, and the parsing was done ad hoc rather than using **yacc**, because the overhead of using these tools for such simple problems would have overwhelmed the benefits. Also, we wanted a greater volume of readable code to serve as an example.
- The **classify** module was originally part of the **counter** module. We decide to break it out (and change our design accordingly) to make the **counter** module smaller and simpler.
- We used linked lists rather than arrays to implement count list because in principle there is no way to know how long a count list might be; hence linked list seem more appropriate than arrays. We could have used a circular list for better efficiency, but noncircular lists are simpler, and the program is fast enough. Had it not been fast enough, and analysis indicated count list processing to be a bottleneck, we might have made this change.

A.4 CCOUNT PROJECT CODING STANDARDS

This document lists the guidelines to be used during the coding phase of the **ccount** development effort.

A.4.1 Naming Conventions

- Use of multiword identifiers is encouraged; portions of multiword identifiers should be separated by underscores to enhance readability For example, **max_element**, **current_file**, and so on.

- Use names that describe the roles of variables, functions, types, and constants. For example, use **char_ptr** rather than **p**.
- Use only lowercase characters in variable and type names.
- Use only uppercase characters in macro and enumeration constant names.
- Capitalize initial word parts of function names. For example, **Find_Max_Element**.
- Use the prefix **is_** for boolean variables and functions. Use the suffixes **_type** for type names, and **_ptr** for pointer variables and functions. For example, **is_found** is a boolean variables, **node_type** is a type name, and **node_ptr** is a pointer variable.

These naming conventions allow program readers to recognize many program objects at a glance. For example, **document_type** is a type name; **Is_Empty** is the name of a function returning a boolean value; and **MEMORY_ERROR** is a constant or a macro name.

A.4.2 Types

- Avoid the **float** and **unsigned** types. Use **double** and the signed types instead.
- Use the **char** type only for character data.
- Make type definitions for structure and enumeration types. Complex type definitions should always be factored.

A.4.3 Control Structures

- Avoid the **goto** and **continue** statements.
- Break out of loops early (with the **break** statement) only when there is no reasonable alternative.
- Avoid early function returns.
- Use comments to mark null loop bodies, missing loop parameters, and missing **switch** break statements.

A.4.4 Expressions

- Use parentheses liberally.
- Avoid expressions with side-effects.
- Simplify complex boolean expressions by factoring, and by using DeMorgan's Laws to drive negations inward.
- Use **<=** and **<** instead of **>=** and **>**.
- Put constants on the left in comparisons.
- Make loop termination expressions as weak as possible.

A.4.5 Formatting

- Use standard indentation conventions for block structured languages. Regarding braces, place them alone on lines indented to the same column as the statement(s) they delimit (the Pascal model).

- Place at most one variable declaration, type definition, or statement on a single line of code. Use the rest of the line for comments.

- Use vertical white space to separate code into segments that do parts of a whole task carried out in a block.

- Use horizontal white space to reflect precedence in expressions.

A.4.6 Use of Preprocessor

- Do not use the preprocessor to disguise the C language.

- Fully parenthesize macro definitions.

- Avoid parameterized macros in favor of functions.

A.4.7 Comments

- Use the module and function header comment templates listed subsequently in every module and function definition.

- State program plans in function header comments and reiterate the plan in function bodies.

- If necessary, supplement role information captured in an object's name by a comment at the object's definition or declaration.

- Explain an object's purpose at its point of definition or declaration. Note whether parameters are in, out, or in-out.

- Explain non-role-based operations when they occur.

- Document unexpected side-effects in code segment comments (like header comments), at the point of declaration of the affected object and at the points where the side-effect occurs.

- List calling functions in function header comments.

A.4.8 Error Checking

- Write functions likely to generate errors, particularly those that rely on memory allocation or input-output, so that they either handle errors themselves, or they return an error code to propagate the error to a function that can handle it.

- Check the return codes of functions that return error codes, and handle or propagate any errors indicated by return codes.

A.4.9 Modules and Access to Program Objects

- A file with a ".c" extension is called a *compile module*. Form and name compile modules in an effort to reflect program structure, with emphasis on principles of cohesion, coupling, and information hiding.
- Associate header files with individual compile modules.
- Make the scope of declarations as local as possible.
- Declare functions and nonlocal variables not referenced outside the compile modules in which they are defined `static`.
- Declare functions and nonlocal variables referenced outside the compile modules in which they are defined `extern` in all nondefining declarations.
- Declare functions and nonlocal variables referenced outside the compile modules in which they are defined neither `extern` nor `static` in their unique defining declaration.

A.4.10 Target Metric Values

- Aim for function comment-to-code ratios of at least 0.8.
- Try to write functions with no more than 60 NCSL.
- Try to write compile modules with no more than 500 NCSL.
- Do not exceed a block nesting level of 7.

A.4.11 Code Checks and Inspections

Run all code through `lint`. All errors and warnings found by `lint` must either be fixed or explained.

Inspect each module; if this is not feasible, inspect modules in order from those most to least likely to contain errors, based on the difficulty of their design.

A.4.12 Module Header Comment Template

```
/***************************    module name    *********************************

     Purpose: One or two declarative sentences describing the contents of
              the module, with emphasis on explaining the modularization
              principle(s) governing inclusion of code in this module.

     Provenance:  A record of the update history of the module.

     Notes:  A discussion of the program goal(s) realized by the code in
             this module, and its relation to other modules.  Also included
             are remarks regarding data, module, or code dependencies,
             special features, nonportable features, and so forth.
***/
```

A.4.13 Function Header Comment Template

```
/*FN********************************************************************

               function_name( parameter_list )

    Returns:    data_type -- purpose of the return value.

    Purpose:    A sentence stating the purpose of the function.

    Called by: local_function1, local_function2, ...
               function1, function2, ... in module1.
               function1, function2, ... in module2.
               ...

    Plan:       Part 1:  Goal of part 1 (line_number)
                Part 2:  Goal of part 1 (line_number)
                ...

    Notes:      Notification of side-effects, references to publications,
                specifications, and so on, discussion of any other
                noteworthy features.
***/
```

Note that this function header template incorporates a **ccount** function delimiter string in its first line, namely "**/*FN**." Including the **ccount** function delimiter string in the header template is an easy way to guarantee correct and consistent use of the function delimiter string.

A.5 CCOUNT REGRESSION TEST SCRIPT AND TEST CASES

The following is a regression test script for **ccount**. The test scripts vary only in the test cases used, and in the name of the test output files. Consequently this example can serve as a model for other test scripts.

```
# This shell script runs a regression test on the program ccount

echo  This script tests ccount
echo  comparing output to the expected result in rtst1.output.
echo ""

# run ccount with the test input and capture stderr and stdout

ccount ccount.c > temp.output 2>&1

# test for differences in the output file and the correct answer file
```

```
diff temp.output rtst1.output > diffs.1

# if a difference was found diff will exit with status 1
# this value will be in the shell variable '?'

if test "$?" = 1
then
   echo  An error has been found in ccount.  Following are the
   echo  differences between the actual and expected output.
   cat diffs.1
else
   echo no error found in ccount for this test
   rm diffs.1
   rm temp.output
fi


#run the cumulative nvcc statistics
nvcs -c
```

Regression testing was done by running the family of scripts. A master shell script could be used to automate execution of a large family of test scripts.

The following list summarizes the **ccount** test cases. An initial list was generated from the requirements. This list was increased with other test cases to bring branch coverage above 90 percent. The annotations suggest the input conditions for the test.

1. **ccount ccount.c**	(Correct file, no options).
2. **ccount ccount.c -- ccount.c**	(File before double dash).
3. **ccount -vd ccount.c**	(Illegal and legal options).
4. **ccount -d'/*FN' ccount.c**	(Single quoted string).
5. **ccount noread.c**	(Unreadable file).
6. **ccount -v ccount.c**	(Illegal option).
7. **ccount bogus.c**	(Nonexistent C file).
8. **ccount ccount.o**	(An object file).
9. **ccount -t -d"FB" hello.c**	(Both options, no space).
10. **ccount -t -d "FB" ccount.c**	(Both options, space).
11. **ccount -td"FB" ccount.c**	(Both options, compressed).
12. **ccount -d"FB" < hello.c**	(One option, no space).
13. **ccount hello.c**	(Correct file, no options).
14. **ccount -d"x ... x" < hello.c**	(Oversize delimiter with 65 x's).
15. **ccount - hello.c**	(Missing option).
16. **ccount "" hello.c**	(Empty file name).
17. **ccount -? hello.c**	(Nonalphanumeric option).

18. `ccount -d <hello.c`   (Missing delimiter).
19. `ccount ccount`   (Lexically bad file).

A.6 CCOUNT MANUAL PAGE

A.6.1 Name

ccount—count commentary and noncommentary C source lines

A.6.2 Synopsis

`ccount [ -t ] [ -d delimiter ] [ file ... ]`

A.6.3 Description

A *commentary source line* (CSL) is any source file line containing at least one nonwhite space character inside a comment. A *noncommentary source line* (NCSL) is any source file line containing at least one nonwhite space character outside a comment. The comment-to-code ratio is the ratio of CSL to NCSL. **ccount** reports CSL, NCSL, and comment-to-code ratios for C source files on stdout. Line counts are reported for each function, for lines external to functions, and for the source file as a whole.

    ccount only provides counts for each function when given a function start delimiter string that serves to mark the place where counting for a function should begin. This string must occur as a prefix of a source file line. The source file delimiter string can be placed in a shell variable called **FDELIM**, or it may be specified on the command line.

    C source code input files can be named on the command line or piped in through **stdin**, but not both.

Command line options are:

-t   Produce a tabbed report suitable for piping to other programs. Readable reports for human consumption are produced as the default.

-d delimiter Use delimiter as the delimiter string, possibly over-riding a specification in the environment variable **FDELIM**.

Reports contain a header and a body. The header contains the filename in tabbed format, and the filename, the date, and column headers in nontabbed format. When input comes from **stdin** and the output is in tabbed format, the header is empty. **ccount** report bodies contain four fields: the function name, CSL for the function, NCSL for the function, and the ratio of CSL to NCSL, expressed as a decimal. Fields are separated by a single tab in tabbed format and by spaces in nontabbed format.

ccount assumes that input files are syntactically correct C source files; behavior for incorrect source files is not defined, though usually it is reasonable.

A.6.4 Bugs

The parser may fail if the preprocessor is used to hide source structure information (like braces) or if complex parenthesized function declarators are used.

REFERENCES

1. Thomas, R., L. Rogers, and J. Yates, *Advanced Programmer's Guide to UNIX System V.* New York: McGraw-Hill, 1986.

B

ccount Source Code

This appendix contains source code for our example software metrics program **ccount** including the following:

- Three **ccount** prototypes written in UNIX shell and **awk**.
- The **ccount** Makefile.
- The C source code for **ccount**.

The code is taken directly from a listing of the program on a computer where it was compiled and tested.

```
#
#     ccount.awk
#
#   This awk script counts the commentary source lines in a C source file,
#   and approximates a count of the non-commentary source lines.  It counts
#   lines per function, lines external to any function, and total lines for
#   the file.
#
#   These counts are used in a report of CSL, NCSL, and the ratio of CSL
#   to NCSL.  The report is presented in tabbed format if the variable F
#   is externally set to "TABBED", and non-tabbed format if F is set to
#   anything else.
#
```

```
BEGIN                {
                     DELIM = "Z";                              # marks start of function
                     in_comment = 0;                           # non-zero inside comment
                     in_func = 0;                              # non-zero inside function
                     t_ncsl = 0; t_csl = 0;                    # total counters
                     e_ncsl = 0; e_csl = 0;                    # external counters
                     f_ncsl = 0; f_csl = 0;                    # per-function counters
                     f_name = ""                               # searched for when empty
                     }

                        # set the output format string
                     {
                     if ( F == "TABBED" )
                        FORMAT = "%s %d        %d        %4.2f\n"
                     else
                        FORMAT = "%20s %6d %6d %8.2f\n"
                     }

                        # skip blank lines
/^[ \t]*$/           { next }

                        # reset function counters at delimiter
                     {
                     if ( $0 == DELIM )
                        {
                        t_ncsl += 1;
                        f_ncsl = 1;
                        f_csl = 0;
                        in_func = 1;
                        braces = 0;
                        next
                        }
                     }

                        # classify the current line
                        # starting classification of the current line
                     {
                     if ( in_comment )
                        {
                        is_csl = 1;
                        is_ncsl = 0;
                        }
                     else
                        {
                        is_csl = 0;
                        is_ncsl = 1;
                        }
                     }

                        # handle a comment opening line
/\/\*/               {
                     is_csl = 1;

                     if ( $1 ~ /\/\*/ )
                        is_ncsl = 0;
                     else
                        is_ncsl = 1;
                     in_comment = 1;
                     }

                        # handle a comment closing line
```

```
/\*\//               {
                     is_csl = 1;
                     in_comment = 0;
                     }

                        # count the current line
                     {
                     if ( is_csl )
                        {
                        t_csl += 1;
                        if ( in_func ) f_csl += 1; else e_csl += 1;
                        }

                     if ( is_ncsl )
                        {
                        t_ncsl += 1;
                        if ( in_func ) f_ncsl += 1; else e_ncsl += 1;
                        }
                     }

                        # pick off the function name if a function in process
                     {
                     if ( in_func )
                        {
                        if ( f_name == "" )
                           for ( i = 1; i <= NF; i++ )
                              if ( $i ~ /.*\(/ )
                                 {
                                 f_name = $i;
                                 while ( f_name ~ /.*\(/ )
                                    f_name = substr(f_name,1,(length(f_name)-1));
                                 }

                           # keep track of the curly bracket count
                        if ( $0 ~ /{/ ) braces += 1;
                        if ( $0 ~ /}/ ) braces -= 1;
                        }
                     }

                        # dump totals at the end of a function
                     {
                     if ( in_func && ($0 ~ /}/) && (braces == 0) )
                        {
                        f_name = substr( f_name, 1, 20 );
                        printf( FORMAT, f_name, f_csl, f_ncsl, f_csl/f_ncsl );
                        f_name = "";
                        in_func = 0;
                        }
                     }

                        # print totals
END                  {
                     printf( FORMAT, "external", e_csl, e_ncsl, e_csl/e_ncsl );
                     printf( FORMAT, "total",    t_csl, t_ncsl, t_csl/t_ncsl );
                     }
```

```
#
#        Makefile for ccount source metrics program
#
```

```
OBJECTS = ccount.o params.o counter.o classify.o report.o list.o error.o
SOURCES = ccount.c params.c counter.c classify.c report.c list.c error.c
HEADERS = ccount.h params.h counter.h classify.h report.h list.h error.h
CFLAGS  =

ccount:          $(OBJECTS)
        $(CC) $(CFLAGS) $(OBJECTS) -o ccount

ccount.o:       ccount.h params.h counter.h report.h list.h

params.o:       ccount.h params.h error.h

counter.o:      ccount.h counter.h list.h error.h

classify.o:     ccount.h classify.h error.h

report.o:       ccount.h report.h list.h

list.o:         ccount.h list.h error.h

error.o:        ccount.h error.h

#
#       Create a cpio output file for distributing ccount
#       Read it back with:
#           cat ccount.cpio | cpio -icvdum
#

ccount.cpio:    $(SOURCES) $(HEADERS) Makefile ccount.man
        ls $(SOURCES) $(HEADERS) Makefile ccount.man | cpio -oc > ccount.cpio
```

```
/******************************* ccount.h ********************************

    Purpose:    To insure consistent usage of program-wide definitions
                for standard identifiers.

    Provenance: Written and tested by C. Fox, February 18, 1989.

    Notes:      None.
**/

/****************** Environment Dependent Definitions ********************/

#define SYSTEM_V                      /* alternatives: SUN_OS, DOS_MSC */

/*********************** Public Definitions *************************/

#define SUCCEED                 0
#define FAIL                    1

#define FALSE                   0
#define TRUE                    1

#define EOS                     '\0'

            /* typical value for maximum source code line size */
#define MAX_LINE                256

            /* reasonable value for a maximum identifier size */
#define MAX_IDENT               64
```

```
/*****************************    ccount.c    *********************************

    Purpose:    Program main function.

    Provenance: Finished and tested by C. Fox, February 18, 1989.

    Notes:      This program is composed of the following modules:

                    ccount.c   - main program module
                    params.c   - check cmnd line and env for program params
                    counter.c  - count the CSL and NCSL in a file
                    classify.c - classify lines to see how to count them
                    report.c   - make a report of counts to stdout
                    error.c    - deliver error messages on stderr
                    list.c     - count list data type implementation

                Each module has a header file declaring the public
                functions of the module, any public data types the
                module may have, and defining public constants.

                The program's strategy is simple: after obtaining program
                parameters from the command line and the function delimiter
                environment variable, each source file is opened, its lines
                counted, the file is closed, and a report is generated.
                The line counting mechanism is also straightforward: a line
                is read from the C source file, classified as CSL, NCSL,
                both, or neither, and apportioned to a function or external,
                and the appropriate counters are incremented.  These counters
                are duly appended to a list of counts on a per-function
                basis, and external and total counts are added in at the
                end of file.

                The only algorithms at all difficult are those for parsing,
                which are rather ad hoc but apparently correct.

                The only somewhat non-portable feature of the program is its
                use of specific names for error codes generated when a file
                open operation fails.  The program requirements say that
                error messages must distinguish between open failures due
                to non-existent files, and those due to unreadable files.
                This requires that the exact cause of the error be known,
                which in turn requires that the error code placed in the
                global variable errno be examined and classified. These
                error codes are fairly standard, but there are minor
                differences between implementations.
**/

#include <stdio.h>

#ifdef __STDC__
#    include <stdlib.h>
#endif

#include "ccount.h"          /* program-wide definitions */
#include "list.h"            /* count list data type public declarations */
#include "params.h"          /* Get_Params declaration */
#include "counter.h"         /* Count_Lines declaration */
#include "report.h"          /* Report_Metrics declaration */

/*********************    Declared Functions    ***************************/

/* extern void main( int argc, char *argv[] ); */

/*********************    Public Procedures    ****************************/
```

```
/*FN*********************************************************************

          main( argc, argv )

     Returns: void

     Purpose: Program main function.

     Plan:    Grab and check program parameters with Get_Params, then
              loop through the files counting lines and reporting the
              results.

     Notes:   Count_Lines creates a count list that Report_Metrics destroys.
              Hence the count list is an out parameter for Count_Lines and
              an in/out parameter for Report_Metrics.
**/

void
main( argc, argv )
   int argc;               /* in: how many command line arguments */
   char *argv[];           /* in: the command line arguments */
   {
   int is_tabbed;          /* TRUE if tabbed output requested, FALSE otherwise */
   char *delimiter,        /* string used to mark function start points */
        **file;            /* array of files; last element is NULL */
   count_list counts;      /* list of line count data */

   (void)Get_Parameters( argc, argv, &is_tabbed, &delimiter, &file);
   do
      {
      Count_Lines( *file, delimiter, &counts );
      Report_Metrics( *file, is_tabbed, &counts );
      if ( NULL != *file ) file++;
      }
   while ( NULL != *file );

   } /* main */
```

```
/****************************    params.h    ****************************

     Purpose:    Header for program parameter fetching module.

     Provenance: Written and tested by C. Fox, February 18, 1989.

     Notes:      None.
**/

/************************    Public Routines    *************************/

#ifdef __STDC__

extern int Get_Parameters( int argc, char *argv[], int *is_tabbed,
                           char **delimiter, char ***files );

#else

extern int Get_Parameters();        /* fetch parameters from cmd line, env */

#endif
```

```
/******************************     params.c     ******************************/

     Purpose:     Obtain program parameters from the command line and
                  the environment.

     Provenance: Written and unit tested by C. Fox, February 18, 1989.

     Notes:       The code comprising Clean_Command_Line and its subsidiary
                  routines is modified from "Advanced Programmer's Guide to
                  UNIX System V" by Rebecca Thomas, Lawrence Rogers, and
                  Jean Yates, Osborne McGraw-Hill, 1986, 135-138.  Although
                  this routine is a bit long, it was not altered significantly
                  so as to obviate the need for extensive testing.
**/

#include <stdio.h>
#include <ctype.h>
#include <malloc.h>

#ifdef __STDC__
#    include <stdlib.h>
#endif

#include "ccount.h"              /* program-wide definitions */
#include "params.h"              /* header for this module */
#include "error.h"               /* error functions and messages */

/*********************     Declared Functions     *****************************/

#ifdef __STDC__

static int Check_Options( char *options, char *optionargs );
static int Clean_Command_Line( char *options, char *optionargs,
                               int *argc, char **argv[] );

#else

static int Check_Options();          /* make sure option letters are ok */
static int Clean_Command_Line();     /* check, rearrange command line args */

#endif

/****************     Private Defines and Data Structures     ******************/

#define DELIM_VAR               "FDELIM"  /* delimiter environment variable */
#define DASH                    '-'       /* standard for identifying options */
#define END_OPTIONS             "--"      /* standard for ending option list */

/***********************     Private Routines     *****************************/

/*FN********************************************************************************

          Check_Options( options, optionargs )

     Returns: int -- FAIL(1) on error, SUCCEED(0) otherwise.

     Purpose: Check that all options to be recognized are letters,
              and that all options with arguments are marked as
              options.  This is an internal consistency check.

     Plan:    Part 1: Make sure the options are all characters
              Part 2: Make sure the optionargs are options
              Part 3: Return an indication of success
```

```
Notes:   This function goes with Clean_Command_Line--see


              notes for that function.
**/

static int
Check_Options( options, optionargs )
    char *options,       /* in: identifies the valid option letters */
         *optionargs;    /* in: identifies the options that take arguments */
    {
    char *ch_ptr;        /* for scanning through the option strings */

            /* Part 1: Make sure the options are all characters */
    for ( ch_ptr = options; *ch_ptr; ch_ptr++ )
       if ( !isalpha(*ch_ptr) ) return( Error(BAD_OPTION,NULL) );

            /* Part 2: Make sure the optionargs are options */
    for ( ch_ptr = optionargs; *ch_ptr; ch_ptr++ )
       if ( NULL == strchr(options, *ch_ptr) ) return( Error(BAD_OPTION,NULL) );

            /* Part 3: Return an indication of success */
    return(SUCCEED);

    } /* Check_Options */

/*FN*************************************************************************

         Clean_Command_Line( options, optionargs, argc, argv )

    Returns: int -- FAIL(1) on error, SUCCEED(0) otherwise.

    Purpose: This routine checks the command line and rearranges it
             into a standard form.

    Plan:    Part 1: Make sure that the options requested are ok
             Part 2: Initialize counters and accumulators
             Part 3: Collect a list of options, arguments, and files
             Part 4: Skip past the option ending double dash
             Part 5: Add the option ending double dash
             Part 6: Add file names from file list and end of argv
             Part 7: Assign the new argv and argc for return
             Part 8: Free any space used for file names
             Part 9: Return an indication of success

    Notes:   This code is modified from "Advanced Programmer's
             Guide to UNIX System V" by Rebecca Thomas, Lawrence
             Rogers, and Jean Yates, Osborne McGraw-Hill, 1986,
             135-138.  The overall strategy and algorithms are
             the same, but comments have been added, names changed,
             and a few other things done to improve readability.

             This routine checks the following:
                 - all allowable options must be alphabetic
                 - options with arguments must be valid options
                 - actual options must be valid options
                 - options with arguments must actually have arguments

             This routine alters argv and argc so that:
                 - argv is rearranged so that all options appear before all
                   file names
                 - options are separated from file names by two dashes
                 - strings of option letters are broken apart into separate
                   entries in argv
```

```
                    - arguments to options always follow options in argv
                    - the terminating file list ends with a NULL pointer

               This routine differs from the original in that arguments can
               immediately follow option letters without intervening white
               space.
**/

static int
Clean_Command_Line( options, optionargs, argc, argv )
     char *options,        /* in: identifies the valid option letters */
          *optionargs,     /* in: identifies the options that take arguments */
          **argv[];        /* in/out: the option strings may be changed */
     int *argc;            /* in/out: the number of options may be changed */
     {
     char **new_argv,      /* this will replace the argv passed in */
          **files,         /* for accumulating a list of files form argv */
          *ch_ptr;         /* for looping through a string of options */
     int new_argc,         /* this will replace the argc passed in */
         num_files,        /* for keeping track of the files accumulated */
         arg_index,        /* for looping through the options in argv */
         file_index;       /* for looping through file names */

             /* Part 1: Make sure that the options requested are ok */
     if ( FAIL == Check_Options(options, optionargs) ) return(FAIL);

             /* Part 2: Initialize counters and accumulators */
     num_files = 0;
     files     = NULL;
     new_argc  = 0;
     new_argv  = (char**)malloc( sizeof(char*) );
     if ( NULL == new_argv ) return( Error(MALLOC_FAILURE,NULL) );

             /* Part 3: Collect a list of options, arguments, and files */
     new_argv[new_argc++] = (*argv)[0];    /* first element is the command name */

     for ( arg_index = 1;
           (arg_index < *argc) && strcmp((*argv)[arg_index],END_OPTIONS);
           arg_index++ )

        if ( (DASH == (*argv)[arg_index][0]) && (NULL != (*argv)[arg_index][1]) )

               /* process an option or list of options */
            for ( ch_ptr = (*argv)[arg_index]+1; *ch_ptr; ch_ptr++ )
               {
               /* add the option to the new argv array */
               if ( NULL == strchr(options, *ch_ptr) )
                  return( Error(BAD_OPTION,NULL) );

               new_argv = (char**)realloc( (char*)new_argv,
                                          (unsigned)(new_argc+1)*sizeof(char*) );
               if ( NULL == new_argv ) return( Error(MALLOC_FAILURE,NULL) );

               new_argv[new_argc] = (char*)malloc( 3 * sizeof(char) );
               if ( NULL == new_argv[new_argc] )
                  return( Error(MALLOC_FAILURE,NULL) );

               new_argv[new_argc][0] = DASH;
               new_argv[new_argc][1] = *ch_ptr;
               new_argv[new_argc][2] = EOS;
               new_argc++;

                  /* grab the argument for an option with an argument */
               if ( NULL != strchr(optionargs, *ch_ptr) )
```

```
                {
                new_argv = (char**)realloc((char*)new_argv,
                                  (unsigned)(new_argc+1)*sizeof(char*) );
                if ( NULL == new_argv ) return( Error(MALLOC_FAILURE,NULL) );

                if ( EOS == *(ch_ptr+1) )
                    {
                    arg_index++;
                    if ( arg_index < *argc )
                        new_argv[new_argc++] = (*argv)[arg_index];
                    else
                        return( Error(MISSING_DELIMITER,NULL) );
                    }
                else
                    {
                    ch_ptr++;
                    new_argv[new_argc++] = ch_ptr;
                    ch_ptr += strlen(ch_ptr)-1;
                    }
                }
            }
    else
        /* process a file name */
        {
        if ( 0 == num_files )
            files = (char**)malloc( sizeof(char*) );
        else
            files = (char**)realloc( (char*)files,
                              (unsigned)((num_files+1)*sizeof(char*)) );
        if ( NULL == files ) return( Error(MALLOC_FAILURE,NULL) );

        files[num_files++] = (*argv)[arg_index];
        }

            /* Part 4: Skip past the option ending double dash */
if ( arg_index < *argc ) arg_index++;

            /* Part 5: Add the option ending double dash */
new_argv = (char**)realloc( (char*)new_argv,
                    (unsigned)(sizeof(char*)
                        *(new_argc+num_files+(*argc-arg_index+2))) );
if ( NULL == new_argv ) return( Error(MALLOC_FAILURE,NULL) );

new_argv[new_argc++] = END_OPTIONS;

            /* Part 6: Add file names from file list and end of argv */
for ( file_index = 0; file_index < num_files; file_index++ )
    new_argv[new_argc++] = files[file_index];

while ( arg_index < *argc )
    new_argv[new_argc++] = (*argv)[arg_index++];

new_argv[new_argc] = NULL;

            /* Part 7: Assign the new argv and argc for return */
*argc = new_argc;
*argv = new_argv;

            /* Part 8: Free any space used for file names */
if ( files ) free( (char*)files );

            /* Part 9: Return an indication of success */
return(SUCCEED);
```

```
    } /* Clean_Command_Line */

/*************************    Public Routines    *****************************/

/*FN***********************************************************************

            Get_Parameters( argc, argv, is_tabbed, delimiter, files )

    Returns: int -- FAIL(1) on error, SUCCEED(0) otherwise
        Purpose: Obtain program parameters from the command line and
                 the environment.

        Plan:     Part 1: Check and clean up the command line
                  Part 2: Process the options from the command line
                  Part 3: Grab the file list from the command line
                  Part 4: If no delimiter string, check the environment
                  Part 5: Trash the delimiter if it is the null string
                  Part 6: Return an indication of success

        Notes:    The interface to this routine (and hence this module) is as
                  follows:
                    - argc and argv are passed in from the command line by
                      way of main;  the original values of these variables
                      are not altered by this routine, though the local
                      versions are;
                    - is_tabbed is set to TRUE if -t occurs as an option on the
                      command line, otherwise it is set to FALSE;
                    - delimiter is set to the value of the user-specified
                      function start delimiter string, if any; if a delimiter
                      is specified in the command line using the -d option,
                      then that string is used;  if no delimiter is specified
                      in the command line, then the string stored in DELIM_VAR
                      (if any) is used;  if no string is specified, or the
                      empty string is specified, then delimiter is set to NULL.
                    - files is set to contain an array of strings, with the
                      last element of the array being a NULL pointer;  these
                      strings are the input file names from the command line.
                    - if an error is encountered, processing is aborted and the
                      function returns FAIL(1),  otherwise it returns
                      SUCCEED(0).

                  The processing in this module allocates some memory that is
                  not freed;  however, it is at most a few hundred bytes, and
                  probably not worth recovering.
    **/

    int
    Get_Parameters( argc, argv, is_tabbed, delimiter, files )
        int argc;           /* in: argument count from the command line */
        char *argv[];       /* in: arguments from the command line */
        int *is_tabbed;     /* out: TRUE iff report to be in tabbed mode */
        char **delimiter;   /* out: function delimiter string */
        char ***files;      /* out: NULL terminated list of files to process */
        {
        char *getenv();     /* returns string value of an environment variable */
        register int i;     /* for looping through command line options */

                    /* Part 1: Check and clean up the command line */
        if ( FAIL == Clean_Command_Line("td", "d", &argc, &argv) ) return( FAIL );

                    /* Part 2: Process the options from the command line */
        *is_tabbed = FALSE;              /* non-tabbed mode is the default */
        *delimiter = NULL;               /* assume no delimiter to start */
```

```
    i = 1;                              /* skip the command name argument */

while ( (NULL != argv[i]) && (DASH == argv[i][0]) )
   {
   switch ( argv[i][1] )
      {
      case 't' : *is_tabbed = TRUE; break;
      case 'd' : i++; *delimiter = argv[i]; break;
      case '-' : /* no action */ break;
      default  : return( Error(BAD_OPTION,NULL) ); break;
      }

      i++;
      }

          /* Part 3: Grab the file list from the command line */
   *files = &(argv[i]);

          /* Part 4: If no delimiter string, check the environment */
   if ( NULL == *delimiter ) *delimiter = getenv( DELIM_VAR );

          /* Part 5: Trash the delimiter if it is the null string */
   if ( (NULL != *delimiter) && (0 == strlen(*delimiter)) ) *delimiter = NULL

             /* Part 6: Return an indication of success */
   return( SUCCEED );

   } /* Get_Parameters */
```

```
/****************************** counter.h ******************************

   Purpose:    Header for line parsing and counting module.

   Provenance: Written and tested by C. Fox, February 18, 1989.

   Notes:      The data collected by Count_Lines is returned to
               the client in a lined list of structures called a
               count_list.  This data structure must therefore be
               shared between this module and its clients.
**/

/************************* Public Routines ************************/

#ifdef __STDC__

extern void Count_Lines(char *file, char *delimiter, count_list *line_counts);

#else

extern void Count_Lines();      /* count lines in file, result in count list */

#endif
```

```
/****************************** counter.c ******************************

   Purpose:    Count CSL and NCSL per function in a C source file.

   Provenance: Written and tested by C. Fox, February 18, 1989.
```

```
     Notes:        None.
**/

#include <stdio.h>
#include <malloc.h>
#include <string.h>

#ifdef __STDC__
#   include <stdlib.h>
#endif

#include "ccount.h"                 /* program-wide definitions */
#include "error.h"                  /* error function and types */
#include "list.h"                   /* count list manipulation routines */
#include "counter.h"                /* header for this module */
#include "classify.h"               /* classifier def's and declarations */

/*************************   Declared Routines   **************************/

/*************************   Public Routines    **************************/

/*FN*********************************************************************

            Count_Lines( file, delimiter, counts )

     Returns: void

     Purpose: Generate the metrics needed for the program report.

     Plan:      Part 1: Create a new count list.
                Part 2: Open the input source file
                Part 3: Process the file or report an error
                Part 4: Main Loop: Count each line of the file
                Part 5: Append list elements for external and total
                Part 6: Close the source input file

     Notes:     This routine calls Classify_Line to take care of
                classifying lines as CSL, NCSL, both, or neither, and to
                determine whether the line is external, and if not, what
                the function name is.  It relies on Create_List and
                Append_Element to manage the count list it builds.
                File input and counter management are the province of
                this routine.
**/

void
Count_Lines( file, delimiter, counts )
    char *file;                 /* in: file to process */
    char *delimiter;            /* in: function start delimiter string */
    count_list *counts;         /* out: linked list of line counts for file */
    {
    long total_CSL   = 0,       /* for output as the total CSL count */
         total_NCSL  = 0,       /* for output as the total NCSL count */
         extern_CSL  = 0,       /* for output as the external CSL count */
         extern_NCSL = 0,       /* for output as the external NCSL count */
         func_CSL    = 0,       /* for output as the CSL for each function */
         func_NCSL   = 0;       /* for output as the NCSL for each function */
    char *func_name;            /* recorded with per-function counts */
    int is_CSL,                 /* TRUE iff current line is a CSL */
        is_NCSL,                /* TRUE iff current line is a NCSL */
        is_extern,              /* TRUE iff current line outside function def */
        is_func_end;            /* TRUE iff current line ends a function */
    FILE *input;                /* stream pointer for the input source file */
```

```
char line[MAX_LINE+1];    /* buffer for the current source file line */

                /* Part 1: Create a new count list */
Create_List( counts );

                /* Part 2: Open the input source file */
input = (NULL == file) ? stdin : fopen(file, "r");

            /* Part 3: Process the file or report an error */
if ( NULL == input )
    (void)Error( ACCESS_ERROR, file );
else
    {
        /* Part 4: Main Loop: Count each line of the file */
    while ( (NULL != fgets(line,MAX_LINE+1,input)) && !feof(input) )
        {
        Classify_Line( line, delimiter, &is_CSL, &is_NCSL,
                       &is_extern, &is_func_end, &func_name );

            /* increment CSL counters as appropriate */
        if ( is_CSL )
            {
            if ( is_extern )
                extern_CSL++;
            else
                func_CSL++;
            total_CSL++;
            }

            /* increment CSL counters as appropriate */
        if ( is_NCSL )
            {
            if ( is_extern )
                extern_NCSL++;
            else
                func_NCSL++;
            total_NCSL++;
            }

            /* make a list entry at a function's end;  reset counters */
        if ( is_func_end )
            {
            Append_Element( counts, func_name, func_CSL, func_NCSL );
            func_CSL = 0;
            func_NCSL = 0;
            }
        }

        /* Part 5: Append list entries for external and total */
    Append_Element( counts, "external", extern_CSL, extern_NCSL );
    Append_Element( counts, "total", total_CSL, total_NCSL );

            /* Part 6: Close the source input file */
    (void)fclose( input );
    }

} /* Count_Lines */
```

```
/****************************** classify.h ******************************

    Purpose:    Header for parser module.

    Provenance: Written and tested by C. Fox, February 18, 1989.

    Notes:      None.
**/

/************************* Public Routines *****************************/

#ifdef __STDC__

extern void Classify_Line( char *line, char *delimiter,
                           int *is_CSL, int *is_NCSL,
                           int *is_extern, int *is_func_end,
                           char **func_name );

#else

extern void Classify_Line();   /* parse and classify a line of source input */

#endif




/****************************** classify.c ******************************

    Purpose:    Parse a line of C source and decide what it is.

    Provenance: Written and tested by C. Fox, February 18, 1989.

    Notes:      This module might be divided into lower level lexical
                analysis objects, and higher level parsing objects.  The
                lexical analysis objects include the character class type
                char_class, the token type token_type, and the tokenizer
                routines Start_Tokenizer and Get_Token.  All this machinery
                converts input source file lines to a stream of tokens for
                use by the various components of the parser.

                The parser objects include the main parsing routine
                Classify_Line, and the subsidiary function
                Find_Function_Name.  Find_Function_Name keeps track of the
                latest function name encountered.  Most of the parsing is
                done by Classify_Line, a line-oriented function that figures
                out whether the current line is a CSL, NCSL, or both, whether
                it is internal or external to a function, and whether the
                current line ends a function definition.  All the parsing
                routines rely on the tokens delivered by the tokenizer to
                do their jobs.

                Both the tokenizer and parser algorithms are ad hoc routines
                developed for this application.  Many are simple finite
                state machines.
**/

#include <stdio.h>
#include <malloc.h>
#include <string.h>

#ifdef __STDC__
#   include <stdlib.h>
#endif
```

```
#include "ccount.h"                      /* program-wide definitions */
#include "classify.h"                    /* header for this module */
#include "error.h"                       /* error functions and messages */

/************************** Private Data Types  **************************/

        /*********************************************************/
        /*   - From Characters to Character Classes to Tokens -  */
        /* Input characters are first categorized as to character */
        /* class.  Values of type char_class drive the finite    */
        /* state machine that recognizes and identifies tokens.  */
        /* This finite state machine returns a stream of values  */
        /* of type token_type.  The initial conversion from char */
        /* to char_class is made by indexing the input character */
        /* into an array pre-loaded with character classes.      */
        /*********************************************************/

typedef enum token_enum         /* all tokens recognized by this prgm */
        {       ID_TKN,                 /* identifier or key word   */
                BEG_CMNT_TKN,           /* comment begin delimiter  */
                END_CMNT_TKN,           /* comment end delimiter    */
                L_PAREN_TKN,            /* left parenthesis         */
                R_PAREN_TKN,            /* right parenthesis        */
                L_BRACE_TKN,            /* left brace               */
                R_BRACE_TKN,            /* right brace              */
                EOL_TKN,                /* end of line              */
                OTHER_TKN               /* anything else            */

        } token_type;

typedef enum char_class_enum    /* the recognized character classes */
        {       WHITE_CH,               /* any white space but newline */
                EOL_CH,                 /* the newline                 */
                LETTER_CH,              /* any letter, underscore      */
                DIGIT_CH,               /* any digit                   */
                STAR_CH,                /* the asterisk *              */
                SLASH_CH,               /* the forward slash /         */
                L_PAREN_CH,             /* the left parenthesis (      */
                R_PAREN_CH,             /* the right parenthesis )     */
                L_BRACE_CH,             /* the left brace or bracket { */
                R_BRACE_CH,             /* the right brace or bracket } */
                OTHER_CH                /* any other character whatever */
        } char_class;

/************************** Declared Functions  **************************/

#ifdef __STDC__

static void Start_Tokenizer( char *line, char *delimiter,
                             int *is_func_start, int *is_cpp_line );
static token_type Get_Token( void );
static void Find_Function_Name( token_type token );

#else

static void Start_Tokenizer();          /* set up line, preliminary classify */
static token_type Get_Token();          /* return the next token from input */
static void Find_Function_Name();       /* find the next function name */

#endif

/************************** Private Data Structures  **************************/
```

```
static char_class class[128] =    /* for rapid character classification */
        {       /* NUL */ EOL_CH,        /* ^A  */ OTHER_CH,
                /* ^B  */ OTHER_CH,      /* ^C  */ OTHER_CH,
                /* ^D  */ OTHER_CH,      /* ^E  */ OTHER_CH,
                /* ^F  */ OTHER_CH,      /* ^G  */ OTHER_CH,
                /* ^H  */ WHITE_CH,      /* ^I  */ WHITE_CH,
                /* ^J  */ EOL_CH,        /* ^K  */ WHITE_CH,
                /* ^L  */ WHITE_CH,      /* ^M  */ EOL_CH,
                /* ^N  */ OTHER_CH,      /* ^O  */ OTHER_CH,
                /* ^P  */ OTHER_CH,      /* ^Q  */ OTHER_CH,
                /* ^S  */ OTHER_CH,      /* ^S  */ OTHER_CH,
                /* ^T  */ OTHER_CH,      /* ^U  */ OTHER_CH,
                /* ^V  */ OTHER_CH,      /* ^W  */ OTHER_CH,
                /* ^X  */ OTHER_CH,      /* ^Y  */ OTHER_CH,
                /* ^Z  */ OTHER_CH,      /* ^[  */ OTHER_CH,
                /* ^\  */ OTHER_CH,      /* ^]  */ OTHER_CH,
                /* ^^  */ OTHER_CH,      /* ^_  */ OTHER_CH,
                /*     */ WHITE_CH,      /* !   */ OTHER_CH,
                /* "   */ OTHER_CH,      /* #   */ OTHER_CH,
                /* $   */ OTHER_CH,      /* %   */ OTHER_CH,
                /* &   */ OTHER_CH,      /* '   */ OTHER_CH,
                /* (   */ L_PAREN_CH,    /* )   */ R_PAREN_CH,
                /* *   */ STAR_CH,       /* +   */ OTHER_CH,
                /* ,   */ OTHER_CH,      /* -   */ OTHER_CH,
                /* .   */ OTHER_CH,      /* /   */ SLASH_CH,
                /* 0   */ DIGIT_CH,      /* 1   */ DIGIT_CH,
                /* 2   */ DIGIT_CH,      /* 3   */ DIGIT_CH,
                /* 4   */ DIGIT_CH,      /* 5   */ DIGIT_CH,
                /* 6   */ DIGIT_CH,      /* 7   */ DIGIT_CH,
                /* 8   */ DIGIT_CH,      /* 9   */ DIGIT_CH,
                /* :   */ OTHER_CH,      /* ;   */ OTHER_CH,
                /* <   */ OTHER_CH,      /* =   */ OTHER_CH,
                /* >   */ OTHER_CH,      /* ?   */ OTHER_CH,
                /* @   */ OTHER_CH,      /* A   */ LETTER_CH,
                /* B   */ LETTER_CH,     /* C   */ LETTER_CH,
                /* D   */ LETTER_CH,     /* E   */ LETTER_CH,
                /* F   */ LETTER_CH,     /* G   */ LETTER_CH,
                /* H   */ LETTER_CH,     /* I   */ LETTER_CH,
                /* J   */ LETTER_CH,     /* K   */ LETTER_CH,
                /* L   */ LETTER_CH,     /* M   */ LETTER_CH,
                /* N   */ LETTER_CH,     /* O   */ LETTER_CH,
                /* P   */ LETTER_CH,     /* Q   */ LETTER_CH,
                /* R   */ LETTER_CH,     /* S   */ LETTER_CH,
                /* T   */ LETTER_CH,     /* U   */ LETTER_CH,
                /* V   */ LETTER_CH,     /* W   */ LETTER_CH,
                /* X   */ LETTER_CH,     /* Y   */ LETTER_CH,
                /* Z   */ LETTER_CH,     /* [   */ OTHER_CH,
                /* \   */ OTHER_CH,      /* ]   */ OTHER_CH,
                /* ^   */ OTHER_CH,      /* _   */ LETTER_CH,
                /* `   */ OTHER_CH,      /* a   */ LETTER_CH,
                /* b   */ LETTER_CH,     /* c   */ LETTER_CH,
                /* d   */ LETTER_CH,     /* e   */ LETTER_CH,
                /* f   */ LETTER_CH,     /* g   */ LETTER_CH,
                /* h   */ LETTER_CH,     /* i   */ LETTER_CH,
                /* j   */ LETTER_CH,     /* k   */ LETTER_CH,
                /* l   */ LETTER_CH,     /* m   */ LETTER_CH,
                /* n   */ LETTER_CH,     /* o   */ LETTER_CH,
                /* p   */ LETTER_CH,     /* q   */ LETTER_CH,
                /* r   */ LETTER_CH,     /* s   */ LETTER_CH,
                /* t   */ LETTER_CH,     /* u   */ LETTER_CH,
                /* v   */ LETTER_CH,     /* w   */ LETTER_CH,
                /* x   */ LETTER_CH,     /* y   */ LETTER_CH,
                /* z   */ LETTER_CH,     /* {   */ L_BRACE_CH,
                /* |   */ LETTER_CH,     /* }   */ R_BRACE_CH,
                /* ~   */ OTHER_CH,      /* ^?  */ OTHER_CH       };
```

```
        /**********************************************************/
        /* The tokenizer consumes a buffer of characters which are */
        /* a line of input.  This buffer should be terminated by   */
        /* a newline and a null character.  The next token is      */
        /* returned every time Get_Token() is called, meaning      */
        /* that the current buffer position must be retained.      */
        /* Also, the text of identifiers must be retained until    */
        /* requested.  This implies two static variables: an       */
        /* input buffer pointer, and an identifier buffer.         */
        /**********************************************************/

static char *ch_ptr;                    /* for scanning through input buffer */
static char identifier[MAX_IDENT+1]; /* identified by the tokenizer */

        /**********************************************************/
        /* The function name finder finds and keeps track of the */
        /* current function name until it is asked for it at the */
        /* end of a function.  This implies a static buffer for  */
        /* holding the function name.                            */
        /**********************************************************/

static char function_name[MAX_IDENT+1]; /* identified by the function finder */

/*************************    Private Routines    **************************/

        /******************************************************/
        /*           --- Tokenizer Routines ---             */
        /* The tokenizer accepts a line of text and sends */
        /* back a stream of tokens.  It also collects the */
        /* text of identifiers for use when asked for it. */
        /* The tokenizer has two constituent routines:    */
        /*    - Start_Tokenizer accepts a line as grist   */
        /*      for the tokenizer mill.  It also does a    */
        /*      preliminary scan to see whether the line   */
        /*      is a function start line, and whether it   */
        /*      is a preprocessor line.                    */
        /*    - Get_Token returns the next token in the    */
        /*      line.  It returns values of token_type.    */
        /******************************************************/

/*FN*********************************************************************************

        Start_Tokenizer( line, delimiter, is_func_start, is_cpp_line )

    Returns: void

    Purpose: Set up the tokenizer, check the line

    Plan:    Part 1: Start the buffer pointer at the beginning of the line
             Part 2: Check for the function delimiter string
             Part 3: Scan past any initial white space
             Part 4: See if the line is a preprocessor line

    Notes:   None.
**/

static void
Start_Tokenizer( line, delimiter, is_func_start, is_cpp_line )
    char *line,             /* in: line to be scanned */
         *delimiter;        /* in: function start delimiter string */
    int *is_func_start,     /* out: TRUE iff line starts with delimiter */
        *is_cpp_line;       /* out: TRUE iff first non-white space char is # */
    {
```

```
        /* Part 1: Start the buffer pointer at the beginning of the line */
    ch_ptr = line;

            /* Part 2: Check for the function delimiter string */
    if ( NULL == delimiter )
        *is_func_start = FALSE;
    else
        *is_func_start = !strncmp( delimiter, line, strlen(delimiter) );

            /* Part 3: Scan past any initial white space */
    while ( WHITE_CH == class[*ch_ptr] ) ch_ptr++;

            /* Part 4: See if the line is a preprocessor line */
    *is_cpp_line = ('#' == *ch_ptr);

    } /* Start_Tokenizer */

/*FN*************************************************************************

        Get_Token()

    Returns: token_type -- the next token from the input.

    Purpose: Grab the next token.

    Plan:    Part 1: Error check: return at the end of the buffer
             Part 2: Scan past any initial white space
             Part 3: Collect the body of whatever kind of token
             Part 4: Append a terminator to the identifier buffer
             Part 5: Return the next token found in the buffer

    Notes:   This is a very simple finite state machine that identifies a
             subset of C tokens: those necessary to identify function
             headers, the ends of functions, and comments.  To do this
             task it converts input characters to their character class,
             then collects further characters as necessary to complete
             a token.  It incidentally collects the text of all identifiers
             if finds so that they may be made available when a function
             name is needed.
**/

static token_type
Get_Token()
    {
    token_type token;   /* the value eventually returned */
    char *id_ptr;       /* for collecting identifiers */

        /* Part 1: Error check: return at the end of the buffer */
    if ( EOS == *ch_ptr ) return( EOL_TKN );

            /* Part 2: Scan past any initial white space */
    while ( WHITE_CH == class[((unsigned)*ch_ptr) % 128] ) ch_ptr++;

        /* Part 3: Collect the body of whatever kind of token */
    id_ptr = identifier;
    switch ( class[*(id_ptr++) = *(ch_ptr++)] )
        {
        case LETTER_CH :
            while ((LETTER_CH == class[*ch_ptr]) || (DIGIT_CH == class[*ch_ptr]))
                *(id_ptr++) = *(ch_ptr++);
            token = ID_TKN;
            break;
```

```
        case STAR_CH :
           if ( SLASH_CH == class[*ch_ptr] )
              {
              ch_ptr++;
              token = END_CMNT_TKN;
              }
           else token = OTHER_TKN;
           break;

        case SLASH_CH :
           if ( STAR_CH == class[*ch_ptr] )
              {
              ch_ptr++;
              token = BEG_CMNT_TKN;
              }
           else token = OTHER_TKN;
           break;

        case L_PAREN_CH :
           token = L_PAREN_TKN; break;

        case R_PAREN_CH :
           token = R_PAREN_TKN; break;

        case L_BRACE_CH :
           token = L_BRACE_TKN; break;

        case R_BRACE_CH :
           token = R_BRACE_TKN; break;

        case EOL_CH :
           token = EOL_TKN; break;

        case DIGIT_CH : /* this is some other token--we don't care what */
        case OTHER_CH :
           while ((DIGIT_CH == class[*ch_ptr]) || (OTHER_CH == class[*ch_ptr]))
              ch_ptr++;
           token = OTHER_TKN;
           break;

     default : /* we should never get here--we're lost */
        (void)Error( INTERNAL_ERROR, NULL ); break;
     }

        /* Part 4: Append a terminator to the identifier buffer */
   *id_ptr = EOS;

        /* Part 5: Return the next token found in the buffer */
   return( token );

} /* Get_Token */

        /***************************************************/
        /*       --- Function Name Finding Routine ---     */
        /* - Find_Function_Name does its own parsing job   */
        /*   recognize function names.                     */
        /***************************************************/

/*FN*****************************************************************************

        Find_Function_Name( token )

   Returns: void
```

Purpose: Find function names and during parsing.

Plan: Execute a finite state machine

Notes: This routine executes a simple finite state machine to parse
          tokens in searching for function names. The machine is
          represented in the following transition diagram:

```
      state |  identifier        (        )           {       other
      --------------------------------------------------------------
        0   |      1             0        0           0         0
        1   |      1             2        0           0         0
        2   |      2             2        3           2         2
        3   |    1(A)          0(D)     0(D)        0(A)      0(D)
```

          The A means "accept" and the D "do not accept." In addition,
          the transition from state 2 to state 3 is only made if the
          count of unmatched left parentheses is 0. Finally, whenever
          a transition is made to state 1 on an identifier, the text of
          the identifier is saved. The saved text is returned when an
          accepting state is encountered.

          The idea of the finite state machine is simple: watch for
          identifiers, and save them as candidate function names. Once
          an identifier is encountered, look for an argument list
          followed by an identifier or a left curly bracket.

          Note finally that this parser relies on being called outside
          the body of a function (hat is, when the unmatched left
          brace count is 0), outside a comment, and not a preprocessor
          line.
**/

```c
static void
Find_Function_Name( token )
   token_type token;      /* in: the latest token */
   {
   static int
    state = 0,            /* current state of the DFA */
    num_parens = 0;       /* count of unbalanced left parentheses */
                          /* -- used to find the end of the argument */
                          /* -- list in a function header or call     */
static char
  candidate[MAX_IDENT+1];    /* candidate function name identifier */

               /* Execute a finite state machine */
switch ( state )
   {
   case 0 : /* watching for a candidate identifier */
      if ( ID_TKN == token )
         {
         (void)strcpy( candidate, identifier );
         num_parens = 0;
         state = 1;
         }
      break;

   case 1 : /* looking for a left parenthesis */
      if ( L_PAREN_TKN == token )
         {
         num_parens++;
         state = 2;
         }
```

```
                 else if ( ID_TKN == token )
                    (void)strcpy( candidate, identifier );
                 else
                    state = 0;
                 break;

           case 2 : /* scanning through an argument list */
                 if ( L_PAREN_TKN == token )
                    num_parens++;
                 else if ( R_PAREN_TKN == token )
                    {
                    num_parens--;
                    if ( 0 == num_parens ) state = 3;
                    }
                 break;

           case 3 : /* watching for identifiers and left braces */
                 if ( (ID_TKN == token) || (L_BRACE_TKN == token) )
                    (void)strcpy( function_name, candidate );
                 if ( ID_TKN == token )
                    {
                    (void)strcpy( candidate, identifier );
                    state = 1;
                    }
                 else
                    state = 0;
                 break;
           }

     } /* Find_Function_Name */

/*************************  Public Routines  ***************************/

/*FN*********************************************************************

           Classify_Line( line, delimiter, is_CSL, is_NCSL,
                                is_extern, is_func_end, func_name )

     Returns: void

     Purpose: Parse and classify a line of source code

     Plan:    Part 1: Send current line to the tokenizer
              Part 2: Set presumptive flag and accumulator values
              Part 4: Parse the current line ad hoc

     Notes:   This parsing routine is entirely ad hoc and somewhat complex,
              but is short, fast, and seems to work.
**/

void
Classify_Line( line, delimiter, is_CSL, is_NCSL,
                                is_extern, is_func_end, func_name )
    char *line,            /* in: source code line to be parsed */
         *delimiter;       /* in: function start delimiter string */
    int *is_CSL,           /* out: TRUE iff line counts as a CSL */
        *is_NCSL,          /* out: TRUE iff line counts as a NCSL */
        *is_extern,        /* out: TRUE iff line is outside a function def */
        *is_func_end;      /* out: TRUE iff line ends a function definition */
    char **func_name;      /* out: function name at end of definition */
    {
    token_type token;          /* succession of tokens in the line */
    int is_func_start,         /* TRUE iff current line has delimiter */
        is_cpp_line;           /* TRUE iff current line a preprocessor line */
```

```
static int
    in_function = FALSE,    /* TRUE between function start delimiter */
                            /* and the end of a function definition  */
    in_comment = FALSE,     /* TRUE between comment delimiters */
    num_braces = 0;         /* it is the end of a function definition */
                            /* when this goes to 0 on a right brace   */

        /* Part 1: Send line to tokenizer; get preliminary story */
Start_Tokenizer( line, delimiter, &is_func_start, &is_cpp_line );
if ( is_func_start ) in_function = TRUE;

                /* Part 2: Make initial classification */
*is_CSL     = FALSE;
*is_NCSL    = FALSE;
*is_extern  = !in_function;
*is_func_end = FALSE;

                /* Part 3: Parse the current line ad hoc  */
while ( EOL_TKN != (token = Get_Token()) )
    {
    if ( in_comment )
            /* ignore everything but the end of comment delimiter */
        {
        *is_CSL = TRUE;
        if ( END_CMNT_TKN == token ) in_comment = FALSE;
        }

    else if ( BEG_CMNT_TKN == token )
            /* mark the start of a comment */
        *is_CSL = in_comment = TRUE;

    else
            /* do more complex processing for a line of code */
        {
        *is_NCSL = TRUE;

        /* watch for the function name */
        if ( (0 == num_braces) && !is_cpp_line ) Find_Function_Name( token );

        /* count braces to find the end of a function */
        if ( L_BRACE_TKN == token )
            num_braces++;
        else if ( R_BRACE_TKN == token )
            {
            num_braces--;
            if ( 0 == num_braces )
                    /* bingo! -- the end of a function */
                {
                if ( in_function )
                    {
                    *func_name = function_name;
                    *is_func_end = TRUE;
                    }
                in_function = FALSE;
                }
            }
        }
    }

} /* Classify_Line */
```

```
/****************************** report.h  ******************************

     Purpose:    Header for report writing module.

     Provenance: Written and tested by C. Fox, February 18, 1989.

     Notes:      None.
**/

/************************** Public Routines  ***************************/
#ifdef __STDC__

extern void Report_Metrics( char *file, int is_tabbed, count_list *counts );

#else

extern void Report_Metrics();                /* write metrics report to stdout */

#endif
```

```
/****************************** report.c  ******************************

     Purpose:    Deliver reports about the collected metrics.

     Provenance: Written and tested by C. Fox, February 18, 1989.

     Notes:      This routine makes use of the count list passed in
                 to it from the main routine.  It destroys the count
                 list as it uses it to generate its report.
**/

#include <stdio.h>
#include <time.h>
#include <malloc.h>

#include "ccount.h"              /* program-wide definitions */
#include "list.h"                /* count list data type declarations */
#include "report.h"              /* header for this module */
#include "error.h"               /* error functions and messages */

#ifdef __STDC__
#    include <stdlib.h>
#endif

/*********************** Defined Functions  ***************************/

/*********************** Private Definitions  ***************************/

/*********************** Private Routines  ***************************/

/*********************** Public Routines  ***************************/

/*FN***********************************************************************

          Report_Metrics( file_name, is_tabbed, counts )

     Returns: void

     Purpose: Dump the metrics report to stdout.
```

```
    Plan:    Part 1: Return immediately if there is no data
             Part 2: Dump the header and set the printf format string
             Part 3: Allocate a buffer for the name to be copied into
             Part 4: Run through the list of counts and print report body
             Part 5: Free space allocated for the name

    Notes:   This function incorporates highly specific stuff about how
             the output should look, so all sorts of peculiar constants
             appear in the code.

             An empty count list signals that there should be no output.
             A NULL file_name signals that data is from stdin.

             Note that this routine destroys the count list as it
             moves through it.
**/

void
Report_Metrics( file_name, is_tabbed, counts )
    char *file_name;      /* in: current file reported on */
    int is_tabbed;        /* in: TRUE if report is to be tabbed */
    count_list *counts;   /* in/out: list of counts for file */
    {
    long time_value,      /* milliseconds since 1970 for tabbed output */
         CSL,             /* a count of CSL from a count list element */
         NCSL;            /* a count of NCSL from a count list element */
    char *name,           /* a function name from a count list element */
         *ratio_fmt,      /* printf format string when ratio exists */
         *no_ratio_fmt;   /* printf format string when no ratio exists */

            /* Part 1: Return immediately if there is no data */
    if ( Is_Empty_List(*counts) ) return;

            /* Part 2: Dump the header and set printf format strings */
    if ( is_tabbed )
        {
        if ( NULL != file_name )
            {
            (void)printf( "%s\n", file_name );
            ratio_fmt    = "%s      %ld      %ld      %.2f\n";
            no_ratio_fmt = "%s      %ld      %ld      -\n";
            }
        }
    else
        {
        time_value = time( NULL );
        if ( NULL == file_name ) file_name = "stdin";
        (void)printf( "%s       %s\n", file_name, ctime(&time_value) );
        (void)printf( "   Function         CSL   NCSL   CSL/NCSL\n" );
        (void)printf( "-------------------------------------------\n" );
        ratio_fmt    = "%20.20s %6ld %6ld %8.2f\n";
        no_ratio_fmt = "%20.20s %6ld %6ld      -\n";
        }

        /* Part 3: Allocate a buffer for the name to be copied into */
    name = malloc( MAX_IDENT );
    if ( NULL == name ) (void)Error( MALLOC_FAILURE, NULL );

      /* Part 4: Run through the list of counts and print report body */
    while ( !Is_Empty_List(*counts) )
        {
        Delete_Element( counts, name, &CSL, &NCSL );
        if ( 0 < NCSL )
```

```
        (void)printf(ratio_fmt, name, CSL, NCSL, ((double)CSL/(double)NCSL));
    else
        (void)printf( no_ratio_fmt, name, CSL, NCSL );
    }

            /* Part 5: Free space allocated for the name */
    free( name );

    } /* Report_Metrics */
```

```
/******************************  list.h  ******************************

    Purpose:     Header for count list abstract data type module.

    Provenance: Written and tested by C. Fox, February 18, 1989.

    Notes:       The count list module is an implementation of an abstract
                 data type which is a list of elements consisting of a
                 string, and two long values.  The string is intended to
                 be the function name;  the long values are the CSL and
                 NCSL counts for the function.

                 The count list data type has four operations:

                     Create_List    -- make a new empty count list
                     Is_Empty_List  -- TRUE iff a list is empty
                     Append_Element -- add count element to tail of list
                     Delete_Element -- remove counts from head of list

                 No other operations are required for this application.
**/

/************************  Public Data Type  ************************/

typedef struct count_struct *count_list; /* pointer to linked list of counts */

/************************  Public Routines  ************************/

#ifdef __STDC__

extern int Is_Empty_List( count_list list );
extern void Create_List( count_list *list );
extern void Append_Element(count_list *list, char *name, long CSL, long NCSL );
extern void Delete_Element(count_list *list, char *name, long *CSL,long *NCSL);

#else

extern int Is_Empty_List();      /* check whether a count list is empty */
extern void Create_List();       /* create a new count list */
extern void Append_Element();    /* add an element to the tail of a list */
extern void Delete_Element();    /* remove an element from the head of a list */

#endif
```

```
/******************************  list.c  ******************************

    Purpose:    Provide count list manipulation routines.
```

```
        Provenance: Written and tested by C. Fox, February 18, 1989.

        Notes:           This module is an implementation of an abstract data type
                         which is a list of elements consisting of a string, and two
                         long values.  The string is intended to be the function name;
                         the long values are the CSL and NCSL counts for the function.
                         The count list data type has four operations:

                             Create_List     -- make a new empty count list
                             Is_Empty_List   -- TRUE iff a list is empty
                             Append_Element  -- add count element to tail of list
                             Delete_Element  -- remove counts from head of list

                         No other operations are required for this application.

                         The count lists are implemented as linked lists of structures.
                         Space allocated for the structures and strings is reclaimed
                         when the nodes are destroyed.
**/

#include <stdio.h>
#include <malloc.h>
#include <string.h>

#ifdef __STDC__
#    include <stdlib.h>
#endif

#include "ccount.h"                        /* program-wide definitions */
#include "list.h"                          /* header for this module */
#include "error.h"                         /* error functions and messages */

/****************** Private Definitions and Declarations  ******************/

struct count_struct {           /* an element of a count list */
          char *name;                      /* function whose lines counted */
          long CSL,                        /* commentary source lines */
               NCSL;                       /* non-commentary source lines */
          count_list next;                 /* link to following count structure */
          };

/************************  Declared Functions   ************************/

#ifdef __STDC__

static count_list Create_Node( char *name, long CSL, long NCSL );
static void Destroy_Node( count_list ptr );

#else

static count_list Create_Node( /* char *name, long CSL, long NCSL */ );
static void Destroy_Node( /* count_list ptr */ );

#endif

/************************  Private Routines   ************************/

/*FN**********************************************************************

        Create_Node( name, CSL, NCSL )
```

```
        Returns: count_list -- pointer to a new list node.

        Purpose: Allocate and fill the fields of a new count list node.

        Plan:    Part 1: Allocate the space for the new list node
                 Part 2: Allocate the space for the name string
                 Part 3: Copy the field values into their respective fields
                 Part 4: Return a pointer to the new node

        Notes:   This is a standard linked list node allocation routine.  Note
                 that is fills in all fields, including the link field, which
                 is set to the NULL pointer.
**/

static count_list
Create_Node( name, CSL, NCSL )
    char *name;       /* in: string value placed in the name field of new node */
    long CSL,         /* in: value placed in the CSL field of new node */
         NCSL;        /* in: value placed in the NCSL field of new node */
    {
    count_list ptr;  /* pointer to the newly created list node */

            /* Part 1: Allocate the space for the new list node */
    ptr = (count_list)malloc( (unsigned)sizeof(struct count_struct) );
    if ( NULL == ptr ) (void)Error( MALLOC_FAILURE, NULL );

               /* Part 2: Allocate the space for the name string */
    ptr->name = malloc( (unsigned)strlen(name)+1 );
    if ( NULL == ptr->name ) (void)Error( MALLOC_FAILURE, NULL );

       /* Part 3: Copy the field values into their respective fields */
    (void)strcpy( ptr->name, name );
    ptr->CSL = CSL;
    ptr->NCSL = NCSL;
    ptr->next = NULL;

               /* Part 4: Return a pointer to the new node */
    return( ptr );

    } /* Create_Node */

/*FN*********************************************************************************

            Destroy_Node( ptr )

    Returns: void

    Purpose: Free the space for an count unneeded list node.

    Plan:    Free the space for the name field and the node itself

    Notes:   Note that the link is set to NULL before deallocation
             in an attempt to contain dangling reference errors.
**/

static void
Destroy_Node( ptr )
    count_list ptr;    /* in: node to be deleted */
    {

            /* Free the space for the name field and the node itself */
    if ( NULL != ptr )
        {
```

```
        if ( NULL != ptr->name ) free( (char *)ptr->name );
        ptr->next = NULL;
        free( (char *)ptr );
        }

  } /* Destroy_Node */


/*************************    Public Routines    *****************************/

/*FN*************************************************************************

        Is_Empty_List( list )

    Returns: int -- TRUE if the list is empty, FALSE otherwise.

    Purpose: See if a count list is empty.

    Plan:    Check whether the pointer is NULL.

    Notes:   None.
**/

int
Is_Empty_List( list )
  count_list list;    /* in: linked list of counts to check */
  {

  return( NULL == list );

  } /* Is_Empty_List */

/*FN*************************************************************************

        Create_List( list )

    Returns: void

    Purpose: Create a new empty count list.

    Plan:    Set the list pointer to NULL.

    Notes:   None.
**/

void
Create_List( list )
  count_list *list;    /* out: new empty count list */
  {

  *list = NULL;

  } /* Create_List */

/*FN*************************************************************************

        Append_Element( list, name, CSL, NCSL )

    Returns: void

    Purpose: Add a new count entry to the end of a count list.
```

```
     Plan:       Add to the front of the list if it is empty, otherwise
                 track to the end and add the node there.

     Notes:      Note that the list head parameter is changed if the
                 input list is empty.
**/
void
Append_Element( list, name, CSL, NCSL )
   count_list *list;    /* in/out: the count list appended to */
   char *name;          /* in: the function name */
   long CSL,            /* in: count of the CSL */
        NCSL;           /* in: count of the NCSL */
   {
   count_list ptr;      /* for tracking to the end of the input list */

   if ( NULL == *list )
      *list = Create_Node( name, CSL, NCSL );
   else
      {
      ptr = *list;
      while ( NULL != ptr->next ) ptr = ptr->next;
      ptr->next = Create_Node( name, CSL, NCSL );
      }

   } /* Append_Element */

/*FN******************************************************************************

          Delete_Element( list, name, CSL, NCSL )

     Returns: void

     Purpose: Remove a count entry from the head of a count list.

     Plan:       Part 1: Return if the list is empty
                 Part 2: Remove the first node from the list
                 Part 3: Grab the data values
                 Part 4: Reclaim the node's space

     Notes:      None
**/

void
Delete_Element( list, name, CSL, NCSL )
   count_list *list;    /* in/out: the count list removed from */
   char *name;          /* out: the function name */
   long *CSL,           /* out: count of the CSL */
        *NCSL;          /* out: count of the NCSL */
   {
   count_list ptr;      /* for tracking to the end of the input list */

                    /* Part 1: Return if the list is empty */
   if ( NULL == *list ) return;

                /* Part 2: Remove the first node from the list */
   ptr = (*list);
   *list = ptr->next;

                    /* Part 3: Grab the data values */
   (void)strcpy( name, ptr->name );
   *CSL = ptr->CSL;
   *NCSL = ptr->NCSL;
```

```
                        /* Part 4: Reclaim the node's space */
        Destroy_Node( ptr );

    } /* Delete_Element */
```

```
/****************************  error.h  ****************************

    Purpose:    Declare error functions and define an error type.

    Provenance: Written and tested by C. Fox, February 18, 1989.

    Notes:      None.
**/

/**************************** Error Messages ****************************/

typedef enum {
            BAD_OPTION,
            MISSING_DELIMITER,
            ACCESS_ERROR,
            MALLOC_FAILURE,
            INTERNAL_ERROR,
        } error_type;

/**************************** Public Routines ****************************/

#ifdef __STDC__

extern int Error( error_type indication, char *file_name );

#else

extern int Error();            /* deliver error messages and perhaps abort */

#endif
```

```
/****************************  error.c  ****************************

    Purpose:    Localization of error messages and functions.

    Provenance: Written and tested by C. Fox, February 18, 1989.

    Notes:      This module contains routines that deliver various classes
                of error message.
**/

#include <stdio.h>
#include <errno.h>

#include "ccount.h"                    /* program-wide definitions */

#ifdef __STDC__
#   include <stdlib.h>
#endif
#ifdef SUN_OS
#   include <sys/file.h>
#endif
```

```
#ifdef SYSTEM_V
#    include <fcntl.h>
#endif
#ifdef DOS_MSC
#    include <fcntl.h>
#    include <sys\types.h>
#    include <sys\stat.h>
#    include <io.h>
#endif

#include "error.h"                      /* header for this module */

/************************* Private Definitions  *************************/

#define USAGE                "\nUsage: ccount [-t] [-d <string>] [<file> ...]\n"

/************************* Defined Functions   *************************/

/************************* Public Routines   *************************/

/*FN********************************************************************

          Error( indication, file_name )

      Returns: int -- FAIL(1) for propagating an error indication.

      Purpose: Issue error and usage messages and perhaps abort the program.

      Plan:    Part 1: Generate an error message and decide whether to abort
               Part 2: Abort the program if necessary
               Part 3: Return a failure value for propagation

      Notes:   None.
**/

int
Error( indication, file_name )
    error_type indication;    /* in: the error code */
    char *file_name;          /* in: file that the message is about */
    {
    int return_code;   /* to make sure that opening a file fails */
    int is_abort;      /* TRUE iff error leads to a program abort */

       /* Part 1: Generate an error message and decide whether to abort */
    switch ( indication )
        {
        case BAD_OPTION :
        case MISSING_DELIMITER :
           (void)fprintf( stderr, USAGE );
           is_abort = TRUE;
           break;

        case ACCESS_ERROR :
            /* generate errno and return code by trying an open */
           return_code = open( file_name, O_RDONLY );
           if ( -1 == return_code ) switch ( errno )
              {
#ifdef SUN_OS
              case ENAMETOOLONG :
              case ELOOP :
              case ENOTDIR :
#endif
#ifdef SYSTEM_V
```

```
            case ENOTDIR :
#endif
            case EINVAL :
            case ENOENT :
                (void)fprintf(stderr, "\nccount: No such file %s\n", file_name);
                is_abort = FALSE;
                break;
#ifdef SUN_OS
            case EISDIR :
            case ENFILE :
            case ENXIO :
#endif
#ifdef SYSTEM_V
            case EISDIR :
            case ENFILE :
            case ENXIO :
#endif
            case EACCES :
            case EMFILE :
                (void)fprintf( stderr,
                              "\nccount: Cannot read file %s\n", file_name );
                is_abort = FALSE;
                break;
            }
        else
            {
            (void)fprintf( stderr, "\nccount: Internal error\n" );
            is_abort = TRUE;
            }
        break;

    case MALLOC_FAILURE :
        (void)fprintf( stderr, "\nccount: Memory allocation failure\n" );
        is_abort = TRUE;
        break;

    case INTERNAL_ERROR :
        (void)fprintf( stderr, "\nccount: Internal error\n" );
        is_abort = TRUE;
        break;
    }

            /* Part 2: Abort the program if necessary */
    if ( is_abort ) exit(-1);

            /* Part 3: Return a failure value for propagation */
    return(FAIL);


    } /* Error */
```

C

Engineering Document Templates

This appendix contains templates for several engineering documents including the following:

- Concept Exploration Document.
- Requirements Document.
- Design Document.
- Project Summary Document.

C.1 CONCEPT EXPLORATION DOCUMENT

C.1.1 Problem Definition

Describe the problem to be solved by the projected system.

C.1.2 System Justification

Justify a computerized solution to the problem, explaining why the product should be provided. Justify the need to build rather than buy a system.

C.1.3 User Characteristics

Profile the user population for the product. This profile might include the size of the potential user population (important for assessing feasibility), the skill level (important

234

for user interface design), the importance of the problems the product will solve to the user population, and so on.

C.1.4 Features and Functions

Sketch the major features and functions of the projected system, explaining how they fit together to provide a useful product for the target user population.

C.1.5 Goals for System and Project

Describe the projected effects that the product and the development project will have on its user population, the user organization, the developers, and the development organization. For example, a goal for the system might be to cut the time spent on some task by users in half; a goal for the project might be to assess a new design method.

C.1.6 Constraints on System and Project

State the financial, environmental, and political constraints on the system and project. For example, the system might need to be priced under $100 to be competitive.

C.1.7 Development, Operation, and Maintenance Environment

Describe the target environment, and the environment needed to develop and maintain the product.

C.1.8 Solution Strategy

Outline the steps to be taken to settle any further questions about feasibility, to generate requirements, to develop the product, and to deploy and maintain the product.

C.1.9 Feasibility Analysis

Demonstrate that the system is both technologically and politically feasible.

C.2 REQUIREMENTS DOCUMENT

C.2.1 Product Overview

Describe the major functions and components of the system in general terms. Summarize the rationale for building the system.

C.2.2 Development, Operation, and Maintenance Environments

Describe the hardware and software resources and tools necessary to build and maintain the product. Indicate the target hardware and software environment, including the optimal and minimal configurations for use of the product.

C.2.3 Conceptual Model

Present the conceptual model of the system (a high-level view showing the major services or components of the model and their relationships with each other). Graphical notations are usually preferred for this task, but other mechanisms such as clear English, decision tables, grammars, and so on may be used.

C.2.4 User Interface Specifications

Describe screens, windows, graphics, and other visual aspects of the system. State key bindings (that is, explain what each keystroke does). Specify the interaction or dialogue conventions governing the interface.

C.2.5 Functional Requirements

Describe the services, operations, and data transformations provided by the system. This portion of the requirements document is usually the largest, because all functionality of the system must be described carefully, precisely, and in full detail. A variety of formal methods and notations may be employed for this purpose.

C.2.6 Nonfunctional Requirements

State the constraints under which the software must operate. Typical nonfunctional requirements have to do with efficiency, reliability, portability, memory size constraints, quality standards, response time, problem size, and so on.

C.2.7 External Interfaces and Database Requirements

If the system must interface with other systems, describe its interfaces to the external systems. Describe the logical organization of databases used by the system.

C.2.8 Exception Handling

Indicate the anticipated exceptional conditions and error conditions, and responses to these conditions.

C.2.9 Foreseeable Modifications and Enhancements

State any foreseeable modifications and enhancements for the benefit of the designers and implementers, who must take this information into account in their work. Such changes generally involve anticipated alterations owing to hardware evolution, changing user needs, the introduction of other systems in the operating environment, and so on.

C.2.10 Design Hints and Guidelines

State any design features, constraints, or pitfalls obvious at this time for the benefit of the designers and implementers.

C.2.11 Glossary

Define all software engineering technical terms for the benefit of customers, and all application technical terms for the benefit of the software engineers.

C.2.12 Index

Provide a standard alphabetic index. Other kinds of indexes may be provided as an aid to traceability and maintenance of the requirements document.

C.3 DESIGN DOCUMENT TEMPLATE

C.3.1 Design Overview

Provide a high-level description of the system's structure with a small collection of top-level modules. This description should identify each major module by name, state its purpose, and discuss how it interacts with other modules.

C.3.2 Architectural Model

Present the system's architectural model; an *architectural model* of a system is a description of the top-level modules, and the data and control flow between them. Graphical notations are preferred for this task, but concise, well-written text may suffice.

C.3.3 Module Descriptions

A *module* is any part or subsystem of a larger system. A module may itself be decomposable into other modules that each provide part of the parent module's functionality and hide some of the parent module's secrets. A module decomposable into other modules is called an *internal module*; a module that is not decomposable into other modules is called a *leaf module*. Internal modules tend not to have internal computational structure, serving instead as grouping mechanisms for their component modules. Leaf modules, conversely, have a rich internal computational structure. Certain information must be supplied for every module in a module description, but some information is only needed to document the richer internal structure of leaf modules. Information that should be provided for every module includes the following:

- *Module behavior*. Explanation of a module's behavior includes (1) a catalog of the operations it provides, with descriptions of their input and output and their externally visible effects, and (2) a catalog of the data types and objects that the module provides.
- *Assumptions*. A module's assumptions are the conditions that must be satisfied for an implementation of the module to work. For example, a file processing module might assume that a file passed to it is open and readable.

- *Secrets.* The implementation details hidden from other modules inside the module under discussion must be listed.

- *Constraints and limitations.* The constraints and limitations governing implementation of the module, such as performance requirements, maximum memory usage requirements, numerical accuracy requirements, and so on, must be stated.

- *Error handling.* Errors and exceptional conditions that may be encountered by the module must be listed, along with their causes, and the strategy used to handle them.

- *Expected changes.* Any changes expected by the designers of the module are listed, with ideas about how the changes might be made.

- *Related requirements.* Reference should be made to the requirements satisfied by the module to help trace requirements through the design to the code.

In addition to this information, leaf module descriptions should also include the following:

- *Module packaging.* All invokable functions provided by the module should be listed, with their types, and the types of all their input and output parameters. The externally visible effects of each function should be explained, and any side-effects noted and explained. The salient features of any data types and objects provided by the module should be discussed in detail.

- *Internal structure.* Hidden data types and objects should be listed and their use explained. Internal functions should be listed with their types, the types of their parameters, and their effects. If particular sorts of algorithms are supposed to be used to implement some function, this should be stated and justified. If some algorithm is particularly crucial or tricky, it may be written down in pseudocode.

C.3.4 Uses Relationships

A module *uses* another module if some function provided by the latter is called somewhere in the implementation of the former. Uses relationships are important because they show the modules on which each module depends for its correctness.

C.3.5 Rationale

This section explains design decisions, listing the alternatives explored, and justifies the design decisions that were made.

C.3.6 Glossary

As in other development documents, a glossary should be provided to minimize confusion about technical terms.

C.4 PROJECT SUMMARY DOCUMENT

C.4.1 Product Description

Outline the system that was the goal of the development project, emphasizing features salient to the rest of the discussion.

C.4.2 Current Project Status and Future Plans

Discuss the current status of the project including staffing, budget, support, user attitude, and so on. Sketch future plans, particularly changes planned for the maintenance phase.

C.4.3 Initial Expectations and Actual Progress

Summarize the initial estimates of effort, personnel, development time, system size, required resources, target environment, cost, and so on. Contrast this with the actual effort, personnel, development time, and so forth. Mention parts of the system that were expected to be particularly troublesome that turned out to be easy, or parts that were expected to be easy that turned out to be difficult.

C.4.4 Retrospective Schedule

Present a timeline indicating the progress of the development effort over time.

C.4.5 Successful and Unsuccessful Project Aspects

Discuss the most successful aspects of the development effort and why they were important. List the most serious failures during the development effort and why they were important.

C.4.6 Lessons Learned

Based on the previous discussions, draw conclusions about what to do and not to do during product development. These will typically be both managerial and technical lessons.

C.4.7 Recommendation for Further Projects

Make any suggestions that others might find helpful in later development projects.

D

Rules of C Programming
Practice

This appendix lists the rules of good C programming practice discussed in Chapters 4 through 6.

Names and Declarations.

- Name objects to indicate their roles.
- Use uppercase characters for macro names.
- Make sure names differ in their first 6 to 8 characters.
- Do not begin names with underscores.
- Distinguish words in long names with underscores or case.
- Use prefixes and suffixes to encode information in names.
- Name multiply occurring structure, union, and enumeration types.

Control Structures.

- Use a **do-while** loop when the loop body is always executed at least once; otherwise use a **while**-loop or a **for**-loop.
- Use a **switch** statement only when the **switch** will contain more than two alternatives.
- Avoid the **goto** and **continue** statements, breaking out of loops, and early function returns.

Rules about Revealing Program Structure.

- Indent statements at the same block level to the same column.
- Indent substatements with respect to their main statement.

- Use vertical white space to separate code into segments that do parts of a whole task carried out in a block.
- Use horizontal white space to reflect precedence in expressions.
- Use standard block bracketing conventions.
- Mark null loop bodies, missing loop parameters, and missing **switch** break statements with comments.
- Adopt a functional style of programming.

Commenting.

- State program goals in module and function header comments, and in banner comments about groups of functions that work together.
- State program plans in function header comments and reiterate the plan in function bodies.
- If necessary, supplement role information captured in an object's name by a comment at the object's definition or declaration.
- Explain an object's purpose at its point of definition or declaration. Note whether parameters are in, out, or in-out parameters.
- Explain nonrole-based operations when they occur.
- Document side-effects in code segment comments (like header comments) at the point of declaration of the affected object, and at the point where the side-effect occurs.
- List calling functions in function header comments.

Size, Complexity, and Comment Density.

- Aim for function comment-to-code ratios of at least 0.8.
- Try to write functions with no more than 60 NCSL.
- Try to write compile modules with no more than 500 NCSL.
- Try to write functions with cyclomatic complexity of no more than 10.
- Do not exceed a block nesting level of 7.
- Do not write boolean expressions with more than 4 components.
- Do not exceed a conditional expression nesting level of 2.
- Avoid pointers to pointers.
- Factor complex declarations using type definitions.

Parameterization.

- Parameterize application specific values, environment specific values, tuning values, data-type limits, data-structure limits, internal codes, bit masks, offsets, operations, and types.

- Use function arguments to parameterize application specific values, data-type and data-structure limits, and operations.
- Use preprocessor macros to parameterize application and environment specific values, tuning values, bit masks, and offsets.
- Use enumeration types to parameterize internal codes.
- Use type definitions to parameterize types.

Preprocessor.

- Do not use the preprocessor to disguise the C language.
- Fully parenthesize macro definitions.
- Avoid parameterized macros in favor of functions.

Function Libraries.

- Use C library functions whenever possible.
- Use libraries and functions that conform to standards whenever possible.

Expressions.

- Use parentheses liberally.
- Avoid expressions side-effects.
- Avoid bitwise operations.
- Simplify complex boolean expressions by factoring, and by using DeMorgan's Laws to drive negations inward.
- Use `<=` and `<` instead of `>=` and `>`.
- Put constants on the left in comparisons.
- Make loop termination expressions as weak as possible.

Types.

- Use the **void** and enumeration types.
- Never default types.
- Use signed types in preference to unsigned types.
- Use the **char** type only with character data.
- Always use **double** instead of **float**.
- Do not mix and convert pointer types, and NEVER use **int** variables for pointers.
- **struct** and enumeration types should be given type definitions.

Coding Efficiency.

- Do not try to write efficient code unless performance requirements are not met.
- Use program performance analyzers to find bottlenecks.

- Improve bottlenecks with accepted optimization techniques.
- Analyze changes to ensure that they are improvements.
- Stop optimizing when performance requirements are met.

Modules and Access to Program Objects.

- Form and name compile modules in an effort to reflect program structure, with emphasis on principles of cohesion, coupling, and information hiding.
- Associate header files with individual source files, and use them to share declarations and definitions between source files.
- Make the scope of declarations as local as possible.
- Do not hide declarations by redeclaring the same name in a nested scope.
- Use function parameters and return values in preference to widely accessed variables to pass data.
- Declare functions and nonlocal variables not referenced outside the compile modules in which they are defined **static**.
- Declare functions and nonlocal variables referenced outside the compile modules in which they are defined **extern** whenever giving a nondefining declaration.
- Declare functions and nonlocal variables referenced outside the compile modules in which they are defined neither **extern** nor **static** in their unique defining declaration.

Error Checking.

- Write functions likely to generate errors, particularly those that rely on memory allocation or I/O, so that they either handle errors themselves, or they return an error code to propagate the error to a function that can handle it.
- Check the return codes of functions that return error codes, and handle or propagate any errors.

E

Code Inspection Checklist

This appendix contains a checklist for inspecting C programs as discussed in Chapter 8.

Data-Declaration Errors.

1. Is each data structure correctly typed?
2. Is each data structure properly initialized?
3. Are descriptive data structure names used?
4. Could global data structures be made local?
5. Have all data structures been explicitly declared?
6. Is the initialization of a data structure consistent with its type?
7. Are there data structures that should be defined in a type definition?
8. Are there data structures with confusingly similar names?

Data-Reference Errors.

1. Is a variable referenced whose value is uninitialized or not set to its proper value?
2. For all array references, is each subscript value within the defined bounds?
3. For pointer references, is the correct level of indirection used?
4. For all references through pointers, is the referenced storage currently allocated?
5. Are all defined variables used?
6. Is the **#define** construct used when appropriate instead of having hard-wired constants in functions?

Computation Errors.

1. Are there missing validity tests (e.g., is the denominator not too close to zero)?
2. Is the correct data being operated on in each statement?
3. Are there any computations involving variables having inconsistent data types?
4. Is overflow or underflow possible during a computation?
5. For expressions containing more than one operator, are the assumptions about order of evaluation and precedence correct?
6. Are parentheses used to avoid ambiguity?
7. Do all variables used in a computation contain the correct values?

Comparison Errors.

1. Is the "=" expression used in a comparison instead of "=="?
2. Is the correct condition checked (e.g., **if (FOUND)** instead of **if !FOUND**)?
3. Is the correct variable used for the test (e.g., **X == TRUE** instead of **FOUND == TRUE**)?
4. Are there any comparisons between variables of inconsistent types?
5. Are the comparison operators correct?
6. Is each boolean expression correct?
7. Are there improper or unnoticed side-effects of a comparison?
8. Has an "**&**" inadvertently been interchanged with a "**&&**" or a "**|**" for a "**||**"?

Control-Flow Errors.

1. Are null bodied **if**, **else**, or other control structure constructs correct?
2. Will all loops terminate?
3. Is there any unreachable code?
4. Do the most frequently occurring cases in a **switch** statement appear as the earliest cases?
5. Is the most frequently exercised branch of an **if-else** statement the **if** statement?
6. Are there any unnecessary branches?
7. Are **if** statements at the same level when they do not need to be?
8. Are **goto**'s avoided?
9. Are out-of-boundary conditions properly handled?
10. When there are multiple exits from a loop, is each exit necessary? If so, is each exit handled properly?
11. Is the nesting of loops and branches correct?
12. Are all loop terminations correct?

13. Does each **switch** statement have a **default** case?

14. Are there **switch case**'s missing **break** statements? If so, are these marked with comments?

15. Does the function eventually terminate?

16. Is it possible that a loop or condition will never be executed (e.g., **flag = FALSE; if (flag == TRUE)**)?

17. For a loop controlled by iteration and a boolean expression (e.g., a searching loop), what are the consequences of falling through the loop? For example, consider the following while statement:

```
while ( !found && (i < LIST_SIZE) )
```

What happens if **found** becomes **TRUE**? Can **found** become **TRUE**?

18. Are there any "off by one" errors (e.g., one too many or too few iterations)?

19. Are there any "dangling elses" in the function (recall that an **else** is always associated with the closest unmatched **if**)?

20. Are statement lists properly enclosed in **{ }**?

Input-Output Errors.

1. Have all files been opened before use?

2. Are the attributes of the open statement consistent with the use of the file (e.g., read, write)?

3. Have all files been closed after use?

4. Is buffered data flushed?

5. Are there spelling or grammatical errors in any text printed or displayed by the function?

6. Are error conditions checked?

Interface Errors.

1. Are the number, order, types, and values of parameters received by a function correct?

2. Do the values in units agree (e.g., inches versus yards)?

3. Are all output variables assigned values?

4. Are call by reference and call by value parameters used properly?

5. If a parameter is passed by reference, does its value get changed by the function called? If so, is this correct?

Comment Errors.

1. Is the underlying behavior of the function expressed in plain language?

2. Is the interface specification of the function consistent with the behavior of the function?

3. Do the comments and code agree?

4. Do the comments help in understanding the code?

5. Are useful comments associated with each block of code?

6. Are there enough comments in the code?

7. Are there too many comments in the code?

Modularity Errors.

1. Can the underlying behavior of the function be expressed in plain English?

2. Is there a low level of coupling among functions (e.g., is the degree of dependency on other functions low)?

3. Is there a high level of cohesion among functions (e.g., is there a strong relationship among functions in a module)?

4. Is there repetitive code (common code) throughout the function(s) that can be replaced by a call to a common function that provides the behavior of the repetitive code?

5. Are library functions used where and when appropriate?

Storage Usage Errors.

1. Is statically allocated memory large enough (e.g., is the dimension of an array large enough)?

2. Is dynamically allocated memory large enough?

3. Is memory being freed when appropriate?

Performance Errors.

1. Are frequently used variables declared with the **register** construct?

2. Can the cost of recomputing a value be reduced by computing the function once and storing the results?

3. Can a more concise storage representation be used?

4. Can a computation be moved outside a loop without affecting the behavior of the loop?

5. Are there tests within a loop that do not need to be done?

6. Can a short loop be unrolled?

7. Are there two loops that operate on the same data that can be combined into one loop?

8. Is there a way of exploiting algebraic rules to reduce the cost of evaluating a logical expression?

9. Are the logical tests arranged such that the often successful and inexpensive tests precede the more expensive and less frequently successful tests?

10. Is code written unclearly for the sake of "efficiency"?

Maintenance Errors.

1. Is the function well enough documented that someone other than the implementer could confidently change the function?
2. Are any expected changes missing?
3. Do the expected changes require much change?
4. Is the style of the function consistent with the coding standards of the project?

Traceability Errors.

1. Has the entire design been implemented?
2. Has additional functionality beyond that specified in the design been implemented?

F

References

1. *An American National Standard IEEE Standard Glossary of Software Engineering Terminology*, ANSI/IEEE Standard 729, 1983.

2. AT&T Bell Laboratories, *UNIX System V: User Reference Manual*. Murray Hill, N.J.: AT&T Bell Laboratories, 1983.

3. AT&T, *OPEN LOOK Graphical User Interface Style Guide*. New York: AT&T, 1989.

4. Abbott, R. J., "Program Design by Informal Descriptions," *Communications of the ACM*, 26, no. 11 (November 1983), 882–894.

5. Adobe Systems Incorporated, *Postscript Language Reference Manual*. Reading, Mass.: Addison-Wesley, 1985.

6. Agresti, W. (ed.), *Tutorial: New Paradigms for Software Development*. Los Angeles: IEEE Computer Society Press, 1986.

7. Aho, A., B. Kernighan, and P. Weinberger, *The AWK Programming Language*. Reading, Mass.: Addison-Wesley, 1988.

8. Aho, A., R. Sethi, and J. Ullman, *Compilers: Principles, Techniques, and Tools*. Reading, Mass.: Addison-Wesley, 1986.

9. Arnold, R., D. Parker, "Using Post Facto Validation for Gathering Empirical Data on Software Maintenance," *Proceedings of the Eighteenth Annual Hawaii International Conference on System Science* (January 1985), 435–446.

10. Babich, W. A., *Software Configuration Management*. Reading, Mass.: Addison-Wesley, 1986.

11. Belanger, D., G. Bergland, and M. Wish, "Some Research Directions for Large-Scale Software Development," *AT&T Technical Journal*, 67, no. 4 (July-August 1988), 77–92.

12. Bentley, J. L., *Writing Efficient Programs*. Englewood Cliffs, N.J.: Prentice Hall, 1982.

13. Bernstein, P. A., "Database System Support for Software Engineering," *Proceedings of the Ninth International Conference on Software Engineering* (March 1987), 166–178.

14. Berry, J., *C++ Programming*. New York: Howard Sams and Company, 1988.

15. Boehm, B., *Software Engineering Economics*. Englewood Cliffs, N.J.: Prentice Hall, 1981.

16. Boehm, B., "Software Engineering—R&D Trends and Defense Needs," in *Research Directions in Software Technology*, pp. 44–86, ed. P. Wegner. Cambridge, Mass.: M.I.T. Press, 1979.

17. Boehm, B., "The Spiral Model of Software Development and Enhancement," *IEEE Computer*, 21, no. 5 (May 1988), 61–72.

18. Bolsky, M. I., *VI User's Handbook*. Piscataway, N.J.: AT&T Bell Laboratories, 1984.

19. Bolsky, M. I., and D. G. Korn, *The KornShell*. Englewood Cliffs, N.J.: Prentice Hall, 1989.

20. Booch, G., "Object-Oriented Development," *IEEE Transactions on Software Engineering*, SE-12, no. 2 (February 1986), 211–221.

21. Booch, G., *Software Components with Ada*. Reading, Mass.: Benjamin/Cummings, 1987.

22. Booch, G., *Software Engineering with Ada* (2nd ed.). Reading, Mass.: Benjamin/Cummings, 1983.

23. Borland, *Turbo C User's Guide*. Scotts Valley, Cal.: Borland International, 1987.

24. Britton, K. H., and D. L. Parnas, *A-7E Software Module Guide*, Naval Research Laboratory, NRL Memorandum Report 4702, December 1981.

25. Buck, F. O., *Indicators of Quality Inspections*, IBM Technical Report IBM TR21.802 (September 1981).

26. Caine, S. H., and E. K. Gordon, "PDL—A tool for Software Design," *Proceedings of AFIPS Conference*, 33 (October 1975), 271–276.

27. Card, D., G. Page, and F. McGarry, "Criteria for Software Modularization," *Proceedings of Eighth International Conference on Software Engineering*, New York: IEEE Computer Society Press, 1985.

28. Chen, P. P., "The Entity-Relationship Model—Toward a Unified View of Data," *IEEE Transactions on Software Engineering*, SE-1, no. 3 (March 1976), 9–36.

29. Chen, Y., N. Nishimoto, and C. Ramamoorthy, "The C Information Abstraction System," *IEEE Transactions on Software Engineering*, SE-16, no. 3 (March 1990), 325–334.

30. Clocksin, W. F., and C. S. Mellish, *Programming in Prolog* (3rd ed.). New York: Springer-Verlag, 1986.

31. Conklin, E. J., "Hypertext: An Introduction and Survey," *IEEE Computer*, 2, no. 9 (September 1987), 17–41.

32. Conte, S., H. Dunsmore, and V. Shen, *Software Engineering Metrics and Models*. Reading, Mass.: Benjamin/Cummings, 1986.

33. Cox, B., *Object Oriented Programming*. Reading, Mass.: Addison-Wesley, 1986.

34. Crawford, S., A. A. McIntosh, and D. Pregibon, "An Analysis of Static Metrics and Faults in C Software," *Journal of Systems and Software*, 5, no. 3 (March 1985), 37–48.

35. Crawford, S. G., and M. H. Fallah, "Software Development Process Audits—A General Procedure," *Eighth International Conference on Software Engineering* (August 1985), 137–141.

36. Davis, A. M., "A Comparison of Techniques for the Specification of External System Behavior," *CACM*, 31, no. 9 (September 1988), 1098–1115.

37. DeMarco, T., *Structured Analysis and System Specification*. Englewood Cliffs, N.J.: Prentice Hall, 1979.

38. DeMarco, T., and T. Lister, *Controlling Software Projects: Management, Measurement, and Evaluation*. Seminar Notes. New York: Atlantic Systems Guild, 1984.

39. DeMillo, R., R. Lipton, A. Perlis, "Social Processes and Proofs of Theorems and Programs," *Communications of the ACM*, 22, no. 5 (May 1979), 271–280.

40. Dowson, M., "Integrated Project Support with ISTAR," *IEEE Computer*, 4, no. 6 (June 1987), 6–15.

41. Dunn, R., *Software Defect Removal*. New York: McGraw-Hill, 1984.

42. Dunsmore, H. E., "The Effect of Comments, Mnemonic Names, and Modularity: Some University Experiment Results," in *Empirical Foundations of Information and Software Science*, pp. 189–196, ed. J. C. Agrawal and P. Zunde. New York: Plenum Press, 1985.

43. Earhart, S. (ed), *The UNIX Programmers Manual* (vol. 1). New York: Holt, Rinehart, and Winston, 1986.

44. Fagan, M. E., "Advances in Software Inspections," *IEEE Transactions on Software Engineering*, SE-12, no. 7 (July 1986), 744–751.

45. Fagan, M. E., "Design and Code Inspections to Reduce Errors in Program Development," *IBM Systems Journal*, 15, no. 3 (March 1976), 219–248.

46. Feldman, S. I., "Make—A Program for Maintaining Computer Programs," *Software Practice and Experience*, 9, no. 4 (April 1979), 255–265.

47. Frakes, W. B. and Fox, C. J., "CEST: An Expert System Subroutine Library for the UNIX/C Environment," *The AT&T Technical Journal*, 67, no. 2 (March-April 1988), 95–106.

48. Frakes, W. B., "A Software Engineering Methodology for the UNIX/C Environment," *Proceedings of the AT&T Bell Laboratories Software Quality Symposium*, Holmdel, New Jersey, 1985.

49. Frakes, W. B., and Myers, D. M., "Using Expert Systems Components to Add Intelligent Help and Guidance to Software Tools," *Information and Software Technology*, 31, no. 7 (September 1989), 366–370.

50. Frame Technology Corp., *FrameMaker Reference Manual*. San Jose, Cal.: Frame Technology, 1989.

51. Freedman, D., and G. M. Weinberg, *Handbook of Walkthroughs, Inspections, and Technical Reviews* (3rd ed.). Boston: Little, Brown and Company, 1982.

52. Gallo, F., R. Minot, and I. Thomas, "The Object Management System of PCTE as a Software Engineering Database Management System," *Proceedings of ACM SIGSoft/SIGPlan Software Engineering Symposium on Practical Software Development Environments* (December 1986), 12–15.

53. Gane, C., and T. Sarson, *Structured Systems Analysis*. Englewood Cliffs, N.J.: Prentice Hall, 1979.

54. Gansner, E., et al., "Syned: A Language Based Editor for an Interactive Programming Environment," *COMPCON Proceedings* (March 1983).

55. Gardner, M., *Logic Machines and Diagrams*. Chicago: University of Chicago Press, 1982.

56. Garg, P., and W. Scacchi, "A Hypertext System to Manage Software Life Cycle Documents," *Proceedings of the Twenty-First Annual Hawaii International Conference on System Sciences* (January 1988), 337–346.

57. Gries, D., *The Science of Programming*. New York: Springer-Verlag, 1982.

58. Grinthal, E. T., "Software Quality Assurance and CAD User Interfaces," *IEEE Proceedings of the International Conference on Computer Design: VLSI in Computer* (1985), 95–98.

59. Halstead, M., *Elements of Software Science*. New York: Elsevier North-Holland, 1977.

60. Harbison, S., and G. Steele Jr., *C: A Reference Manual* (2nd ed.). Englewood Cliffs, N.J.: Prentice Hall, 1987.

61. Harel, D., "STATEMATE: A Working Environment for the Development of Complex Systems," *Proceedings of the Tenth International Conference on Software Engineering* (April 1988), 396–406.

62. Hatley, D., and I. Pirbhai, *Strategies for Real-Time System Specification*. New York: Dorset House, 1987.

63. Hecht, A. and M. Harris, "A CASE Standard Interchange Format: Proposed Extension of EDIF 2.0.0," *Proceedings of Twelfth Structured Methods Conference* (August 1987), 112–123.

64. Heitz, M., *HOOD: Hierarchical Object-Oriented Design for Development of Large Technical and Real-Time Software*, CISI Ingenierie, Direction Midi Pyrennes, November 1987.

65. Henniger, K., J. Kallander, D. Parnas, and J. Shore, *Software Requirements for the A7-E Aircraft*, NRL Memorandum 3876, November 1978.

66. Hetzel, W., *The Complete Guide to Software Testing*. Wellesley, Mass.: QED Information Sciences, 1984.

67. Hopgood, F. R., D. A. Duce, J. R. Gallop, and D. C. Sutcliffe, *Introduction to the Graphical Kernel System (GKS)*. New York: Academic Press, 1983.

68. Horgan, J., and D. Moore, "Techniques for Improving Language Based Editors," *Proceedings of the ACM SIGSoft/SIGPlan Software Engineering Symposium on Practical Software Development Environments* (April 1984).

69. Hudson, S. E., and R. King, "The Cactis Project: Database Support for Software Environments," *IEEE Transactions on Software Engineering*, SE-14, no. 6 (June 1988), 709–719.

70. Hurley, R. B., *Decision Tables in Software Engineering*. New York: Van Nostrand Reinhold, 1983.

71. Interleaf, Inc., *Interleaf Sun Reference Manual, TPS 4.0*. Cambridge, Mass: Interleaf, 1989.

72. Iverson, K., *A Programming Language*. New York: Wiley, 1962.

73. Jackson, M.A., *Principles of Program Design*. Orlando, Fla.: Academic Press, 1975.

74. Jackson, M.A., *System Development*. Englewood Cliffs, N.J.: Prentice Hall, 1983.

75. Johnson, S. C., *Yacc: Yet Another Compiler Compiler*, Computing Science Technical Report 32, AT&T Bell Laboratories, Murray Hill, N.J., 1975.

76. Juran, J. M., *Juran's Quality Control Handbook* (4th ed.). New York: McGraw-Hill, 1988.

77. Kernighan, B., and R. Pike, *The UNIX Programming Environment*. Englewood Cliffs, N.J.: Prentice Hall, 1984.

78. Kernighan, B. W., and P. J. Plauger, *The Elements of Programming Style*. New York: McGraw-Hill, 1978.

79. Kernighan, B. W., and R. Pike, *The UNIX Programming Environment*. Englewood Cliffs, N.J.: Prentice Hall, 1984.

80. Kishimoto, Z., "Testing in Software Maintenance and Software Maintenance from the Testing Perspective," *Proceedings of the Software Maintenance Workshop* (1983), 166–177.

81. Knuth, D. E., "An Empirical Study of FORTRAN Programs," *Software Practice and Experience*, 1, no. 2 (April-June 1971), 105–133.

82. Koenig, A., *C Traps and Pitfalls*. Reading, Mass.: Addison-Wesley, 1989.

83. Kolman, B., and R. C. Busby, *Discrete Mathematical Structures for Computer Science*. Englewood Cliffs, N.J.: Prentice Hall, 1984.

84. Leblang, D. B., and R. P. Chase, "Parallel Software Configuration Management in a Network Environment," *IEEE Software*, 4, no. 6 (November 1987), 28–35.

85. Ledgard, H., *Programming Practice*. Reading, Mass.: Addison-Wesley, 1987.

86. Lesk, M. E., *Lex—A Lexical Analyzer Generator*, Computing Science Technical Report 39, AT&T Bell Laboratories, Murray Hill, N.J., 1975.

87. Letovsky, S., and E. Soloway, "Delocalized Plans and Program Comprehension," *IEEE Software*, 3, no. 3 (May 1986), 41–49.

88. Lientz, B., and E. Swanson, *Software Maintenance Management*. Reading, Mass.: Addison-Wesley, 1980.

89. Liskov, B., and J. Guttag, *Abstraction and Specification in Program Development*. Cambridge, Mass.: M.I.T. Press, 1986.

90. MacLennan, B. J., *Principles of Programming Languages: Design, Evaluation, and Implementation*. New York: Holt, Rinehart and Winston, 1986.

91. Macdonald, N. H., L. T. Frase, P. S. Gingrich, and S. A. Keenan, "The WRITER'S WORKBENCH: Computer Aid for Text Analysis," *IEEE Transactions on Communications*, 30, no. 1 (January 1982), part 1, 105–110.

92. Marcotty, M., and H. Ledgard, *Programming Language Landscape* (2nd ed.). Chicago: Science Research Associates, 1986.

93. Martin, J., and C. McClure, *Software Maintenance: The Problem and Its Solutions*. Englewood Cliffs, N.J.: Prentice Hall, 1983.

94. McCabe, T., "A Complexity Measure," *IEEE Transactions of Software Engineering*, SE-2, no. 4 (April 1976), 308–320.

95. Myers, G. J., *The Art of Software Testing*. New York: Wiley, 1979.

96. Myers, G. L., *Reliable Software Through Composite Design*. New York: Petrocelli/Charter, 1975.

97. Neal, D., *NVCC Tutorial*, Department 45327 Technical Report, AT&T Bell Laboratories, August 1988.

98. Nejmeh, B., "NPATH: A Measure of Execution Path Complexity and Its Applications," *Communications of the ACM*, 31, no. 2 (February 1988), 188–200.

99. Nejmeh, B. A., and H. Dunsmore, "A Survey of Program Design Languages," *Proceedings of IEEE COMPSAC '86* (October 1986), 447–455.

100. Open Software Foundation, *OSF/Motif Style Guide*, Englewood Cliffs, N.J.: Prentice Hall, 1990.

101. Orlin, P., and J. Heath, "Easy C," *Byte*, 11, no. 5 (May 1986), 137–148.

102. Parnas, D. L. and P. C. Clements, "A Rational Design Process: How and Why to Fake It," *IEEE Transactions on Software Engineering*, SE-12, no. 2 (February 1986), 251–257.

103. Parnas, D. L., "Designing Software for Extension and Contraction," *Proceedings of the Third International Conference on Software Engineering* (May 1978), 264–277.

104. Parnas, D. L., "On the Criteria to be Used in Decomposing Programs into Modules," *Communications of the ACM*, 15, no. 12 (December 1972), 1053–1058.

105. Parnas, D. L., and D. M. Weiss, "Active Design Reviews: Principles and Practices," *Eighth International Conference on Software Engineering* (August 1985), 132–136.

106. Penedo, M. H., and W. E. Riddle, "Guest Editors' Introduction: Software Engineering Environment Architectures," *IEEE Transactions on Software Engineering*, SE-14, no. 6 (June 1988), 689–696.

107. Potier, D., "Experiments with Computer Software Complexity and Reliability," *Proceedings of the 6th International Conference on Software Engineering* (October 1982), 92–102.

108. Rajani, P. "Syntax Directed Editors," *The C Journal*, 2, no. 2 (Summer 1986).

109. Rochkind, M. J., "The Source Code Control System," *IEEE Transactions on Software Engineering*, SE-1, no. 4 (April 1975), 255–265.

110. Royce, W. W., "Managing the Development of Large Software Systems: Concepts and Techniques," *Proceedings WESCON* (August 1970), 1–6.

111. Rubinstein, R., and H. Hersh, *The Human Factor*. Bedford, Mass.: Digital Press, 1984.

112. Scheifler, R. W., J. Gettys, and R. Newman, *The X Window System C Library and Protocol Reference*. Bedford, Mass.: Digital Press, 1988.

113. Schneidewind, N. F., "The State of Software Maintenance," *IEEE Transactions on Software Engineering*, SE-13, no. 3 (March 1987), 303–310.

114. Seidowitz, E., and M. Stark, *General Object-Oriented Software Development*, Report SEL-86–002, NASA Goddard Space Flight Center, 1986.

115. Selby, R. W., V. R. Basili, and F. T. Baker, "Cleanroom Software Development: An Empirical Evaluation," *IEEE Transactions on Software Engineering*, SE-13, no. 9 (September 1987), 1027–1037.

116. Sheppard, S. B., M. A. Borst, B. Curtis, and T. Love, *Predicting Programmers' Ability to Modify Software*, TR 78–388100–3, General Electric Company, May 1978.

117. Shooman, M., *Software Engineering*. New York: McGraw-Hill, 1983.

118. Smith, J., and S. Weiss, "Hypertext," *Communications of the ACM*, 31, no. 7 (July 1988), 816–819.

119. Sommerville, I., *Software Engineering* (2nd ed.). Reading, Mass.: Addison-Wesley, 1985.

120. Stallman, R., *GNU Emacs Manual*. Cambridge, Mass.: Free Software Foundation, 1987.

121. Stanat, D. F., and D. F. McAllister, *Discrete Mathematics in Computer Science*. Englewood Cliffs, N.J.: Prentice Hall, 1977.

122. Steffen, J. L., "Interactive Examination of a C Program with Cscope," *Proceedings of the USENIX Winter Conference* (1985), 170–175.

123. Strang, J., *Programming with Curses*. Newton, Mass.: O'Reilly & Associates, 1986.

124. Stroustrup, B., *The C++ Reference Manual*. Reading, Mass.: Addison-Wesley, 1986.

125. Sun Microsystems, *Commands Reference Manual*, Mountain View, Cal.: Sun Microsystems, 1986.

126. Teitelbaum, T. and T. Reps, "The Cornell Program Synthesizer: A Syntax-Directed Programming Environment," *Communications of the ACM*, 24, no. 9 (September 1981), 563–573.

127. Thomas, R., L. R. Rogers, and J. L. Yates, *Advanced Programmer's Guide to UNIX System V*. New York: McGraw-Hill, 1986.

128. Tichy, W., "RCS—A System for Version Control," *Software Practice and Experience*, 15, no. 7 (July 1985), 637–654.

129. Tichy, W., "What Can Software Engineers Learn From Artificial Intelligence," *IEEE Computer*, 20, no. 11 (November 1987), 43–54.

130. Ward, P. T., and S. J. Mellor, *Structured Development for Real-Time Systems* (vols. 1–3). Englewood Cliffs, N.J.: Yourdon Press, 1985–1986.

131. Wasserman, A., P. Pircher, and B. Muller, "An Object-Oriented Structured Design Method for Code Generation," *ACM SIGSoft Software Engineering Notes*, 14, no. 1 (January 1989), 32–55.

132. Wasserman, A., "Extending State Transition Diagrams for the Specification of Human-Computer Interaction," *IEEE Transactions on Software Engineering*, SE-11, no. 8 (August 1985), 699–713.

133. Wasserman, A., and P. A. Pircher, "A Graphical, Extensible Integrated Environment for Software Development," *Proceedings of Practical Software Development Environments Conference* (December 1986), 131–142.

134. Weinberg, G., *The Psychology of Computer Programming*. New York: Van Nostrand Reinhold, 1971.

135. Weiner, R., and R. Sincovec, *Software Engineering with Modula-2 and Ada*. New York: Wiley, 1984.

136. Wirth, N., "Program Development by Stepwise Refinement," *Communications of the ACM*, 14, no. 4 (April 1971), 221–227.

137. Wirth, N., *Systematic Programming*. Englewood Cliffs, N.J.: Prentice Hall, 1973.

138. Wood, J., *Joint Application Design*. New York: Wiley, 1989.

139. Woodfield, S. N., H. E. Dunsmore, and V. Y. Shen, "The Effect of Modularization and Comments on Program Comprehension," *Proceedings of the Fifth International Conference on Software Engineering* (March 1981), 215–223.

140. Yourdon, E., and L. Constantine, *Structured Design*. Englewood Cliffs, N.J.: Prentice Hall, 1979.

Index